ISLAM IN EUROPE

MIGRATION, MINORITIES AND CITIZENSHIP SERIES

Series Editors: Zig Layton-Henry, *Professor of Politics and Head of the Centre for Research in Ethnic Relations, University of Warwick*; and Danièle Joly, *Lecturer in Politics, Centre for Research in Ethnic Relations, University of Warwick.*

This series has been developed to promote books on a wide range of topics concerned with migration and settlement, immigration policy, refugees, the integration and engagement of minorities, dimensions of social exclusion, racism and xenophobia, ethnic mobilisation, ethnicity and nationalism. The focus of the series is multidisciplinary and international. The series will publish both theoretical and empirical works based on original research. Priority will be given to single-authored books but edited books of high quality will be considered.

Titles include:

Naomi Carmon (*editor*)
IMMIGRATION AND INTEGRATION IN POST-INDUSTRIAL SOCIETIES
Theoretical Analysis and Policy-Related Research

Danièle Joly
HAVEN OR HELL?
Asylum Policies and Refugees in Europe

John Rex
ETHNIC MINORITIES IN THE MODERN NATION STATE
Working Papers in the Theory of Multiculturalism and Political Integration

Islam in Europe

The Politics of Religion and Community

Edited by

Steven Vertovec
Principal Research Fellow
Centre for Research in Ethnic Relations
University of Warwick
Coventry

and

Ceri Peach
Professor of Social Geography
University of Oxford

in association with
CENTRE FOR RESEARCH IN ETHNIC RELATIONS
UNIVERSITY OF WARWICK

First published in Great Britain 1997 by
MACMILLAN PRESS LTD
Houndmills, Basingstoke, Hampshire RG21 6XS and London
Companies and representatives throughout the world

A catalogue record for this book is available from the British Library.

ISBN 0–333–68702–7 hardcover
ISBN 0–333–68703–5 paperback

First published in the United States of America 1997 by
ST. MARTIN'S PRESS, INC.,
Scholarly and Reference Division,
175 Fifth Avenue, New York, N.Y. 10010

ISBN 0–312–16598–6

Library of Congress Cataloging-in-Publication Data
Islam in Europe : the politics of religion and community / edited by
Steven Vertovec and Ceri Peach.
    p.   cm. — (Migration, minorities, and citizenship)
Most of the papers included in this volume were presented at the
Oxford Conference on "Islam in Europe: Generation to Generation"–
–CIP galley.
Includes bibliographical references and index.
ISBN 0–312–16598–6
1. Muslims—Europe—Congresses.   I. Vertovec, Steven.   II. Peach,
Ceri.   III. Series.
D1056.2.M87I85   1997
940'.08'82971—dc20
                                                    96–43151
                                                        CIP

Contents

List of Figures

List of Tables

Acknowledgements

The editors gratefully acknowledge the grants from the Leverhulme Trust (Grant F 697) and the Alexander von Humboldt Stiftung towards the work on which much of this volume is based. They gratefully acknowledge the grants from the Spalding Trust and the British Association for Central and Eastern Europe towards the costs of running the Oxford Conference on 'Islam in Europe: Generation to Generation' at which most of the papers included in this volume were presented. The Oxford Centre for Islamic Studies made a grant towards the translation costs of several of the papers. Marian FitzGerald acted as interpreter at the conference and advised on the written translations. The editors also wish to record their thanks to Rita Hughes and Caroline Carpenter at St Catherine's College, Oxford, Pat Woodward, Alisdair Rogers and Marie McAllister at the School of Geography, and to Rachel Reeve, Geoff Roberts, Valery Rose, Annabelle Buckley, Astrid Gräfe and Katie Peach for help in running the conference and producing the book.

STEVEN VERTOVEC and CERI PEACH

Notes on the Contributors

Stefano Allievi is Instructor of Urban Sociology at the University of Milan and a PhD candidate at the University of Trento. His main research interests concern Islam in Europe and cultural and religious problems related to migration. He is author of *La sfida dell'immigrazione* (Emi, 1991), *Médias et minorités ethniques: Le cas de la guerre du Golfe* (Academia, 1992)(with A. Bastenier, A. Battegay and A. Boubeker), *Le parole della Lega* (Garzanti, 1992), *Il libro dell'altro: il Vangelo secondo lo straniero* (Edb, 1995), and editor of *L'occidente di fronte all'islam* (Franco Angeli, 1995).

Valérie Amiraux is a PhD student in political science at the Centre d'Études et de Recherches Internationales (CERI), Paris, and a research fellow at the Deutsches-Französisches Forschungszentrum in Berlin. Her research concerns identity and politics among Turkish Muslims in Germany. She has published a number of articles in this field, including 'Les transformations de l'identité islamique turque en Allemagne' in *Exils et Royaumes*, edited by G. Kepel (Presses FNSP, 1994).

Yannis Frangopoulos is a PhD candidate in sociology at the Université Catholique de Louvain. He has also studied theology at Aristotle University, Thessaloniki and ethnology at l'École des Hautes Études en Sciences Sociales, Paris. His doctoral research has involved religion, politics and identity among Pomaks in the Greek–Bulgarian border region, and he is author of several articles concerning Muslims in Greece.

Gilles Kepel is Senior Researcher at CNRS and teaches at the Institut d'Etudes Politiques de Paris. He is a specialist in North African Islamic societies and Muslim communities in France. He is author of *The Prophet and the Pharaoh: Muslim Extremism in Egypt* (University of California Press, 1985), *Les Banlieues de l'Islam: Naissance d'une reli-*

gion en France (Seuil, 1987), and *The Revenge of God: The Resurgence of Islam, Christianity and Judaism in the Modern World* (Blackwell, 1994, which is a translation of *La Revanche de Dieu*, Seuil, 1991), editor of *Exils et Royaumes* (Presses FNSP, 1994), and co-editor (with Rémy Leveau) of *Les musulmans dans la société française* (Presses FNSP, 1988).

John King is a writer, researcher, journalist and broadcaster working principally with the BBC Arabic Service, where he produces programmes on both politics and religion. His research interests are primarily in the field of Middle East politics, international relations and the politics of Islam. He is the editor of *Morocco: The Journal of the Society of Moroccan Studies*, and is author of *Three Asian Associations in Britain* (Centre for Research in Ethnic Relations, 1994), *Handshake in Washington: The Beginning of Middle East Peace* (Ithaca, 1994), *Conflict in the Middle East* (Wayland, 1993) and *Bedouin* (Wayland, 1992).

Nico Landman is Assistant Professor of Oriental Languages and Cultures at Utrecht University. His research interests are contemporary Islam, especially in Turkey and among immigrants in Western Europe. He is author of *Van mat tot minaret: De institutionalisering van de islam in Nederland* (VU Uitgeverij, 1992).

Rémy Leveau is Professor of Political Science at the Institut d'Études Politiques de Paris and Associate Research Fellow at the Centre d'Études et de Recherches Internationales (CERI), Paris. He is currently on leave at the Centre Marc Bloch in Berlin. His research interests concern the contemporary Arab/Muslim world, Islam in Europe, and migration. He is author of *Le Fellah marocain défenseur du Trône* (Presses FNSP, 1985, 2nd edn), *Le sabre et le turban* (Francis Bourin, 1993), editor of *L'Algérie dans la guerre* (Camplexe, 1995), and co-editor (with Gilles Kepel) of *Les musulmans dans la société française* (Presses FNSP, 1988).

Philip Lewis is Advisor on Inter-Faith issues to the Anglican Bishop of Bradford and lectures in the Department of Theology and Religious Studies at the University of Leeds. He spent six years in Pakistan studying Sufism, South Asian Islam and Christian–Muslim relations. His research interests focus on how religious communities respond to religious and ideological diversity. His most recent publication is *Islamic Britain: Religion, Politics and Identity among British Muslims* (I. B. Taurus, 1994).

Jørgen S. Nielsen is Director and Principal Lecturer at the Centre for the Study of Islam and Christian–Muslim Relations (CSIC), Selly Oak Colleges, Birmingham. His research interests are Islamic law and history and the place of religious minorities in Europe and the Arab world. He is general editor of the annual *International Documents on Palestine* (Institute for Palestine Studies), author of *Secular Justice in an Islamic State* (Netherlands Institute for the Near East, 1985), and *Muslims in Western Europe* (Edinburgh University Press, 1995, 2nd edn), editor of *Religion and Citizenship in Europe and the Arab World* (Grey Seal, 1992), and co-editor of *Christian Arabic Apologetics during the Abbasid Period (750–1258)* (E. J. Brill, 1994).

Ceri Peach is Professor of Social Geography at Oxford University and Fellow of St Catherine's College. His research interests are in patterns of migration, settlement and segregation. He is author of *West Indian Migration to Britain: A Social Geography* (Oxford University Press, 1968), editor of *Urban Social Segregation* (Longman, 1975), and co-editor of *Ethnic Segregation in Cities* (Croom Helm, 1981) (with Susan Smith and Vaughan Robinson); *Geography and Ethnic Pluralism* (Allen & Unwin, 1984) (with Colin Clarke and David Ley); *South Asians Overseas: Migration and Ethnicity* (Cambridge University Press, 1990) (with Colin Clarke and Steven Vertovec).

Alexandre Popovic is Director of Research at the Centre National de la Recherche Scientifique, Chargé de Conférences at l'École Pratique des Hautes Études (Section: Sciences Historiques et Philologiques) and a research programme leader for CNRS and l'École des Hautes Études en Sciences Sociales, Paris. He is a specialist on Muslim communities and Sufism in the Balkans. He is author of several books, including *l'Islam balkanique: Les musulmans du sud-est européen dans la période post-ottomane* (Otto Harrassowitz, 1986), *Les Musulmans yougoslaves (1945–1989): Médiateurs et métaphores* (L'Age d'Homme, 1990), *Les*

Musulmans des Balkans à l'époque post-ottomane: Histoire et politique (Editions Isis, 1994) and *Cultures musulmanes balkaniques* (Editions Isis, 1994).

Åke Sander is Associate Professor of Religious Studies and Director of the Centre for the Study of Cultural Contact and International Migration (KIM) at Göteborg University. His research interests include phenomenology, encounters between religions, and Islam in Sweden and Western Europe. He is author of *En Tro–En Livsvärld: En fenomenologisk undersökning av religiös erfarenhet, religiöst medvetande och deras roller i livsvälds-konstitutionenen* (Göteborg, 1988), *Kan Koranskolan i Göteborg Fungera som Medium för Traditionsförmedling?* (Göteborg, 1988), *I vilken utsträckning är den svenske muslimen religiös?* (Göteborg, 1993), and co-editor of *Multiculturality: Welfare or Well-fare?* (Göteborg, 1993).

Werner Schiffauer is Professor and Chair of Comparative Social and Cultural Anthropology at the European University Viadrina in Frankfurt (Oder). Having conducted ethnographic research in Turkey and Germany, his major fields of interest are anthropology of religion with particular reference to Islam, migration and urban anthropology. He is author of *Die Gewalt der Ehre* (Suhrkamp, 1983), *Die Bauern von Subay* (Klett-Cotta, 1986), *Die Migranten aus Subay* (Klett-Cotta, 1991) and *Kultur und Differenz* (Suhrkamp, forthcoming).

Bogdan Szajkowski is Professor of Pan-European Politics at the University of Exeter, where he is also Director of the Centre for European Studies. He is a leading authority on the former Communist countries of Europe and their transition from authoritarianism to democracy. His research interests include social, political, economic and religious conflicts, religious minorities, politicised ethnicity and political parties. His most recent books include *Encyclopaedia of Conflicts, Disputes and Flashpoints in Eastern Europe, Russia and the Successor States* (Longman, 1994) and *Political Parties of Eastern Europe, Russia and the Successor States* (Catermill, 1995). He is also co-editor of *Muslim Communities in the New Europe* (Ithaca, 1996) (with Tim Niblock and Gerd Nonneman).

Steven Vertovec is Principal Research Fellow at the ESRC Centre for Research in Ethnic Relations (CRER), University of Warwick. His research interests surround theories of ethnicity and culture, multicul-turalism and religious minorities in Europe. He is author of *Hindu Trinidad: Religion, Ethnicity and Socio-Economic Change* (Macmillan, 1992), editor of *Aspects of the South Asian Diaspora* (Oxford University Press, 1991), and co-editor of *South Asians Overseas: Migration and Ethnicity* (Cambridge University Press, 1990) (with Colin Clarke and Ceri Peach) and *The Urban Context: Ethnicity, Social Networks and Situational Analysis* (Berg, 1995)(with Alisdair Rogers).

Chapter Summaries

Chapter 2:   Islamic Groups in Europe: Between Community Affirmation and Social Crisis

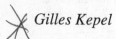 *Gilles Kepel*

Gilles Kepel argues that the perception of Muslims in Europe changed radically in the mid-1980s, largely as a result of seeds sown in the 1970s. The 1973 Arab–Israeli War, the subsequent economic disruption of the West and the rise of the Ayatollah Khomeini gave at once a change in the economic situation of Muslims in the West and a focus for their political and cultural organisation. Muslims changed from transients to settlers in Europe and at the same time experienced rejection by the society in which they were settling. Their children, in particular, became alienated in this transitional state. Islam was re-invented, Kepel argues, as a contingent identity of protest. There was a selective adoption of traditional forms, but with meanings rather different from those in the societies of origin. The headscarf affair in France and the Rushdie Affair in Britain characterised this reformulation. Both Britain, which has a policy of multiculturalism, and France, which has traditionally been hostile to communalism, have failed to reach an accommodation with Islam.

Chapter 3:   The Balkan Muslim Communities in the Post-Communist Period

Alexandre Popovic

Alexandre Popovic's chapter examines the position of Muslim groups in the Balkans, Greece and Hungary in the aftermath of the fall of Communism. The chapter is organised on a country-by-country basis, indicating that the situation varies considerably. Hungary has hardly any Muslims, although the Ahmadiyas and Bahais, who had a presence before 1939, are re-establishing themselves. The Greek Muslims are concentrated in the northern part of the country and are largely repressed. Albanian Muslims, who constitute a majority of the population, are emerging from the period of atheistic suppression. In Bulgaria, the change in regime has produced a return flow of many of the Turkish Muslims who fled the country at the time of enforced Bulgarisation in the late 1980s. The really violent changes affecting the Muslims are currently concentrated, not surprisingly, in former Yugoslavia, mainly in Bosnia-Herzegovina, but also in Kosovo.

Chapter 4: Religion, Identity and Political Conflict in a Pomak Village in Northern Greece

Yannis Frangopoulos

Yannis Frangopoulos's chapter is an anthropological account of religious and political contestation in a Muslim village in Thrace, northern Greece. Public life takes place in the cafes, which are essentially male domains. Each cafe has a distinctive character and set of views. In one of the cafes on the main square, the imam holds court; in another it is the mayor. The most open discussions, however, take place in the cafes of young men in the side streets. These cafes coincide with political views and attitudes to the state, highlighted by certain political events. The imam's cafe represents a 'Turkish' ethnic view of Islam, while the Mayor's cafe represents Greek secular power, despite its members being Muslim. The youth cafes, on the other hand, represented a kind of apolitical view of the state.

Chapter 5: The Muslim Minority in Poland

Bogdan Szajkowski

Muslims in Poland represent a small, almost forgotten population whose influence on the wider culture – particularly that in military circles – was historically significant. Islam was brought to Lithuanian Poland with the Tatars in the fourteenth century. Originally comprised of only a small number of relocated prisoners, the Tatar population grew considerably over over the following centuries. By the early seventeenth century, they numbered over 100 000 Muslims who prayed at some 400 mosques. In this chapter Bogdan Szajkowski traces the history of Muslim Tatars in Poland from their origins to the present day, from a period of widespread nobility and martial renown, through cultural assimilation and population decline, to a time and context of virtual obscurity.

Chapter 6:   The Bradford Council for Mosques and the Search for Muslim Unity

Philip Lewis

This chapter explores the significance, locally and nationally, of the Bradford Council for Mosques from its establishment in 1981 through the turbulent period of the Rushdie Affair. This study includes a brief history of migration, settlement and consolidation of Muslim communities in Bradford, a review of the Council's activities surrounding issues of *halal* food, educational matters and the Honeyford Affair. There emerges a detailed picture of extensive Muslim involvement in local political affairs. This is followed by an extensive account of events following the publication of the *The Satanic Verses*, when the Bradford Council for Mosques was catapulted onto the national stage. Philip Lewis demonstrates how the Council's personnel were active both in seeking to translate anger and outrage at the novel into institutional unity at a national level, and to begin a debate on a range of issues exercising Muslims across Britain.

Chapter 7:   Tablighi Jamaat and the Deobandi Mosques in Britain

John King

Tablighi Jamaat is an international movement dedicated to reaffirming the basic principles of Islam and to drawing back into the fold of the religion Muslims who may have strayed, while at the same time confirming and strengthening the faith of the Tablighi missionaries themselves. Tabligh is professedly a non-political organisation, and because it operates entirely within the Muslim community, it is relatively invisible to outsiders. It is especially linked with the Deobandi school of Islam among South Asians in Britain, but is attracting increasing attention in Europe particularly among Maghrebi Muslims of North African origin. The implication is that the version of Muslim solidarity expressed through and engendered by Tabligh is capable of transcending not only profound cultural and linguistic differences but also internal divisions within the learned tradition of the Muslim community, since North Africans follow the Maliki madhhab of Islamic law while the Indian tradition is Hanafi.

John King traces the origins of the differences between the Deobandi and Barelvi approaches to Islam. In summary, Barelvis profess a populist Islam, more infused with superstition and syncretism, which characterises the religious beliefs of the peasantry. Deobandis, on the other hand, represent a more austere and intellectual form of belief. Barelvis, however, are much more numerous in Britain than Deobandis so that part of the proselytising drive of the Tabligh in Europe may stem from difficulty in making converts among their Barelvi rivals.

Chapter 8:   The Political Culture of the *'Beurs'*

Rémy Leveau

Rémy Leveau examines whether the Islamic identity adopted by the second generation Maghrebians has developed with positive feelings about religion or with negative feelings of exclusion. He sees the religious discourse as nothing more than an ideological camouflage. Through an examination of opinion poll data, he concludes that it is to do with exclusion rather than religion *per se*. Religion was of little consequence for North Africans before the economic situation worsened, bringing threats to employment and before family reunification meant confronting the racism of French society from the perspective of a settler rather than a transient. However, despite the adoption of headscarves by many young women as a means of asserting group membership, the attitude of the younger generation was strongly accepting of French values, particularly in relation to sexual relations with young French people. The Muslim identity of North African settlers is, paradoxically, part of their strategy for integration and the recognition of their rights.

Chapter 9: Islamic Vision and Social Reality: The Political Culture of Sunni Muslims in Germany

Werner Schiffauer

The history of Islam in Augsburg, Germany, is conflict-ridden, a history characterised by coups, fissions and takeovers of Islamic institutions. This study by Werner Schiffauer concerns four 'fundamentalist' groups in the city (that is, groups which fight for the reintroduction of the *seriat* or system of Islamic law): the National Sight, the Süleymancı, the Nurcu, and the Annunciation Movement. The four groups are generally oriented toward society in Turkey while showing 'a marked disinterest with regard to German society'. Nevertheless, their contrasting systems of belief, practice and organisation have been at the core of conflict in their German setting. Schiffauer analyses the ideological reasons for socio-political conflicts which are largely grounded in differential religious assumptions concerning the ideal relationship between individual and society and the ideal strategy for bringing about religious–political change.

Chapter 10: To What Extent is the Swedish Muslim Religious?

Åke Sander

For a thousand years, Sweden has had an extremely homogeneous population, so that foreign immigration since the 1960s had resulted in a profound shock to the system. Out of a population of about 8.4 million, 1.3 million are foreigners and of these about 200 000 come from countries that are predominantly Muslim in faith. The Swedish Protestant Church is an established part of the state. However, legislation allows state funds to be allocated to recognised non-state religions, basically in proportion to the numbers of their faithful that they serve. The amount of money to be distributed is fixed so that increase in the allocation to one religion is at the expense of all other participants. Under these circumstances, the size of the Muslim population is a matter of contestation.

Sander's paper examines the various levels of Islamic observation among people in Sweden originating from Muslim countries. He takes two samples, one from Göteborg, the other a national sample. Sander's method of measuring the degree of religious observation was to administer a 'thermometer-type' questionnaire to the Göteborg sample. With increasing degrees of commitment, he defines *cultural*, *ethnic* and *religious* Muslims.

Using a somewhat different methodology, measurement of Friday prayer attendance during Ramadan for Sweden as a whole, he found that around 35 per cent of the total Muslim population, measured in terms of frequency of prayer hall visiting, could be considered to be religious in a fairly exclusive sense of the term and that about an additional 18.5 per cent, giving a total of 53.5 per cent, could be said to be religious using a more inclusive definition. The remaining 46.5 per cent is, then, non-religious. Since religiosity measured according to the variable 'mosque visiting' gave a lower proportion of religious people than measurements according to the other suggested variables, he concludes that the results from the two indices for measuring religiosity suggest that 60 per cent of the Muslim population could be called religious.

Chapter 11: Muslim Minorities in Italy and their Image in Italian Media

Stefano Allievi

Having only become a country of immigration rather recently, Italy is home to some of the newest Muslim communities in Europe. This settlement is, of course, actually a return of Islam to Italy, since Muslims lived in parts of the territory throughout medieval times. In this chapter, Stefano Allievi provides a 'morphology' of the contemporary Muslim presence in Italy, which is comprised of variously organised groups from several ethnic and national backgrounds. Subsequently, he points to ways in which Italian media treatment of Muslim issues – particularly newspaper coverage of the Gulf War, inter-faith pronouncements of the Catholic Church, and the explusion of a Muslim student leader – play upon a popular fear/desire among non-Muslims regarding the new Muslim presence and the constructed image of the Arab Muslim terrorist.

Chapter 12:   The Islamic Broadcasting Foundation in the Netherlands: Platform or Arena?

Nico Landman

The history of the Dutch Islamic Broadcasting Foundation (IBF) reflects a complex picture of institutionalisation processes, Muslim experiences of liaison with government authorities, inter-ethnic relations within a European-based Muslim population, and vexed questions of representation and 'representativeness' among Muslim organisations and in the media. Since its establishment, Nico Landman demonstrates, the IBF has functioned as an arena in which individuals and organisations contested for power and the right to represent both ethnic (Turkish, Moroccan, Surinamese) and general Muslim interests. However, as shown by its programme framework, the IBF has also served as a platform on which Muslims could independently present their ideas and show the lives of their communities to a large Muslim and non-Muslim public.

Chapter 13:   Turkish Islamic Associations in Germany and the Issue of European Citizenship

Valérie Amiraux

In light of a new political context in which measures contained within the Maastricht Treaty will create a status of European citizenship, Valérie Amiraux describes views among leaders of the three largest Turkish-Islamic associations in – Avrupa Milli Görüs Teskilatları (AMGT), Süleymancı and Dyanet Isleri Türk Islam Birligi (DITIB) – and within one prominent local organisation, the Islamic Federation of Berlin (IFB).

One generally negative view emerges, by which the construction of 'Europe' is perceived to hold a mass regionalisation of the local structural problems which Muslims face in German towns and cities, particularly after the fall of the Berlin wall and the mass arrival of 'ethnic Germans' who automatically gain a host of rights denied other, long settled, immigrant minorities. This is countered simultaneously by a positive view of new European political frameworks which looks to potential benefits of multiculturalist policies, the emergence of new gates of entry into common public space, and the creation of a broad ground for the exercise of new modes of collective mobilisation available to Muslims.

Chapter 14: Muslims in Europe into the Next Millennium

Jørgen S. Nielsen

Jørgen S. Nielsen argues that, at the end of the millennium, we are experiencing a period of change of historical proportions. The collapse of Communism and the sudden flurry of attempts to settle long-standing tensions, such as those in South Africa and Palestine, combine with the outbreak of new categories of crisis, such as those in Bosnia and Central Asia, to give a sense of an historical turning point. After reviewing the history of the presumed clash of Christendom and Islam, Nielsen argues that Christendom is less accepting of the 'other' than Islam. In an Orwellian sense it is transforming Islam into the enemy that it needs in order to replace its fallen antagonist, Communism. There are, however, countervailing tendencies within the West. Nielsen suggests three levels – European, national and local – at which the West will have to adapt to a Muslim presence.

Part I
Introduction

1 Introduction: Islam in Europe and the Politics of Religion and Community

Steven Vertovec and Ceri Peach

Around the time this volume was being prepared, events which dominated the attention of national and international news media included the bombing of the Israeli embassy in London attributed to Middle East Muslims, the hijacking of an airplane by Algerian Islamicists and the spectacular rescue of hostages in Marseilles, and the bombings in the Paris Metro and the Place Charles de Gaulle believed to be linked with Muslim extremists. Meanwhile, many analyses of the conflict in Bosnia-Herzegovina tended to portray the complexities of conflict there in over-simplified terms of some kind of eternal, tribalised Christian–Muslim duel. Evidence seemingly supporting post-Cold-War worries of an emergent 'clash of civilisations' (Huntington, 1993) pitting the Islamic world against the Christian West were becoming more manifest in Europe itself. Indeed, since the Iranian Revolution public concern and reactionary suspicions throughout Europe have turned toward the increasingly visible and vocal communities of Muslim migrants and their descendants. Are they to be regarded as a menace, some kind of advance unit in Islam's bid for world domination?

As John Esposito (1992) has demonstrated, although the current myth of 'The Islamic Threat' has arisen through a convergence of many factors, it has taken hold of non-Muslim world opinion in a rather monolithic way (cf. Said, 1978, 1981; Sardar and Davies, 1990). Indeed, essentialised images of Islam are now taken by many as a kind of 'common-sense' explanatory factor in world affairs, having been reproduced and amplified in many quarters.

3

For instance, the cover of the 15 June 1992 issue of the international edition of *Time* magazine displayed a photograph of a silhouetted minaret in the background and in the foreground, a robed arm holding an automatic weapon; under the photograph appeared the special issue title 'Islam: Should the World Be Afraid?' (Even though the articles which comprised the cover story largely answered the question with 'No' – countless people in shops and airports the world over doubtless glanced only at the cover and thought to themselves, 'Yes.') Early in 1995, NATO Secretary-General Willy Claes declared militant Islam as the Western world's number one menace following the collapse of Communism, a view shared in think-tanks and government circles throughout the West (see Mazrui, 1991). And when the federal building in Oklahoma City was bombed, much of the world's press immediately engaged in Islam-bashing before further information about the disaster emerged. One of the worst blunders of this kind – given that the bombing turned out to have nothing what so ever to do with Islamic causes – was committed by the British daily *Today*, whose front page of 20 April 1995 was filled with a picture of a fireman at the scene cradling a bloodstained baby, with which the newspaper's banner headline declared 'In The Name of Islam.'

With such widespread and amplifying fear/suspicion/hostility toward Islam, it is not surprising that these feelings have been turned upon the resident Muslim populations of Europe. Hence in European Muslim minorities, right-wing activists have found an easy – it seems, popularly 'acceptable' – quarry in their exclusivist political hunt. 'Stigmatising Islam with everything contradictory to the essential values of Western civilisation has now been proven to be a successful instrument of political mobilisation,' point out W. A. R. Shadid and P. S. van Koningsveld (1995, pp. 71–2): 'Racist ideologies are now succeeding in conveying political views which would have met with fierce resistance if they had not been propagated under the guise of criticising Islam.' The conflation of 'race,' 'nation' and religion – often under the rubric of 'culture' – has become the stock-in-trade of what has been called 'the new racism'. In particular, the contemporary Muslim presence in Europe has effected, in Etienne Balibar's (1991, p. 12) term, a *condensation* of colonial and racist discourses 'so that imagery of racial superiority and imagery of cultural and religious rivalry reinforce each other'.

In Britain such views were encapsulated in views voiced by Winston Churchill MP (grandson of the famous Prime Minister), who scare-

mongered whites and railed against immigrants and immigration policy
by painting a lurid picture of a Britain endangered by too many Muslims:
'Mr Major promises us that 50 years from now, spinsters will still be
cycling to communion on Sunday mornings – more like the muezzin will
be calling Allah's faithful to the High Street mosque', he said (the
Guardian, 29 May 1993). Meanwhile Jean Marie Le Pen leads Le Front
National with calls for a halt to the 'Islamisation' of France, Franz
Schonhuber, leader of the right-wing Republikaner party, declares
'Never will the green flag of Islam fly over Germany', and the
Progressive Party of Denmark campaigns with a promise of 'Denmark
with No Musselmen.' Presented with such rhetoric, Henry Louis Gates
(1993, p. 42) instructively reminds us that today 'the terms of the argu-
ment about the "Muslim factor" are reminiscent of the language in which
the "Jewish question" was debated in England a century and a half ago'.

What is lost sight of is that fact that every day, millions of Muslims
across Europe are participating in the social and economic milieu as
residents, neighbours, pupils and students, workers, professionals – as
de facto Europeans. Yet despite some indications of success, various
forms of socio-economic, political, and physical exclusion abound.
Such forms of exclusion have largely been responsible for producing
conditions of serious deprivation rampant throughout the Muslim population of Europe, a population described in one recent survey as
'divided and traumatized, weakened by unemployment and humiliated
by dependence on social welfare ... a Muslim population stymied by
cultural values it does not share, having done little to integrate over the
years' (Ibrahim, 1995). Muslims in Europe currently face the combined
effects of the swelling of anti-Islam-ism in Europe (itself arguably a
part of a mass upsurge in xenophobic hostility and violence), a tighten-
ing of immigration restrictions which are also related to expanding
racist and culturalist assumptions, widespread unemployment, and fears
of persecution underlined almost daily by news of the plight of Bosnian
Muslims. Although certainly 'It is not easy to be a Muslim in Europe
today', as one British newspaper (the *Independent*, 19 June 1993)
bluntly stated in an editorial, such a configuration of adversities has
prompted, among other things, 'a new self-consciousness for European
Muslims'.

One consequence of such new self-consciousness is a greater willingness among Muslims in Europe to engage, in various ways and on
diverse levels, the broad public sphere of politics, local and national

administration, and the media. Although large numbers of Muslims
have settled in Western Europe since the end of the Second World War
and have over decades established Islamic organisations of many kinds,
it has only been since the late 1980s that Muslims have collectively
engaged with, and had considerable impact upon, the European public
sphere. The 'Rushdie affair' and the *'foulards* [headscarves] affair'
mark watersheds in this respect (see Kepel in this volume).
Unfortunately for Muslims, their strides forward in mobilising themselves with a view to addressing publicly their basic collective concerns, exercise of rights, and elements of discrimination were read by
many non-Muslim Europeans as evidence of an amassing anti-
modernist enemy within.

   The 'Rushdie affair' rapidly broadened and eventually concretised,
in a largely negative fashion, Muslims' place in the public sphere (see
Ruthven, 1990; Samad, 1992; Lewis, 1994; Lewis in this volume). The
nature of media coverage surrounding the Rushdie Affair transformed
the dominant view of Muslims in Britain (Appignanesi and Maitland,
1989). The book-burning in Bradford on 14 January 1989 (orchestrated
by Muslim groups as a media event, yet without much forethought as to
its 1930s Nazi allusion) was seized upon by some quarters of the press
as evidence of an 'uncivilised' and 'intolerant' Muslim nature. The
Ayatollah Khomeini's *fatwa* of 14 February 1989, calling for the death
of Salman Rushdie, was taken as further evidence of this collective
trait, portrayed as a world-wide Muslim threat which had infested the
body Britain. Far less attention was given to Muslims' own perceptions
and feelings of offence and hurt underlying the public demonstrations.
Media treatment of the Rushdie Affair (which, it must be said, included
some irresponsible and inflammatory statements by alleged 'Muslim
leaders') created or bolstered an image of a homogeneous Muslim population (Parekh, 1990) which posed a challenge both to nationalist ideologies of 'Britishness' (Asad, 1990) and to liberal notions surrounding
modernity, freedom and human rights (Modood, 1990).

   Thus by 1990, albeit in a largely undesirable manner, Muslims had
gained a firm place on the national political agenda. Among leading
intellectuals, in the popular press and in much popular opinion, the
main issue surrounding the 'Rushdie affair' was freedom of expression
– although this was often posed in 'singular, monolithic terms' without
reference to authors' responsibilities (Sardar and Davies, 1990, p. 5;
also see Commission for Racial Equality, (CRE), 1990). Other issues

which British Muslim mobilisation raised surrounded the notion of blasphemy (what kinds of offences were included and, most importantly, which religions it covered; CRE, 1989) and whether offences to religious groups (slander, incitement to hatred) were akin to offences relating to 'race' and ethnicity (CRE, 1992). For many, however, the central implicit issue became the question of what to do with those problematic Muslims who didn't 'fit' into an assimilationist model of society which is widespread despite rhetoric praising multiculturalism.

Also in 1989, the '*foulards* affair' in France witnessed Muslims posing in the public sphere essential questions as to the evolving perplexities of French society and French identity, the principles of French republican political philosophy, the nature of *intégrisme* and strategies for managing or assimilating large migrant minorities (see Nielsen, 1992a, pp. 162–4; Husbands, 1995; Kepel, 1995; Shadid and van Koningsveld, 1995, pp. 89–96). After three Muslims girls at a secondary school in Creil insisted on wearing headscarves in contravention of school rules banning overt expressions of religion – rules which were fully in keeping with broader French traditions surrounding the establishment of laicism in public sphere – the girls were barred from attending. Among Muslims this prompted 'a first step towards creating community structures in an adverse social environment' (Kepel, 1995, p. xxi; see also Leveau in this volume). Among non-Muslims throughout France, elements of the intellectual and popular left and right reacted strongly, making strange bedfellows in some cases and seemingly contradicting themselves in others (just as had occurred in Britain over the 'Rushdie affair') while arguing intermittently for the causes 'tolerance', 'secularism', feminism, anti-racism, and Frenchness.

The cacophony eventually prompted responses by the Conseil d'Etat in 1989 and again in 1992, whereby in principle the wearing of religious symbols in French schools was deemed not incompatible with the broad ideals of laicity. However, the 'affair' will not go away. In late 1994 it re-emerged as dozens more schoolgirls were barred from classes in at least four French cities, stimulating a further wave of anti-Muslim, anti-immigrant sentiment upon which the Education Minister François Bayrou has challenged the State Council's rulings. Even the liberal weekly *L'Express* (17–23 November 1994) has come to portray the headscarf as a potent symbol of Islamic conspiracy. 'Thus,' as Ziauddin Sardar (1995, p. 5) observes, 'a French woman with a scarf is chic, but a Muslim woman with a scarf is a threat to civilisation'. The

wearing of headscarves by Muslim schoolgirls has also proved controversial in Germany (Mandel 1989) and Great Britain (*The Times*, 24
January 1990).

The terms 'Muslim' and 'Islamic' increasingly appeared in European
public space with rather rigid images attached to them, whether originating from Muslim or non-Muslim sources. For non-Muslims, such
images rested on assumptions that in the predominantly Muslim-
populated countries of migrants' origins, everyone is thoroughly
steeped in a single and unitary 'Islam' (van Oijen, 1992). This image of
Islam, further, is one of being 'stuck in the Middle Ages', irrational,
suppressive of women, anti-Western, anti-modern, anti-democratic,
controlled by theocracy, and prone to over-emotionalism and mob-like
public outpourings. Further, because such an Islam was presumed to
determine people's behaviour intrinsically, 'common sense' concludes
that the same traits characterise Muslims 'over here' where they are,
therefore, 'out of place.' Conversely, Sardar (1995) observes, some
Muslims in Europe have uncritically constructed a self-image which
assumes a moral superiority and a monopoly on truth, which sustains a
victimisation complex whereby all Muslims' problems are created by
Western corruption, racism and anti-Islam-ism, and which precludes
the possibility of problems being attributed to within their own ranks.

Both images of Islam and Muslim people do gross injustice to the
broad historical and geographical plasticity and creativity of Islamic
writings, social forms, institutions and practices as found in numerous
'schools' of Islamic law, mystical brotherhoods, devotional and popular
traditions, minority Muslim traditions (such as Ismailis, as well as
Ahmadiyyas and Alevis who are often not accepted by the 'mainstream' Muslim population), regional variations of teachings and practices (even in countries of limited size). Such images also mask
contemporary variations in the manifestation of Islamic belief and practice throughout the world which reflect the nature of any local
rural–urban continuum, class and status structures and levels of education, both religious and secular. Compounding such complexity, too,
are differences among individuals and collectives with respect to the
degree Islam is understood as a private faith or as a public activity, as a
conservative doctrine or a revolutionary agenda.

Besides stereotyping adherents of an entire world religion, an often
unasked question concerns 'who is Muslim?' It is widely presumed that
in the context of Europe, 'Muslim' refers to people deriving from coun-

tries with predominantly Muslim populations and an Islamic civilisa-
tional heritage. This is inappropriate for those who do not wish to be
labelled. One survey of 13 000 foreigners living in France, for instance,
remarkably claimed that 68 per cent of Algerians considered themselves to have no religion (*International Herald Tribune*, 6–7 May
1995). A wholesale definition of 'Muslim' may also distort varieties
and variations in forms and degrees of identification and practice. In
chapter 10 of this volume, Åke Sander explores methodological issues
surrounding criteria indicating Islamic religiosity and for enumerating
'who is Muslim?' in Sweden. In a related manner, Rémy Leveau
describes how young Muslims in France, while they maintain a firm
'Muslim' identity, exhibit attitudes and behaviours strikingly different
from their parents' views of what a 'Muslim' should be.

Another consequence of the 'Muslim' label is that non-Muslim
Europeans – even when they (often rather patronisingly) claim to
accept the depth of attachment Muslims have to their (again, assumed
singular) religion – will point to this as grounds for the notion that
Muslims really cannot, and will not, become part of European society:
that Muslims endemically pose problems concerning 'assimilability'
(Husbands, 1995). Or if local government authorities or other mediators
of the public sphere wish to make some gestures toward Muslim 'integration' – in keeping with co-extensive presumptions surrounding the
nature of immigrant 'communities' and 'cultures' which underpin
emergent political ideologies of multiculturalism – there is the notion
that entire minority populations can be represented and funded via
some unelected, usually older, male, 'community leader' (Vertovec,
1996).

The profound diversity of Muslims in Europe – with respect to
national backgrounds, local and linguistic divisions, characteristics surrounding socio-economic, devotional orientations, settlement histories
and so forth – 'makes it impossible', Fred Halliday (1989, p. 387) suggests, 'to form any general picture or "sociology" of Western European
Muslims'. Halliday (ibid.) argues that,

The variety and fluidity under the apparently universal cover of
Islam touches on a recurrent aspect of all study of 'Islamic' society,
whether in Western Europe or in the relevant Third World countries,
namely how far the very designation 'Islam' provides a key to understanding how such groups behave in the social and political arenas.

... The study of Islamic communities cannot be based on a 'sociology of religion' alone, but must involve a sociology of how religion interacts with other, ethnic, cultural and political forces.

Although a sociology of 'Muslims' as a socio-cultural group *per se* may not be possible, recent developments suggest that a kind of political sociology may serve as an appropriate approach to seeking an understanding of, and to assess accommodations surrounding, what seems at first glance to be a broad new social movement. It is clear that in recent years a 'politics of religion and community' has emerged among Muslims in Europe. On the one hand, such a movement can be seen as part of the broad trend among minority groups in Western societies who have come to advocate a 'politics of difference' or 'politics of recognition'. They argue that states should establish special group rights and privileges meant to offset historically produced conditions of exclusion and discrimination (see Rutherford, 1990; Taylor, 1992; West, 1993). On the other hand, some Muslim commentators assert that a new politics of religion and community among Muslims in the West is but part of a world-wide Islamic awakening.

While demographic, historical and anthropological examinations of the Muslim population in Europe reveal it to be characterised by social, cultural, intellectual and political diversity, these findings must not eclipse the fact that, increasingly on local, national and now even European levels, large numbers of Muslims do indeed mobilise, resist and struggle for rights and social benefits *as Muslims* and as an *'Islamic community'*. Still, as Gilles Kepel points out in the opening essay of this volume, such notions of 'community' among Muslims have been produced through processes of identity reconstruction *vis-à-vis* a variety of evolving characteristics marking the encompassing non-Muslim societies themselves.

A key feature of what we are referring to as 'the politics of religion and community' is the strategy of 'ethnic mobilisation', entailing a process through which ethnic groups self-consciously define themselves by specific criteria of 'belonging', compile and co-ordinate financial and symbolic resources, formalise social networks, institutionalise selected social practices (often by way of invoking – or, indeed, 'inventing' – 'tradition'), and engage the wider public sphere in order to advance group-specific causes (see Rex, 1991; Rex and Drury, 1994; Rogers and Vertovec, 1995). Increasingly in recent years, the discourse of 'community' – a vague yet comfortable notion which civic authorities and minority groups both invoke without defining – has become a core feature of ethnic mobilisation. While, on the positive side, 'community' conveys a warm sense of connectedness among group members, on the negative side it supports implicit assumptions – indeed, stereotypes – that all members of a specific category share the same values, behaviours, goals, leadership and resources (Ålund and Schierup, 1992; Vertovec, 1996). Throughout the West, such a discourse has become common, not only through strategies from within ethnic minority populations, but through state administrative structures which favour ready defined, organised and encapsulated collectivities. Thus, Jørgen Nielsen (1992a, p. 124) observes, 'The pressure imposed on Muslim organisations by European official, legal, political and bureaucratic expectations, is such that Islam has to become an ethnic identity.'

Processes involving moblisation, articulation, and the construction of frameworks for liaison with government authorities comprise key features of a broad new politics of religion and community among Muslims in Europe. This volume is comprised of articles by specialists from a number of social science disciplines exploring dimensions of, and developments surrounding, such processes. Prior to such focused studies, some general treatment of the background and nature of Muslim populations in Europe, and the structural and political situations facing them, should be outlined.

THE MUSLIM PRESENCE IN EUROPE: LEGACY

The presence of Islam in Europe is certainly nothing new: Muslims have been living in and travelling throughout the geographical region for a thousand years, practically since the beginning of historical Islam itself (see Nielsen, 1992a). Yet in addition to the ebb and flow of Muslim social and political presence over centuries, most notably in Spain, Sicily and the Balkans, facets of Islamic civilisation have come to imbue intellectual, artistic and other cultural properties in Western Europe – indeed, European civilisation itself. However, due to often wildly constructed images of Islam, elaborated and amplified historically in order to inspire Christian crusades, to legitimate colonial expansions, or generally to convince Europeans of their moral superiority, Europeans particularly (and in many quarters, increasingly, Muslims too) have come to take it for granted that there is a wide and unbridgeable gulf between two distinct 'worlds' which are poised to feud forever.

The work of W. Montgomery Watt, among others, provides an important corrective to widespread views of the relationship between Europe and Islam. Watt's research and writing does much to deconstruct long-standing European misrepresentations of Islamic values, to further the understanding of the nature of Islam's introduction to, and presence in, Europe during medieval times, and to trace the emergence and evolution of the presumed notion of the 'clash of civilisations.'

Among his contributions, Watt describes how Arab/Muslim expansion across north Africa and into Spain occurred more through alliance and federation than by the sword; how a common Hispano-Arabic culture developed among Muslims and Christians alike during a time when Christians and Jews were protected under Islamic authority – the fabled (albeit often over-romanticised) time of the *convivencia*; how the *reconquista* of Spain was politically stimulated and only later legitimised by reference to religious differences between Christianity and Islam; and how Europeans' distorted image of Islam was constructed between the twelfth and fourteenth centuries largely out of an inferiority complex. Watt emphasises that the influence of Islam on Christendom is far greater than usually realised. While pointing specifically to the contributions Arabic/Islamic civilisation made to the progression of European technological production, scientific discoveries, and philosophical development, Watt also suggests there were more general and subtle influences as well:

> First, the contributions of the Arabs to western Europe were chiefly in respect of matters which tended to be the refinement of life and the improvement of its material basis; second, most Europeans had little awareness of the Arab and Islamic character of what they were adopting; third, the 'gracious living' of the Arabs and the literary tradition that accompanied it stimulated the imagination of Europe and not least the poetic genius of the Romance peoples.   (1972, p. 29)

With a similar view, Roger Garaudy (1984) has described Islam as the third, forgotten pillar of Europe alongside Graeco-Roman and Judaeo-Christian pillars, while Claus Leggewie (1993) proposes that modern Europe should thank Arab/Islamic civilisation for assistance in its very birth.

THE MUSLIM PRESENCE IN EUROPE: CIVILISATIONS, MIGRATIONS, EXODUS

In addition to historical influences in cultural style and intellectual pursuit, Muslims have had substantial demographic impact on Europe. Currently there are in total about 23 million Muslims in Europe as a whole – just over 3.5 per cent of its total population. Among these are over 7 million Muslims who live in western Europe – some 2 per cent of the latter region's total population (see Table 1.1). The resident Muslim population of Europe can be described by way of four distinct historical categories.

The first category consists of groups left by the medieval Mongol empire in the European part of the former USSR (west of the Urals). While Islam was officially 'tolerated' under the Communist regime, the Soviets systematically combated ethnic identification based on religion and, particularly after 1941, forcefully suppressed Muslims and their institutions (see Benningsen and Wimbush, 1985; Ramet, 1989; Teheri, 1989). Following the collapse of the Soviet system, the category today accounts for about 11.5 million people, among whom a reconstruction and revitalisation of Islamic identification and practice is underway.

The second major category arises out of the former Ottoman Turkish empire in the remainder of eastern Europe (see Popovich, 1975; Szajkowski, 1988; Irwin, 1989). Currently this population amounts to just over 5 million Muslims. Former Yugoslavia (about 10 per cent of its one-time population of 23 million), Albania (with about 2.24 million Muslims out of an estimated population total of 3.14 million), and Bulgaria (prior to the recent upheavals, about 750 000 out of 8.7 million) have the largest concentrations in (non-former USSR) eastern Europe. Smaller indigenous pockets of Muslims were left in Greece, Romania and even Austria, Hungary and Finland in the wake of post-First-World-War territorial settlements (Nielsen, 1981, pp. 12–21). In this volume Alexandre Popovic surveys the position of Islam and Muslims in countries throughout south-eastern Europe following the collapse of the Communist system, Yannis Frangopoulos provides an ethnographic account of ethnic–religious dynamics affecting the Muslim Pomak minority in northern Greece, and Bogdan Szajkowski describes the long and important, but largely overlooked, presence of Muslim Tatars in Poland.

Table 1.1   Estimated Muslim population in Eastern and Western Europe

Country	Date	Muslims	Total	Source
Belgium	1990	244 000	9 889 000	SOPEMI (1992, Table 8, p. 135)
Denmark	1990	60 000	5 089 000	Nielsen (1992, p. 77)
France	1990	2 619 000	53 086 000	Peach and Glebe (1995)
Germany	1990	2 012 200	79 365 000	German Yearbook (1991)
Greece	1981	140 000	9 165 000	Nielsen (1981, p. 11)
Italy	1991	250 000	56 024 000	SOPEMI (1992, p. 66)
Netherlands	1990	441 900	13 838 000	Netherlands Year Book (1990)
Portugal	1975	30 000	9 449 000	Nielsen (1981, p. 11)
Spain	1990	40 000	36 260 000	SOPEMI (1992)
UK	1991	1 000 000	56 000 000	Peach and Glebe (1995)
European Community		**6 837 100**	**328 165 000**	
Austria	1990	62 000	2 548 000	Peach/SOPEMI (1992, p. 141)
Finland	1980	1 500	4 739 000	Nielsen (1981, p. 11)
Norway	1990	20 000	4 200 000	Nielsen (1992, p. 85)
Sweden	1989	60 000	8 255 000	Nielsen (1992, p. 81)
Switzerland	1990	78 000	6 366 000	Peach/SOPEMI (1992, p. 40)
Other West Europe		**221 500**	**26 108 000**	
Albania		1 750 000	2 548 000	Nielsen (1981, p. 11)
Bulgaria	1978	750 000	8 761 000	Nielsen (1981, p. 11)
Hungary	1977	30 000	10 654 000	Nielsen (1981, p. 11)
Poland	1977	15 000	37 571 000	Nielsen (1981, p. 11)
Romania	1979	35 000	21 446 000	Nielsen (1981, p. 11)
Yugoslavia	1988	2 450 000	23 559 000	German Yearbook (1989)
Eastern non-Soviet Europe		**5 030 000**	**104 539 000**	
European former Soviet Union		**11 500 000**	**186 431 000**	
TOTAL EUROPE		**23 589 600**	**645 153 000**	

The third category of Muslims in Europe refers to the much more recent population in western Europe that has come as immigrant labour from the 1950s to the 1970s. Since 1945, western Europe has experienced successive waves of immigration (Peach, 1992). One involved the post-war phase of returning nationals displaced by new frontiers or by processes of decolonisation. Another phase surrounded the massive flow of workers and later their dependants, who now account for about 15 million persons in the European Community. Finally there has been a flow of refugees, in some cases liberated to travel by the political upheavals of eastern Europe, in some cases claiming political status now that the economic doors have closed, but increasingly cases displaced by the civil wars in the former Yugoslavia. The different flows of migration have overlapped and have interacted with each other. The final two categories characterising Muslims in Europe are embedded in these same, broader processes of post-war movement.

There are about 6.6 million Muslims in the European Union, now outnumbering those in the traditional Eastern European areas outside the former USSR (see Figure 1.1). France, Britain and Germany are the main countries of settlement, but as described briefly below, the size, settlement histories, cultural backgrounds and ethnic identities of the main Muslim groups in each country differ considerably (see Nielsen, 1992a).

French Muslims are overwhelmingly from North Africa, particularly Algeria, though with an increasing sub-Saharan West African element from Senegal and Mali. There is also a significant Turkish population (about 200 000 in 1990 according to SOPEMI, 1992) about half being Kurds (Nielsen, 1992a, p. 9). The French Muslim population is much larger, and arrived earlier, than Britain's, for instance, due to the tighter constitutional attachment of Algeria to France than the British colonial territories to Britain.

French statistics are much more difficult to unravel with regard to ethnicity than those of most other European countries. There is a large number of second and third generation Muslims living in France whom the statistics on foreign birthplace do not enumerate. A French law of 1978 forbids the collection of religious data by government agencies (Nielsen, 1992a, p. 11). The highest estimate of Muslims living in France is a figure of 3.5 million given by the Prime Ministerial Commission on the *Harkis* (Mission de Réfléxion, 1991, p. 24), but with no explanation of the figure's origin. Etienne (1989, p. 30) gives a figure of 2.45 million Muslims, while Nielsen has radically revised his earlier estimate of 2 million in 1979 (Nielsen, 1981, p. 11) to 3 million in the late 1980s (Nielsen, 1992a, p. 11).

· Two sources of difficulty in computing the number of French Muslims are the *Harkis* and the '*Beurs*'. The *Harkis* are Algerians and

16

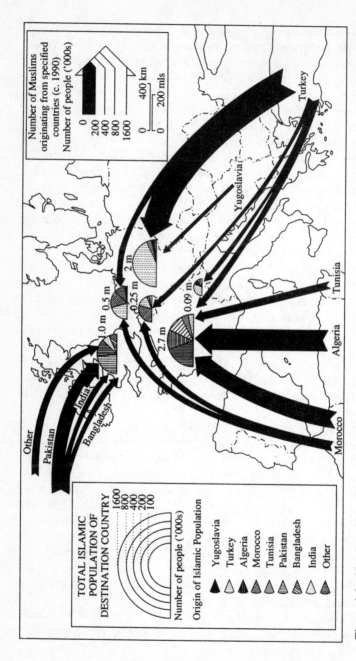

Figure 1.1 Number of Muslims originating from specified countries, total Islamic population of destination countries, c. 1990

Table 1.2 Estimates of the composition of the Muslim population of selected West European countries, by country of origin, 1990

Country of origin / Destination:	Belgium	France	Germany	Netherlands	United Kingdom	Switzerland	Total
Turkey	84.9	201.5	1 675.1	203.5	12.0	64.9	2 241.90
Algeria	10.7	619.9	6.7	0.7	3.6	2.5	644.10
Morocco	141.6	584.7	67.5	156.9	9.0	3.2	962.90
Tunisia	6.3	207.5	25.9	2.6	2.4	2.5	247.20
Yugoslavia*	0.6	5.2	65.3	1.4	1.4	11.7	98.00
Iran		50.0	89.7		3.2		172.00
Afghanistan			30.0				30.00
Pakistan			17.0		475.8		492.80
Bangladesh			23.0		160.3		183.30
India*			12.0		168.2	3.8	184.00
Indonesia				9.5			9.50
Other		1000		67.2	139.2		1 206.40
TOTAL	244.1	2 668.8	2 012.2	441.8	975.40	88.6	6 430.90

* The Yugoslav figures represent the 10 per cent of the population which is thought to be Muslim; the Indian figures represent the 20 per cent of the population which is thought to be Muslim.

Belgium: Based on SOPEMI (1992).

France: Based on SOPEMI (1992). The 'Other' category refers to 100 000 West Africans, 300 000 *Harkis* and 600 000 *Beurs*.

Germany: SOPEMI (1992). The German census of 1987 gives a figure of 1 650 952 Muslims.

Netherlands: SOPEMI (1992). The Netherlands Yearbook (1990) gives a figure of 405 900 Muslims. The Indonesian figure comes from this source. The 'Other' figure is a balancing term to arrive at the Yearbook total.

UK: Based on an update of Peach (1990) and special tabulations from the 1991 census.

Switzerland: These figures are taken from the *Statistisches Jahrbuch der Schweiz* (1992, T1.30, p. 39).

their children who fought for, or were involved with, the French side against the Algerian independence movement and who fled to France at Algerian independence in 1962. The professional classes assimilated into French life, but the rest often languished in camps. They now experience, in many cases, considerable alienation from both the French and other Algerian immigrants (Mission de Réfléxion, 1991). The *Harkis* are estimated by both Etienne (1989, p. 30) and Nielsen (1992a, p. 10) to number up to 450 000. However, given its starting base of 140 000 in 1968 (when last officially enumerated by the Census) and the fact that it cannot be replenished from the outside, 250 000 seems a more reasonable estimate for the early 1990s. The '*Beurs*' – children of Maghrebian immigrants – are estimated to number between 450 000 by Nielsen (1992a, p. 11) and 600 000 by Etienne (1989, p. 30). The higher figure for children born in France seems more likely, amounting to about one-third of the population born in Algeria, Tunisia and Morocco and now living in France.

A final Muslim minority category of significant size is that of West Africans living in France, who are estimated to have numbered some 100 000 in 1989 (Nielsen,1992a, p. 11). Taking all these categories together, the likeliest estimate, then, is about 2.7 million persons with Muslim backgrounds – albeit with diverse identities by way of origins and generation, to name but two variables – living in France in 1990.

The probable Muslim population in Britain in 1951 was about 23 000. By 1961, there were about 82 000 Muslims in Britain, by 1971 about 369 000, by 1981 about 553 000 (Peach, 1990b) and by 1991 about 1 million. These numbers are based on the ethnic origin of the minority population of Britain and about 75 per cent is made up of groups originating in the South Asian sub-continent (see Table 1.2).

There were small communities in Britain, largely in port areas such as Cardiff, Tyneside, Liverpool and London that dated back to the beginning of the century (Little, 1947; Collins, 1957; Halliday, 1992). Many Somali, Yemeni and Bengali seamen had been stranded by their ships in the depression of the inter-war years. The main migrant stream to Britain from Pakistan and India got under way in the late 1950s (see Clarke *et al.*, 1992). The late 1960s and early 1970s saw the expulsion of Asians from East Africa, some 200 000 of whom fled to Britain: about a quarter of their number was Muslim (Brown, 1984), among whom was a significant proportion of Ismailis. The most recent and rapidly growing group arriving in the 1970s and 1980s has been the

Bangladeshis, whose migration to Britain differs from that of many other Muslim groups in that it seems unrelated to economic demand for labour (Peach, 1990a). According to the 1991 census, there were 475 000 ethnic Pakistanis in Great Britain, 160 000 Bangladeshis (Owen, 1993) and 168 000 Indian Muslims (assuming one-fifth of the Indian ethnic population of 840 800) in Britain. This would suggest a total of about 804 000 Muslims from these areas.

In addition to the Muslims of South Asian origin in Britain, there are Arabs and Somalis whose numbers are disputed – but an estimate of about 120 000 is not unreasonable (Halliday, 1992; El-Solh, 1992, 1993; Labour Force Survey, Census, 1991). Estimating numbers from the Middle East in Britain is complicated by the fact that place of birth includes children who were born to members of the British forces serving in Egypt and Libya before British withdrawal from those countries, so that there is no direct relationship between numbers born in Egypt and Libya and those of Muslim identity. Similar problems arise with regard to Cyprus.

Germany has the most recent record of Muslim movement. The numbers are dominated by the Turks whose arrival in substantial numbers began in 1961, regulated by bilateral agreements between the German and Turkish governments. In 1961 there were 6700 Turks in Germany. By 1970 there were 429 000; by 1976 there were over 1 million; by 1981, 1.5 million and the number has fluctuated about that total since then. There were in 1990 1.67 million Turks in Germany; a more recent estimate is just over 2 million (Peach and Glebe, 1995). Not all Turkish nationals are Muslim, of course. Apart from staunch secularists – of whom there are many – there are significant groups of Armenian and Syrian Orthodox Christians. Moreover, the Muslim Turks are ethnically, culturally and linguistically quite heterogeneous (Schmuck, 1982). Among Turkish nationals living in Germany, Kurds, the largest minority living in Turkey, are estimated to be as much as 25 per cent of the population, or about 400 000.

Due to a continuous flow of family members of Turks and other long-standing minorities, to more recent migrations of persons whose origins lay in the Maghreb (often by way of another European country), and particularly to growth in the number of asylum seekers from Muslim states such as Iran, Afghanistan and Pakistan and from states with a large Muslim minority like India and especially Yugoslavia, numbers have continued to grow. In 1990, the Muslim population was estimated at just over 2 million (see Tables 1.1 and 1.2), of whom over 80 per cent had origins in Turkey. The German census of 1987 was the first to record Islam as a religion, giving a figure of 1 650 952 Muslims. However, Nielsen (1992a, p. 26) emphasises that the census included some 100 000 Turks who did not declare themselves to be Muslim (although he does not cite the source for this). Nielsen also states that there are also about 5000 German converts to Islam.

The fourth and final category of Muslims in Europe are refugees. They fall into two groups: those seeking refuge from radical Islamic regimes in the Middle East and those displaced by the upheavals in the former socialist bloc, particularly the victims of 'ethnic cleansing' in the former Yugoslavia. Apart from the expulsion of Greeks and Armenians from Turkey and the expulsion of Turks from Greece in the first part of the century, there have been considerable shifts of Christians and Muslims. A small Turkish Muslim minority (129 000) remains in north-eastern Greece, but under circumstances of considerable discrimination. As mentioned above, in 1962 Algerian independence led to the flight of 1 million former colonial settlers to France. The civil war in Lebanon in the 1970s and 1980s has seen a polarisation of the geographical territories of Christians and Muslims there. Cyprus was partitioned between Turks and Greeks in 1974. An estimated 320 000 Turkish Muslims fled Bulgaria in 1989. In early 1991, at least 3500 Christian Greeks (out of an estimated total of 59 000 in the country) fled from Albania into Greece. From the Shah's downfall in 1979, the number of Iranians in Germany tripled to 90 000 in 1990 (SOPEMI, 1992, p. 136); in France in the late 1980s there were some 50 000 Iranians and 31 000 Iranians in Great Britain in 1991 according to the census. Estimates of the number of Iraqis in Britain (many of them refugees from Saddam's regime) put the figure at about 80 000 (Al Rasheed, 1992).

Probably the most notorious of the displacements, however, has been that of the Yugoslav, especially Bosnian, Muslims. In August 1992, it was estimated that there were 1.98 million Yugoslav refugees within the former Yugoslavia, of whom 681 000 were from Bosnia-Herzegovina (*The Economist*, 19 September 1992). By 1994 estimates suggested that up to a half million refugees from former Yugoslavia had been displaced to other parts of Europe (*The Independent*, 28 January 1994). Among these refugee populations within or outside the borders of former Yugoslavia it is not possible to say how many are 'ethnically Muslim'. This official category formed about 10 per cent of the total population of former Yugoslavia, but areas of Muslim concentration in Bosnia-Herzegovina have been, to say the least, disproportionately affected by the war and the competing strategies of 'ethnic cleansing'. Prospects for the return of Muslim refugee populations to the region of former Yugoslavia appear bleak.

The statistics and problems of enumeration described in the above section reflect, in one way, the diversity of past and present Muslim populations in Europe. Differential histories of settlement, collective organisation and modes of interaction with Western European public authorities, as described below, represent other important, evolving indicators of their complexity.

TRANSFORMATIONS OF STRUCTURES AND STRATEGIES

It is primarily among the category of post-war immigrants in Western Europe that the politics of religion and community have recently arisen, and this particularly in the years following 1973. In the wake of that year's devastating OPEC oil price increases, the onset of a world-wide economic recession, and the consequent creation of new barriers to foreign labour enacted by governments across Europe, there was a dramatic decrease in labour migration into Europe. This, in turn, brought about a significant change in the demographic structure of immigrant, including Muslim, communities. Up to this time, the largest part of the migration was of single men whose strategy was to work temporarily in Europe and invest earned income in their places of origin. With the restrictions upon further labour immigration, men were faced with the decision of returning to less favourable economic conditions in their homelands, or of bringing their families to join them in their countries of immigration. Many returned to their countries of origin, but their numbers in Europe were more than compensated for by the arrival of women and children.

Thus, with the reunion of families especially since the 1970s, the demographic structure of Muslim communities has become more balanced. For example, among Turks in Germany in 1974 the male:female ratio was 180:100 and 139:100 in 1981; in 1987 it was 128:100 for the total Muslim population in Germany. In Great Britain in 1981, the male:female ratio among the Bangladeshi-born population was 201:100 but among the longer established Pakistani population, 131:100. By 1991 the ratio of Bangladeshi-born men to women was 113:100 and for Pakistani-born persons 104:100.

With the change in social structure, it followed that the establishment of religious institutions became increasingly more important to Muslim communities in Europe. This was essentially because of the relatively new and growing responsibilities of rearing children in non-Islamic environments. 'The context into which Muslim families settled in Europe was one where nothing could be taken for granted in terms of access to Islamic facilities', Nielsen (1992a, p. 119) points out: 'The provision of facilities for prayer, teaching Islam to children, access to *halal* food and proper burial – these and many other matters which had been taken for granted at home now had to be consciously sought out.' The realities of permanence, the desire for an assured reproduction of religious traditions, and the will to direct the trajectory of Islamic values and practices among Muslim youth have continued to provide the main motivations for Muslim mobilisations in Europe. 'Many of these campaigns reflect alarm about the maintenance of control within the community', Fred Halliday (1989, p. 387) suggests, 'more than about the threat from a non-Islamic world without: in every country Islamic leaders express concern about the degree to which the second-generation immigrants, by now up to half of the total, will continue to respect the faith.'

In addition to the stimulus of concerns arising from the socio-cultural and demographic shifts following the reunification of families in the 1970s, by this decade Muslim organisational efforts were facilitated by migrants' greater familiarity with procedural and administrative structures in European civic arenas, as well as by the growing role of a generation of Muslims who were born and/or were largely raised and educated in local contexts of Europe. Overall, since the 1970s and particularly in the 1980s, Europe witnessed an upsurge of Islamic socio-religious development which has been fairly well documented by sociologists (see especially Gerholm and Lithman, 1988; Nielsen, 1992a; Rex 1994), often in terms of processes of institutionalisation (Rath *et al.*, 1991; Dwyer and Meyer, 1995, Doomernik, 1995), ethnic mobilisation (Rex, 1991) and public incorporation (Vertovec, 1996).

As Muslim groups have increasingly and more effectively organised themselves to engage with local administrations, national policy frameworks, and other areas of the public domain, they have voiced their concerns by broadening their agendas to address an ever wider set of social and political spheres. These include the construction of mosques, the freedom to exercise religious practices, the pursuit of educational matters, the granting of official 'recognition' and the gaining of political representation. These spheres are themselves variably conditioned by ever evolving contextual considerations including: national political discourses (surrounding, for instance, laicism in France, 'pillarisation' in the Netherlands, federalism in Germany, pluralism in Belgium, 'multiculturalism' in Britain); aspects of national legislation (including those regulating the relationship between religion and the state); specific national and local policies concerning foreigners or citizen minorities; popular racisms and xenophobias and their variable modes of expression and operation; and specific images and prejudices surrounding new, local manifestations of 'anti-Islam-ism' (see Shadid and van Koningsveld, 1995; Nielsen, 1992a).

Elements of the politics of religion and community as engaged by Muslim are also significantly conditioned by differential developments concerning 'race' and ethnic relations in each country, including: policies developed by national and local authorities with regard to discrimination, anti-racism, and 'integration'; the evolving nature of processes, successes and failures involving the mobilisation and public incorporation of non-Muslim minorities; the emergence of official categorisations as well as self-ascriptions of ethnic–national–linguistic groups (which may either recognise 'Muslim' as an identity, or ignore it); and the emergence broad anti-racist political fronts (which also may or may not endorse 'Muslim' identity and Islamic concerns; see, for instance, Modood, 1993a, 1994).

While socio-political activity among Muslim minorities has emerged alongside such broader developments among ethnic minorities in different European contexts, however, Muslims have arguably faced particularly difficulties within a socio-political landscape coloured by the expansion of negative images of Islam in the media (Nielsen, 1994; Dwyer and Meyer, 1995). In this volume, problems and prospects surrounding the representation of Muslims and Islam in European media are addressed by Stefano Allievi and Nico Landman.

Resulting from their campaigns over the past two decades, Muslims have enjoyed a number of successes in lobbying political authorities in several European countries, hardly any in some countries, or – as is most widely the case – a combination of success in some spheres and frustration in others. Recent overviews by Nielsen (1992a) and Shadid and van Koningsveld (1995) have described, country-by-country in the majority of Western European states, the variability of accommodations extended by political authorities to Muslims. What follows here, instead, is but an outline of key issues or spheres of activity which have characterised the politics of religion and community among Muslims in Europe.

THE POLITICS OF RELIGION AND COMMUNITY: KEY SPHERES OF ACTIVITY

The rapid development of Muslim social organisation in Europe can be observed in *creation of Islamic institutions*. Like the general size of the Muslim population, the number of such institutions rose rapidly in the 1970s. This growth is doubtless linked with the reunion of immigrant families during this period. The presence of families stimulated, among the migrants and refugees, thoughts of permanent settlement which, in turn, raised awareness of the need for a variety of forms of communal religious expression: (a) proper mosques for collective prayer; (b) madrassahs and Qur'anic schools for religious education of the young; and (c) formal associations for local and national co-ordination with regard to funding, liaising with government authorities, lobbying for religious accommodations, and safeguarding collective rights.

In Britain, by way of example, Nielsen (1992b, pp. 44–5) points out that in 1963 there was a total of 13 mosques registered with the Registrar–General; by 1970 this increased to 49 mosques, 99 in 1975, 203 in 1980 and 338 by 1985. However, these figures represent only those mosques officially registered: many more, particularly very small ones based in converted houses (sometimes unapproved by local government) do not appear in such figures. One recent survey (conducted by the Religious Resources Centre, University of Derby, UK, and the Inter-Faith Network for the UK) suggests there are at least 849 mosques, registered and unregistered, located in Britain; added to these, the survey names no less than a further 950 British Muslim organisations. These numbers are especially impressive when compared with the relative handful of mosques – and virtual dearth of formal organisations – which existed in Britain in the early 1960s. In Germany, too, the growth has been from practically no mosques in the 1960s to over

800 at present. As Muslim communities have continued to raise funds for the opening of new mosques in many places, they have also campaigned for the establishment of Islamic prayer facilities in workplaces, prisons, schools, universities and hospitals.

While driven by the concerns of local Muslims themselves, Islamic institutionalisation in Europe has often been importantly facilitated by other agents. Kepel (1987) has described the rapid proliferation of mosques and other Muslim places of worship in France which has taken place since the 1970s. This process witnessed a combination of agents and motivations, including not only Muslim migrants and their desire for religious practice, but the French government acting to 'buy social peace' by extending certain provisions to the Muslim minorities, French industrial institutions trying to counter the leftist presence in workplaces, international associations (especially Tablighi Jamaat) looking to gain influence in diaspora Muslim communities, and foreign governments (particularly Algeria, Morocco and Saudi Arabia) wanting to assure themselves of a hand in the developing affairs of Islam in France.

The proliferation of mosques in most European countries has stimulated various forms of anti-Muslim backlash. For example, in Germany, all applications for mosque-building in the city of Hannover have been turned down due to public protests (Antes, 1994). In Britain, Muslim efforts to gain permission to establish mosques have fuelled heated debates about the nature of local 'belonging' and the 'right' to use public space in Tower Hamlets and Ealing (Eade, 1993). French cases include Lebercourt, where the mayor organised an illegal referendum asking citizens if they would tolerate the erection of a mosque, and Charvieu-Chavagneux, where a mosque has actually been destroyed (Cesari, forthcoming).

Although mosques provide a readily visible record of Islamic community development, in the United Kingdom, at least, Muslims first really entered the sphere of public debate in the early 1980s with regard to matters surrounding *aspects of Islamic practice*. One central concern has been the provision of *halal* (sanctioned) food in schools and other public institutions such as prisons and hospitals. Muslim organisations engaged local government and educational authorities with calls for such provision, and this relatively new strength of Muslim purpose was given increasing attention in newspapers and public meetings. One of the key controversies which subsequently arose from such attention

PTO.

was not the provision itself, but the fact that Islamic ritual slaughter (*dhabh*) was abhorred by many non-Muslims since it is often interpreted as prescribing that the animal remain conscious when its throat is slit. The most vocal opponents to Muslim calls for *halal* food provision emerged as the unlikely pairing of animal rights activists, who were against the method of slaughter, and right-wing nationalists, who were against accommodating seemingly alien customs of minorities (see Charlton and Kaye, 1985). The right to engage in ritual slaughter in inspected abattoirs was maintained, largely through the political lobbying of Jewish rather than Muslim groups, and provision of *halal* food soon became standard practice in British public institutions of many kinds, schools not least.

Another kind of ritual slaughter – the killing of sheep by Muslim households on the annual festival of Eid el Kebir – has continued to be controversial in France. While authorities have tended to turn a blind eye to the practice (which accounts for the slaughter of some 60 000 sheep in the Ile-de-France alone) or to make special public arrangements for the day (as in Val-d'Oise département, where authorised sites and Muslim professional sacrificers are provided), here, too, animal rights activists and elements of the far right have allied in a campaign against the 'throat-slitting of French sheep' by immigrants (*Le Monde/Guardian Weekly*, 29 May 1994).

The call for accommodations regarding other forms of Islamic religious practice has also included matters surrounding burial, such as gaining designated areas of public cemeteries for Muslims, obtaining permission for burial in a cloth shroud instead of a coffin, and urging speedy issuing of death certificates for burial within twenty-four hours.

Concerns surrounding the raising of Muslim families in Europe have naturally led to lobbying with regard to aspects of *education* (see Parker-Jenkins, 1995; Joly, 1995). The concerns and needs of Muslim parents which have prompted such lobbying include: expressed preference for single-sex education, especially for girls; modesty in dress and in physical education activities (such as swimming, showers, changing rooms) – again, especially for girls; accommodating Muslim prayer times and religious holidays in the school timetable and calendar; providing *halal* food in school cafeterias; providing for Islamic collective worship among Muslim pupils, or exempting them from Christian-oriented collective worship; being sensitive to Muslim concerns over aspects of curriculum including sex education, aspects of art, dance and music, and of course the entire subject of religious education; and more Muslim staff members and schools' governors.

In only a few European countries have Islamic schools received state support (see Shadid and van Koningsveld, 1995). Claire Dwyer and Astrid Meyer (1995) observed that the outcomes of such calls have been strongly conditioned not only by national legislation but by the variable strength of local (Muslim and non-Muslim) support for such schools, the effectiveness of lobbying efforts by local Muslim groups, and – not least – the influence of constructed representations of 'Muslims' on the local non-Muslim population. Regardless of whether Islamic schools – state or privately funded – exist, in most places for most Muslims Islamic education takes place in supplementary schools which run at mosques or in private homes during evenings and weekends.

Another key public sphere which concerns Muslims in Europe is that of *law* – particularly family law, which includes matters of marriage (including polygamy and arranged marriage), divorce, custody of children, and inheritance. However, as Nielsen (1992a, p.104) points out, 'the perceptions of what is legitimate or illegitimate in family relations among Muslims settled in Europe are related very much to what particular combination of these four areas of Shari'a, custom, modern legislation and current administrative practice they bring with them, as well as the specific content of the four.' Given the breadth of localised Islamic traditions whence Muslims in Europe derive, no unitary Islamic jurisprudence has been presented to state authorities. Moreover, for most Muslims, Nielsen (1992a, p. 106) notes, the complex issues of Islamic and Western law remain irrelevant until such time as specific situations needing legal rulings arise.

Each effort in mobilising and lobbying – whether successful, unsuccessful, or still in process – has brought new experience and, thereby, new confidence in Muslim organisational efforts. This, in turn, has encouraged the engagement in recent years of new spheres of concern and activity around *access to resources* and *social service provision*. Examples of such activity can be seen in applications by Muslim women's groups seeking public funding for education and community activities, the rise of Muslim housing associations and employment advice centres, and calls by Muslims for special promotion of health awareness campaigns and programmes and the provision of suitable hospital facilities (see *British Muslims Monthly Survey*, 1995). Tariq Modood (1993a, pp. 516–17) has pointed to a number of other related areas, in Britain at least, in which forms of disadvantage affecting Muslims still need to be addressed. These include:

same-race adoption and fostering policies which place black Muslims with black Christians, and Asian Muslims with Hindus and Sikhs; social work based on Asian needs which can lead to a Muslim being given a Hindu home-help who does not know about Muslim sensitivities or whose own inhibitions (about meat for example) prevent her from fulfilling her duties; the recent decision by the Housing Corporation to reverse its policy of registering housing associations catering for religious communities in favour of race; recruitment monitoring and targeting in terms of 'Black' or 'Asian' statistics which obscure the level of Muslim disadvantage and under-representation and fail to measure whether the equal opportunity policies are making any difference to the Muslim position; arts funding for anti-Muslim but not Islamic artists; racial harassment figures which fail to register that the majority of victims are Muslims and that there is a specific anti-Muslim harassment which even white Muslims suffer.

In the past two decades and through the present, calls and campaigns for such various kinds of accommodation have been organised largely by formal associations.

TOWARDS ACCOMMODATION: ASSOCIATIONS, 'RECOGNITION', REPRESENTATION AND LEGISLATION

Muslim associations in Europe can be distinguished according to the following rough typology, in categories which are by no means mutually exclusive (see Waardenburg, 1988; Nielsen, 1988, 1992a; Vertovec, 1994; Shadid and van Koningsveld, 1995).

(1) Those which arose as 'grass-roots' organisations to serve perceived needs of a local community – including those specific to certain neighbourhoods, kinship groups, Muslim minority traditions (e.g. Ismailis), national or regional origins, linguistic groups, or social

groups such as youths, women, or students. (2) Those which were set up as an extension of organisations in a country of origin (for example Jamaat-i-Islami, a prominent Islamicist political party in Pakistan tied closely with Muslim organisations in Britain – specifically the Islamic Foundation, the UK Islamic Mission, Young Muslims UK and Dawat-ul-Islam – see Andrews (1993); or the Turkish groups described in this volume by Werner Schiffauer and Valérie Amiraux). (3) Those which are an extension of the government of another country (such as the Turkish Department of Religious Affairs, or Diyanet), (4) have obvious close ties with the government of another country (exemplified by the Grand Mosque of Paris and its connections with Algeria), or (5) which have benefited only financially from contributions by the government of another country (no political or other ties are known to have derived, for instance, from Saddam Hussein's contribution of £2 million for a mosque in Birmingham which still bears his name or from Saudi Arabia's supposed investment of some £50 million in British Islam during the 1980s; *The Economist*, 26 January 1991). (6) Those which are attached to an international Islamic organisation, mystical fraternity or religious movement (such as Tablighi Jamaat, described in chapter 7 by John King). And (7) those which have been set up, co-ordinated or backed by national or local government agencies (an example of the former is the Islamic Cultural Centre in Belgium (see Nielsen, 1992a, pp. 69–75) and of the latter, the Bradford Council of Mosques described by Philip Lewis in chapter 6).

Other kinds of Islamic organisations have been established within Europe as fund-raising outposts of movements elsewhere. As described in a feature article in *The Guardian* (7 February 1994), outside the Regent's Park mosque in London every Friday there are numerous groups gathering donations for various Muslim causes in Algeria, Palestine, Iraq, Egypt and, increasingly, Bosnia. Among the active overseas groups are Al Muntada al Islami (linked with the Middle Eastern Salafi movement), Muslim Welfare House (said to be linked with the Algerian Front islamique du salut, or FIS), and the Palestine and Lebanon Relief Fund (believed linked with the Palestinian Hamas movement). Although perhaps raising the consciousness of some, the role of these Islamicist groups among British Muslims is extremely peripheral and their impact, very limited. In France, by contrast, the underground impact of FIS in particular is doubtless much more significant (see *L'Express*, 6 May 1993).

Summarising the changing nature of Muslim associational activity across Europe, Nielsen (1992b, p. 16) observes that,

> The decade until 1988 had witnessed a major change in the way in which Muslim organisations took part in public life. They had previously been marginal and often timid; they had tended to implicitly present themselves as ethnic minorities as they sought to fit in through the community and race relations structures. By the end of the decade many had laid claim to participation in the public space; they had effectively integrated into the organisational politics of the local scene functioning like most other special interest groups, standing out only by the express Muslim identity.

Indeed, times have changed considerably. Now, not only are matters such as those described above often accommodated routinely, but Muslim organisations are in some cities regularly included in local government consultations regarding community relations matters. On both local and national levels, there have been efforts to create forums, boards or other umbrella organisations to provide a common front in dealing with political authorities. While some successes of this kind are evident (such as the Bradford Council of Mosques and Leicester's Federation of Muslim Organisations; see Lewis in this volume and Vertovec, 1994), however, in most European contexts Islam has been characterised by a failure to forge common fronts among various Muslim associations. And it is such obvious disunity (not surprising given Muslims' complex and diverse origins) to which government authorities across Europe point by way of refusing to respond to Muslims' socio-political overtures.

The lack of effective umbrella organisations has had many consequences in terms of access to public resources and representation. In Germany, to be recognised for public corporate status (*Körperschaft des öffentlichen Rechts*) under Section 14 of the Basic Law, a religion has to fulfil a number of requirements based on assumptions concerning Christian churches: it has to be of a 'permanent character'; it has to be an established organisation, with clearly defined responsibilities of board members and independently appointed priests; and it should be autonomous and free of any kind of external control. German authorities point to the lack of any central organising body among Muslims in Germany as a key factor in denying public corporate status. The lack of 'permanency' with regard to German Muslim organisations acts as an impediment as well: 'However,' Shadid and van Koningsveld (1995, p. 53) point out, 'the lack of permanency ascribed to these organisations seems to be mainly due to the fact that Germany denies the idea of permanency to immigration in general.'

German tax-payers in established churches can nominate their organisation to receive 9 per cent of the income tax gathered from them. Muslims, lacking this status, cannot do so. Religion organisations recognised as public law corporations are not liable for taxation themselves, but rather are entitled to government subsidies. Moreover, 'having obtained the status of a public law corporation means a considerable increase in both prestige and actual possibilities of securing, for instance, the rights of the Muslim minority in matters of educational or cultural policy' (Abdullah, 1989, p. 445).

Yet the quest for recognition and its benefits – as positive as many of these may be – arguably may have had the effect of actually limiting the scope of socio-political activity among Muslims in Germany. According to Peter O'Brien (1988, p. 129),

> The large [Islamic] associations ... show support for rather than resistance to government policy. In their effort to curry favor with the German officials who possess the power to confer the title of officially recognized religious denomination, the associations tone down and/or avoid any critique of German government and society. Thus, each association's charter underscores the given group's respect for the German political order and denies attempts to reject and denounce it.

In some contexts where official 'recognition' has been extended by the state, this has actually stimulated disunity. From the mid-1960s, Muslims in Austria lobbied the government to take the view that imperial laws of 1874 and 1912 recognising Islam were still in force (Nielsen, 1992a, pp. 91–2). They succeeded in 1979, when the Austrian government agreed that the existing laws provided a legal foundation for recognising Islam in the new, post-immigration context. Advantages of this recognition include provision of Islamic religious instruction in Austrian state schools, access to public broadcasting, and certain advantages with regard to taxation. In the wake of official recognition, however, conflicts among various ethnic and political–

religious groups ensued as the makeup and nature of the required national Muslim council was contested. In a related fashion, in Belgium a law of 1870 making provisions for Islam was superseded by government recognition in 1974. But struggles among Muslim groups and in government circles for acknowledging who is to maintain the central role of liaising on behalf of all Muslims has created a kind of stalemate in which no authoritative representative body exists and, therefore, Belgian Muslims do not receive the considerable financial support guaranteed by Belgian law (Shadid and van Koningsveld, 1995, pp. 51–2).

In the Netherlands, the Dutch constitution enshrines equality for all religious groups, so 'recognition' as such is not really an issue. This originally stems from a political philosophy designed to establish parity of Catholics and Protestants, but now it is a convention increasingly relied upon by Muslim and Hindu minorities (Rath *et al.*, 1991). The Dutch legal framework is in stark contrast with the United Kingdom, where there is no such written constitution and where the 'establishment' of the Church of England arguably acts as a barrier to the recognition and equal treatment of Muslim and other religious minorities (Modood, 1994). This situation, coupled with the common problem of perceived 'Muslim community' disunity, has greatly limited the extent of socio-political accommodations for British Muslims. This was apparent in March 1994 when a delegation of British Muslims met with the British Home Secretary, Michael Howard. He curtly rejected their request to consider legislation combating religious discrimination and told them to come back when a united Islamic representative body had been formed so that the government would know with whom it should negotiate. Yet 'The Home Office refused to reply why the Home Secretary felt the Muslim delegation was not representative of the Muslim community when it was the Home Office which invited them as representatives of the Muslims' (*Muslim News*, 25 March 1994).

In France the situation has shifted rather suddenly. Instead of waiting for Muslim groups to come forward with a united front, the government has virtually decreed one. In January 1995 French Interior Minister Charles Pasqua recognised the Conseil représentatif des musulmans de France (CRMF) as the official body which is to speak for Islam in France. This body stems from the highly moderate and intellectual group which comprises the consultative council of the Grand Mosque of Paris, which, in turn, is considered to have close ties to the (also French-backed) government of Algeria (*Le Monde*, 12 January 1995). While some Muslims see Pasqua's measure as essentially something to be welcomed, for it opens new possibilities for the acceptance and socio-political participation of a 'French Islam', it has also been severely criticised by some more activist Muslim organisations who have been excluded from the official Council (*Le Croix*, 12 January 1995). Overall, Pasqua's move was politically very shrewd as it publicly portrayed a major positive gesture toward Muslim minorities only weeks after the Air France hijacking – which fuelled non-Muslims' fears and suspicions of Islam and of Maghrebians – and after months of heavy police crackdowns on foreigners, which had portrayed Pasqua and his ministry as harbouring severe attitudes toward Muslims in France.

Despite some successes in uniting as a single voice so as to liaise with national and local government authorities, fragmentation and lack of a common front has generally plagued the politics of religion and community among Muslims in Europe. Jacques Waardenburg (1991, p. 34) suggests that rivalries underpinning relations among various Muslim groups in Europe have a combination of causes:

> They are due, above all, to socio-psychological forces within and between minority groups: struggles for leadership, the reflex of self-defence against outside interference, fear that a rival group may enjoy more privileges from the state or other institutions. The pressures of unemployment, discrimination and economic and social *déclassement* intensify such conflicts, in which Islam plays no real role but rather hides what happens from outsiders. This accounts at least in part for the fruitlessness of so many efforts to create more cohesion between the many Muslim associations which exist in European countries, on the basis of Islam.

In their wide-ranging review of relevant developments affecting Muslims in Europe, Shadid and van Koningsveld (1995, p. 58) find that 'Spain can be considered to be the only country of the European Union to have legally solved the problem of a representational body of Muslims on a national level.' Since 1992 the Spanish state has officially recognised the Comisión islámica de España as the body responsible for all Muslims in the country. One wonders how or in what ways this commission, which is comprised of two umbrella organ-

isations – one largely of converts, the other of professionals from the
Middle East and Asia – is representative of the interests of poorer,
newer (and often illegal) Muslim immigrants from North Africa.
Nevertheless, the Spanish recognition brings with it significant benefits,
including provisions which: declare mosques and other Muslim places
of worship inviolable; assure pastoral functions of imams; allow for
civil recognition of Islamic marriages; make for certain advantageous
tax advantages; respect food restrictions; and open various possibilities
regarding Islamic religious education at all levels (Antes, 1994,
pp. 49–52).

Besides official recognition of Islam by way of an umbrella organisation and leadership, more effective representation can and should be
encouraged through the political process. But in respective European
countries the ability of, and scope for, Muslim minorities to engage in
representative politics are highly conditioned, of course, by citizenship
status and voting rights. In Germany there is only a small proportion of
persons of Turkish origin who have German citizenship, although a
significant proportion (perhaps as much as 40 per cent) is German born.
Being born in Germany does not entitle one to claim citizenship. Turks
are therefore in a weak political position and this encourages them to
keep a low profile. However, especially after the murderous arson
attacks on Turkish families in 1993, the question of citizenship – in
particular the allowance of double citizenship for those born in
Germany – has again been brought to the forefront of the political
agenda.

It is in Britain where the citizenship and voting rights provide the
greatest prospects for Muslim minorities. In contrast with immigrant-
descent minorities in the majority of European countries, most Blacks
and Asians in Britain today are citizens (that is, in actual British terms,
subjects of the Crown), having originally entered as members of the
Commonwealth or having gained the legal status after being born in
the country. (In 1981 the British Nationality Act removed the right to
automatic citizenship of those born in Britain to immigrant parents; this
must now be applied for.) They have full voting rights in local and
national elections.

In Britain the size and impact of 'the Muslim vote', especially in
local elections, is not insubstantial, but often it is exaggerated (Le
Lohe, 1990). Nevertheless, local politicians are always sure to liaise
with designated Muslim leaders who promise to deliver 'the Muslim

vote'. In 1991 the Islamic Party of Great Britain contested its first seat; however, it has never received much support. It is the Labour Party which receives the bulk of the support of Muslim voters in Britain, and this is particularly evident in the success of Muslim candidates for Labour in local government elections. For example, in 1981 only three of Bradford's 90 councillors were Muslim; by 1992 there were 11 Muslim councillors, including the deputy leader of the ruling group (Lewis, 1994). The city also boasted the country's first Asian, and Muslim, Lord Mayor in 1985–6. The city of Leicester not only has produced a number of Muslim city and country councillors, but also a Muslim Chief Executive (alongside a Muslim Police Superintendent; Vertovec, 1994). In June 1994, Waltham Forest produced the first Muslim woman to be elected mayor. And at the time of writing, there was much talk within the Labour Party of forwarding a Muslim candidate (perhaps from Birmingham Small Heath or Bradford West) for the House of Commons in the next general elections.

In addition to liaison with associations, official recognition and forms of direct political representation, new legal frameworks are needed to ensure that the widespread exclusion of Muslim minorities in Europe is curtailed. In recent years – particularly since the 'Rushdie' and 'headscarves' affairs – the rise of specifically anti-Muslim forms of racism has led to calls for new or extended legislation (see CRE, 1989, 1990a,b; Modood, 1993b; Horton, 1993).

In Britain, although there exist legal frameworks surrounding discrimination with regard to gender, 'race' and ethnicity which are some of the most far-reaching in Europe, at present Muslims-*qua*-Muslims are not protected from discrimination by law. An important ruling by the House of Lords in 1983 (*Mandla* v. *Dowell-Lee*, following a head teacher's refusal to allow a Sikh boy to wear a turban in school) established that Sikhs – and by extension, Jews – are considered an 'ethnic group' and are thus protected by the 1976 Race Relations Act. However, a case in 1988 (*Nyazi* v. *Rymans Ltd*, concerning an employer's refusal to allow an employee time off to celebrate Eid al Fitr) ruled that Muslims do not constitute such a group – and, therefore, are not protected by the act – since their regional and linguistic origins are more diverse. The implications of this ruling were evident in a 1991 case (*Commission for Racial Equality* v. *Precision Engineering Ltd*) after an employer blatantly stated that he refused to employ Muslims because he considered them 'extremist': he was found guilty only of 'indirect discrimination' against Asians (since most British Muslims are of such descent), while his anti-Muslim sentiments were unassailed. More recently, Muslim workers in Yorkshire mills have alleged that Muslims are treated worse than other employees with respect to tasks, pay, and holiday benefits (*The Guardian*, 15 March 1993; *Q-News*, 2–9 April 1993).

With the support of Muslim organisations and Muslim newspapers, the Commission for Racial Equality has advocated measures to redress the situation (CRE, 1992). This includes a call for legislators to consider enacting special laws (as exist in Northern Ireland) on religious discrimination and on incitement to religious hatred, similar to existing laws with regard to racial discrimination and incitement to racial hatred. It also sees the need for change in law concerning blasphemy: at present, only Christianity is protected under such law. The CRE and others believe that either the blasphemy law should be extended to other faiths, or that it should be abolished altogether. (Many Muslims prefer the former option, since this, they say, would therefore remove *The Satanic Verses* from British bookshops.) In its *Second Review of the Race Relations Act 1976*, the UK's Commission for Racial Equality (1992, p. 60) concluded that:

> While the blasphemy law is concerned with certain forms of attacks on *religion* as such, a law of incitement to religious hatred is concerned with stirring up hatred against persons, identified by their religion. Arguments that freedom of speech should include the right to stir up hatred against persons inevitably seem limp, and the more so when this done on grounds of religion, since the freedom to practise the religion of one's choice is itself recognised in international law. No country can be said to guarantee the freedom to practise the religion of one's choice if, at the same time, it permits others lawfully to stir up hatred against those doing just that.

Although discrimination based on sex has been legally addressed, the European Union has not developed any such common laws or frameworks protecting people from racial or religious discrimination. This is despite the fact that such laws should follow from international conventions to which member states are party, such as the International Convention on Civil and Political Rights, the UN Declaration on the Elimination of All Forms of Intolerance and Discrimination based on

Religion or Belief and the UN Convention on the Elimination of All Forms of Racial Discrimination. It is clear that effective EU and national laws along these lines are called for.

Despite the fact that much has been achieved by Muslim groups through their collective engagements with the European public domain, it will take more than a series of structural accommodations to overcome discrimination and exclusion. Transformations of notions concerning 'Europe' and 'European' are needed to begin to produce a flourishing society diverse in its makeup. Similarly, many observers suggest, contemporary conditions require re-evaluations of notions surrounding 'Islam' and 'Muslim'. And, indeed, Muslim communities in Europe are themselves in the process of re-interpreting Islamic concepts, practices, collective strategies and identities.

LIVING IN EUROPE: SOME MUSLIM OPTIONS

How should Muslims express their self-identity in a society and polity which is not Islamic? Muhammad Khalid Masud (1989) reviews historical, Qur'anic and Islamic juristic material in order to explore this question. He finds traditional Islamic precedence in examples and models by way of the following options. Muslims in a non-Muslim polity should either: (1) struggle for the establishment of *dar al-Islam* (the realm of Islam); (2) migrate to *dar al-Islam*; (3) withdraw from or do not co-operate with non-Muslims; or – what appears to be the favoured option evidenced in the recent Muslim politics of religion and community – (4) engage in a kind of pact with the non-Muslim state in order to ensure their own religious freedom (minimally to include the freedoms surrounding public call to prayer, public observance of Friday and Eid prayers, appointment of Muslim judges to rule on their own affairs, provision of Islamic religious education, and observance of dietary restrictions).

Apart from such conscious strategies derived from Islamic precedence, Felice Dassetto (1993) distinguishes several options which already characterise individual Muslims in Europe. He suggests that, regardless of their ethnic origins or migration histories, the bulk of Muslims in Europe – perhaps 60 per cent – fall into the 'undeclared believer' categories of 'agnostic', 'silent indifferent', or 'culturalist' Muslims: that is, people who may be proud to call themselves 'Muslim' but who do not engage in much in terms of religious activity. The balance of the population is comprised of the 'declared believers'. Perhaps 20 per cent of the Muslim population in Europe, Dassetto submits, are 'individualist pietist' by way of their religiosity, undertaking their own private forms of practice while not really engaging in collective mobilising activities. The remaining 20 per cent, he suggests, is comprised of the formal 'ritualists', 'missionaries', 'mystics' and 'militants' who are the most active in promoting or proselytising Islam.

Dassetto's portrait of the Muslim population in Europe does much to dispel the idea that Muslims are collectively bent on controversy, confrontation, and clash – an image which, as we have noted, has been propagated by widespread portrayals of 'the Islamic threat'. It has been easy for some quarters of the media to overlook the majority of Muslims in order to highlight the few who convey a 'seige mentality' (Pickles, 1995; Alibhai-Brown, 1994): among the oft-cited, notorious examples are the leader of the self-proclaimed Muslim Parliament, Kalim Siddiqui, who in January 1992 advised Muslims in Britain to break any law they feel is hostile to their interests as Muslims (*The Times*, 7 January 1992) and the militant youth group called Hizb-ut-Tahrir, which has been trying to recruit Muslim students in some British universities with inflammatory anti-Western, anti-Jewish and anti-homosexual propaganda (*Times Higher Education Supplement*, 25 February 1994). Despite the attention given to those who urge the option of self-exclusion among Muslims and collective confrontation with non-Muslims in Europe, a likely more important and prevalent trend – particularly among young, European-born Muslims – is that of reclaiming and re-interpreting Islamic values and reconstructing Muslim identity itself.

TOWARDS A EUROPEAN ISLAM

As occurs in each of the world's 'great religions', there is nothing new in modifying meanings of, and within, Islam in relation to the sociocultural, political and economic contexts in which Muslims find themselves (see, for instance, Eickelman, 1982). One mode of modifying meanings occurs through a particular kind of self-consciousness which the condition of 'borderlands', 'diaspora' or minority status stimulates. Emblematic of such self-consciousness, Clifford Geertz (1968, p. 61) has described ways in which, in Morocco and Indonesia (representing two margins of the Islamic world) 'the primary question has shifted from "What shall I believe" to "How shall I believe it?"' This shift has entailed, further, 'a distinction between "religiousness" and "religious-mindedness,"between being held by religious convictions and holding them'.

As Nielsen (1992a, pp. 114–15) emphasises, such new modes of religious self-consciousness are certainly stimulated in the Western European context.

> The circumstances of migration, the situation into which Muslims have settled in European cities, and the adaptations which are being made, especially as the young grow up to be the first European Muslim generation, all impose the need to analyse. The old way has to be analysed into discrete parts so that Islam can be identified. The emphasis of the identification of Islam can be on the Qur'an and Qur'anic principles or it can be on aspects of the Shari'a tradition. In either case, one proceeds to 'reassemble' these Islamic components together with the components arising out of the migration and settlement experience into a new complex whole which functions more successfully in European urban, industrial life. As a universal religion with a long historical experience of successfully integrating into new cultures, it would be extremely surprising if Islam were not to follow exactly this kind of path also in Europe.

From the perspective of an Islamic scholar, Omar Khalidi (1989) makes several recommendations with regard to 'reassembling' or integrating new elements. 'There is no inherent clash of interests', he (ibid., p. 430) emphasises, 'between the interests of the Muslim minority and the non-Muslim state.' Calling for 'a new orientation' among Muslim minorities, Khalidi (ibid., pp. 432–3) suggests 'The first step in this direction is to present Islam minus the baggage of local Muslim culture and burden of medieval history, as Muslims are an ideological group and not an ethnic community.' Indeed, throughout Western Europe it has been argued by Muslims and non-Muslims alike that first-generation migrants have too often tried to preserve values and behaviours of villages and towns of eastern Anatolia in Germany, the Maghreb in France, or northern Pakistan in Britain 'as identity markers claiming that all this is typical of and essential to Islam' (Antes, 1994, p. 52).

Such a tendency has been part of, in Margaret Pickles' (1995, p. 107) term, the 'frozen clock syndrome' characterised by migrants who live as though the cultural clock stopped when they left their homeland decades ago and by their children who are brought up in the new context 'synchronous with this frozen parental frame'.

Research by Kim Knott and Sadja Khokher (1993) among young South Asian Muslim women in Britain underscores the emergence of complex, shifting strategies which provide a 'perceptual map' allowing for the situational assertion, rejection, or synthesis of values deemed either 'religious' or 'ethnic'. Many young South Asian Muslim women, they found, are conceptually establishing a firm distinction between 'religion' and 'culture', which were realms largely indistinguishable for their parents. Further, they are rejecting their parents' conformity to ethnic traditions which are considered as emblematic of religiosity (such as manner of dress) while wholly embracing a Muslim identity in and of itself. Among these young women, Knott and Khokher (ibid., p. 596) explain, there is a 'self-conscious exploration of the religion which was not relevant to the first generation.'

Knott and Khokher see such an emerging, critical role for Muslim women generally, which reflects their growing engagement with Western education, textual analysis (here, of the Qur'an), speculative reasoning and wider debates about the role of women in Islam and in Western society. This kind of engagement is evident, too, among new Muslim women's groups in Britain. For example,

> Members of the Al-Nisa women's group in London and grassroots organisations in Bradford, Birmingham and other places, spend hours every week analysing the kind of Islam that would help to empower them instead of limiting their capacities. They talk openly and passionately about contraception, abortion, adoption, rape, the education of their children, how men can be better fathers and husbands, geopolitical changes and ecological problems. (Alibhai-Brown, 1994)

In forging a new European Islam, young Muslim men and women are reclaiming the concept of *ijtihad* – 'interpretation' or 'independent judgement' – not as a special right of scholars but of all Muslims. And the idea of the Muslim 'religious community', or *Ummah*, itself has been subject to fundamental re-thinking.

Anwar Ibrahim (1991) calls for a rediscovery of the meaning and ideal of *Ummah* and for a development and promulgation of '*Ummah* consciousness'. Central to Ibrahim's view is a more open understanding of the notion of the global community of Muslims than many commentators – Muslim and non-Muslim alike – have heretofore proposed. For Ibrahim, 'The *Ummah* is not a cultural entity patterned on the norms of any one dominant group' but it 'exists within and is expressed through diverse cultural groups' demonstrating 'diversity within unity' (ibid., p. 306). This model, he emphasises, can be historically located in Medina during the lifetime of the Prophet.

> Recapturing the meaning of that model would necessitate that Muslims engage with other people, nations, worldviews, religions and ideologies to work for a set of moral objectives that we can and must define together. But it takes us much further. It requires that we respect the *Ummah* of other people. ... The history of the *Ummah* has shown exemplary, almost unique models of multiracial, multicultural, multireligious, pluralist societies. If ever we had need of recovering such an imperative, it is now. (ibid., p. 309)

Such an understanding would likely foster, among young Muslims in Europe, a 'grounded flexibility' in Islam (Pickles, 1995) which would none the less allow for the construction and exercise of multi-faceted, hybrid ethnic and social identities. Further, this would facilitate, as Sardar (1995, p. 12) describes it, 'The evolution of a new identity – distinctly Islamic, clearly Western – that would bring the marginal in, not for assimilation, but for empowerment through a modicum of acculturation and active participation in all walks of life ... through being part of the common landscape of the West.'

At present, however, the European landscape is far from 'common' among Muslims, non-Muslims, minorities and majorities. This was particularly noticeable, Bhikhu Parekh (1990, p. 73) indicates, in the scarcity of 'such values as moral equality, common citizenship, tolerance, diversity, pluralism and dialogue' expressed in public space during the Rushdie Affair. Yet it is in public space – the space of media, political debate and administrative policy, among other things – where the foundations must be laid for the construction of a common landscape designed by way of the values to which Parekh points. The politics of religion and community undertaken by Muslim groups in

Europe over the past two decades can be seen as one way in which minorities have pressed for such a change of social scenery.

BIBLIOGRAPHY

Abdullah, M. S. (1989) 'The Religion of Islam and its Presence in the Federal Republic of Germany', *Journal of the Institute of Muslim Minority Affairs*, 10, pp. 438–49.
Al Rasheed, M. (1992). 'Political Migration and Downward Socio-economic Mobility: The Iraqi Community in London', *New Community*, 18, pp. 537–50
Alibhai-Brown, Y. (1994) 'A New Islam for the West', *The Independent*, 14 February.
Ålund, A. and C. Schierup (1992) *Paradoxes of Multiculturalism: Essays on Swedish Society* (Aldershot: Avebury).
Andrews, A. Y. (1993) 'Sociological Analysis of Jamaat-i-Islami in the United Kingdom', in R. Barot (ed.), *Religion and Ethnicity: Minorities and Social Change in the Metropolis* (Kampen, The Netherlands: Kok Pharos) pp. 68–79.
Antes, P. (1994) 'Islam in Europe', in S. Gill, G. D'Costa and U. King (eds), *Religion in Europe: Contemporary Perspectives* (Kampen, The Netherlands: Kok Pharos) pp. 46–67.
Appignanesi, L. and S. Maitland (1989) *The Rushdie File* (London: Fourth Estate).
Asad, T. (1990) 'Multiculturalism and British Identity in the Wake of the Rushdie Affair', *Politics and Society*, 18, pp. 455–80.
Balibar, E. (1991) 'Is there a "neo-racism"?', in E. Balibar and I. Wallerstein (eds), *Race, Nation, Class: Ambiguous Identities* (London: Verso) pp. 17–28.
Benningsen, A. and S. E. Wimbush (1985) *Muslims of the Soviet Empire* (London: C. Hurst).
British Muslims Monthly Survey (1995) *Review of 1994* (Birmingham: Centre for the Study of Islam and Christian–Muslim Relations).
Brown, C. (1984) *Black and White Britain: The Third PSI Survey* (Aldershot: Gower).
Cesari, J. (forthcoming) 'New Ways of Being Muslim in France', in S. Vertovec (ed.), *Muslim European Youth: Reproducing Religion, Ethnicities, Cultures* (Aldershot: Avebury).
Charlton, R. and R. Kaye (1985) 'The Politics of Religious Slaughter: An Ethno-religious Case Study', *New Community*, 12, pp. 490–503.
Clarke, C., C. Peach and S. Vertovec (eds) (1990) *South Asians Overseas: Migration and Ethnicity* (Cambridge: Cambridge University Press).
Collins, S. (1957) *Coloured Minorities in Britain* (London: Butterworth Press).
Commission for Racial Equality (1989) *Law, Blasphemy and the Multi-Faith Society – Report of a Seminar* (London: CRE and the Inter-Fatih Network for the UK).

Commission for Racial Equality (1990a) *Free Speech – Report of a Seminar* (London: CRE and the Policy Studies Institute).

Commission for Racial Equality (1990b) *Britain: A Plural Society* (London: CRE and the Runnymede Trust).

Commission for Racial Equality (1992) *Second Review of the Race Relations Act 1976* (London: CRE).

Dassetto, F. (1993) 'Islam and Europe', paper presented at the International Conference on Muslim Minorities in Post-Bipolar Europe, Skopje, Macedonia.

Doomernik, J. (1995) 'The Institutionalization of Turkish Islam in Germany and the Netherlands: A Comparison', *Ethnic and Racial Studies*, 18, pp. 46–63.

Dwyer, C. and A. Meyer (1995) 'The Institutionalisation of Islam in the Netherlands and in the UK: The Case of Islamic Schools', *New Community*, 21, pp. 37–54.

Eade, J. (1993) 'The Political Articulation of Community and the Islamisation of Space in London', in Rohit Barot (ed.), *Religion and Ethnicity: Minorities and Social Change in the Metropolis* (Kampen, The Netherlands: Kok Pharos) pp. 27–42.

Eickelman, D. F. (1982) 'The Study of Islam in Local Contexts', *Contributions to Asian Studies*, 17, pp. 1–16.

El-Solh, C. F. (1992) 'Arab Communities in Britain: Cleavages and Commonalities,' *Islam and Christian–Muslim Relations*, 3, pp. 236–58.

El-Solh, C. F. (1993) 'Be True to your Culture: Gender Tensions among Somali Muslims in Britain', *Immigrants and Minorities*, 12, pp. 21–46.

Esposito, J. (1992) *The Islamic Threat: Myth or Reality?* (New York: Oxford University Press).

Etienne, B. (1989) 'Islamic Associations in Europe', *Contemporary European Affairs*, 2, pp. 29–44.

Garaudy, R. (1984) 'The Future of Muslim Workers in Europe', Research paper No. 24 (Birmingham: Centre for the Study of Islam and Christian–Muslim Relations).

Gates, L. H. (1993) 'Blood and Irony: How Race and Religion will shape the Future', *The Economist*, 11 September.

Gerholm, T. and Y. G. Lithman (eds) (1988) *The New Islamic Presence in Western Europe* (London: Mansell).

Geertz, C. (1968) *Islam Observed: Religious Developments in Morocco and Indonesia* (Chicago: University of Chicago Press).

Halliday, F. (1989) 'The Struggle for the Migrant Soul', *Times Literary Supplement*, 14–20 April, pp. 387–8.

Halliday, F. (1992) *Arabs in Exile: Yemeni Migrants in Urban Britain* (London: I. B. Taurus).

Horton, J. (ed.) (1993) *Liberalism, Multiculturalism and Toleration* (London: Macmillan).

Huntington, S. P. (1993) 'The Clash of Civilizations?', *Foreign Affairs*, Summer, pp. 22–49.

Husbands, C. (1995) 'They Must Obey our Laws and Customs!': Political Debate about Muslim Assimilability in Great Britain, France and the Netherlands', in A. G. Hargreaves and J. Leaman (eds), *Racism, Ethnicity and Politics in Contemporary Europe* (Cheltenham: Edward Elgar) pp. 115–30.

Ibrahim, I. (1991) 'The *Ummah* and Tomorrow's World', *Futures*, 26, pp. 302–10.

Ibrahim, Y. M. (1995) 'Muslim Immigrants in Europe: A Population Apart', *International Herald Tribune*, 6–7 May.

Irwin, Z. T. (1989) 'The Fate of Islam in the Balkans: A Comparison of Four State Policies', in P. Ramet (ed.), *Religion and Nationalism in Soviet and East European Politics*, revised edn (Durham, NC: Duke University Press) pp. 387–407.

Joly, D. (1995) *Britannia's Crescent: Making a Place for Muslims in British Society* (Aldershot: Avebury).

Jones, P. N. and M. T. Wild (1992) 'West Germany's "Third Wave" of Migrants: The Arrival of the Aussiedler', *Geoforum*, 23, pp. 1–11.

Kepel, G. (1987) *Les Banlieues de l'Islam: Naissance d'une Religion en France* (Paris: Editions du Seuil).

Kepel, G. (1995) 'Foreword. Between Society and Community: Muslims in Britain and France Today', in D. Joly, *Britannia's Crescent: Making a Place for Muslims in British Society* (Aldershot: Avebury) pp. ix–xxiii.

Khalidi, O. (1989) 'Muslim Minorities: Theory and Experience of Muslim Interaction in Non-Muslim Societies', *Journal of the Institute of Muslim Minority Affairs*, 10, pp. 425–37.

Knott, K. and S. Khokher (1993) 'Religious and Ethnic Identity among Young Muslim Women in Bradford', *New Community*, 19, pp. 593–610.

Le Lohe, M. J. (1990) 'Political Issues', *New Community*, 16, pp. 447–54.

Le Lohe, M. J. (1991) 'Political Issues', *New Community*, 17, pp. 442–7.

Leggewie, C. (1993) *Alhambra: Der Islam im Westen* (Reinbek bei Hamburg: Rowohlt).

Lewis, P. (1994) *Islamic Britain: Religion, Politics and Identity among British Muslims* (London: I. B. Taurus).

Little, K. S. (1947) *Negroes in Britain* (London: Kegan Paul, Trench, Trubner)

Mandel, R. (1989) 'Turkish Headscarves and the 'Foreigner Problem': Constructing Differences through Emblems of Identity', *New German Critique*, 46, pp. 27–46.

Masud, M. K. (1989) 'Being Muslim in a Non-Muslim Polity: Three Alternate Models', *Journal of the Institute of Muslim Minority Affairs*, 10, pp. 118–28.

Mazrui, A. (1991) 'The Resurgence of Islam and the Decline of Communism', *Futures*, 23, pp. 273–89.

Mission de Réfléxion (1991) *Rapport a Madame le Premier Ministre de la Mission de Réfléxion sur la Communauté Repatriée d'Origine Nord-Africaine*, xerox, May.

Modood, T. (1990) 'British Asian Muslims and the Rushdie Affair', *Political Quarterly*, 61, pp. 143–60.

Modood, T. (1993a) 'Muslim Vews on Religious Identity and Racial Equality', *New Community*, 19, pp. 513–19.

Modood, T. (1993b) 'Muslims, Incitement to Hatred and the Law', in J. Horton (ed.), *Liberalism, Multiculturalism and Toleration* (London: Macmillan) pp. 139–56.

Modood, T. (1994) 'Establishment, Multiculturalism and British Citizenship', *Political Quarterly*, 65, pp. 53–71.

Nielsen, J. (1981) 'Muslims in Europe: An Overview', Research Paper No. 12 (Birmingham: Centre for the Study of Islam and Christian–Muslim Relations).

Nielsen, J. (1987) 'Muslims in Britain: Searching for an Identity?', *New Community*, 13, pp. 384–94.

Nielsen, J. (1988) 'Muslims in Britain and Local Authority Responses', in T. Gerholm and Y. G Lithman (eds), *The New Islamic Presence in Western Europe* (London: Mansell) pp. 53–77.

Nielsen, J. (1991) 'A Muslim Agenda for Britain: Some Reflections', *New Community*, 17, pp. 467–75.

Nielsen, J. (1992a) *Muslims in Western Europe* (Edinburgh: Edinburgh University Press).

Nielsen, J. (1992b) 'Islam, Muslims, and British Local and Central Government', CSIC Papers: Europe No. 6 (Birmingham: Centre for the Study of Islam and Christian–Muslim Relations).

Nielsen, J. (1994) 'Islam and Europe', CSIC Papers: Europe No. 13 (Birmingham: Centre for the Study of Islam and Christian–Muslim Relations).

O'Brien, P. (1988) 'Continuity and Change in Germany's Treatment of Non-Germans', *International Migration Review*, 22(3), pp. 109–34.

Owen, D. (1993) 'Ethnic Minorities in Great Britain', 1991 Census Statistical Paper No 2 (Coventry: Centre for Research in Ethnic Relations, University of Warwick).

Parekh, B. (1990) 'The Rushdie Affair and the British Press: Some Salutary Lessons', in *Free Speech – Report of a Seminar* (London: Commission for Racial Equality and the Policy Studies Institute).

Parker-Jenkins, M. (1995) *Children of Islam: A Teacher's Guide to Meeting the Needs of Muslim Pupils* (Stoke-on-Trent: Trentham Books).

Peach, C. (1990a) 'Estimating the Growth of the Bangladeshi Population of Great Britain', *New Community*, 16, pp. 481–91.

Peach, C. (1990b) 'The Muslim Population of Great Britain', *Ethnic and Racial Studies*, 13, pp. 414–19.

Peach, C. (1992) 'Urban Concentration and Segregation in Europe since 1945', in M. Cross (ed.), *Ethnic Minorities and Industrial Change in Europe and North America* (Cambridge: Cambridge University Press).

Peach, C. and G. Glebe (1995) 'Muslim Minorities in Western Europe', *Ethnic and Racial Studies,* 18, pp. 26–45.

Pearl, D. (1987) 'South Asian Communities and English Family Law, 1971–1987', *New Community*, 14, pp. 161–9.

Pickles, M. E. (1995) 'Muslim Immigration Stress in Australia', in S. Z. Abedin and Z. Sardar (eds), *Muslim Minorities in the West* (London: Grey Seal) pp. 106–16.

Popovich, A. (1975) 'Les Musulmans du sud-est européen dans la périod post-ottomane: Problèmes d'approche', *Journal Asiatique*, 263, pp. 317–60.

Ramet, P. (ed.) (1989) *Religion and Nationalism in Soviet and East European Politics*, revised edn (Durham, NC: Duke University Press).

Rath, J., K. Groenendijk and R. Penninx (1991) 'The Recognition and Institutionalization of Islam in Belgium, Great Britain and the Netherlands', *New Community*, 18, pp. 101–14.

Rex, J. (1991) *Ethnic Identity and Ethnic Mobilisation in Britain*, Monographs in Ethnic Relation No. 5 (Coventry: Centre for Research in Ethnic Relations).

Rex, J. (1994) 'The Political Sociology of Multiculturalism and the Place of Muslims in West European Societies', *Social Compass*, 41, pp. 79–92.

Rex, J. and B. Drury (eds) (1994) *Ethnic Mobilization in a Multi-Cultural Europe* (Aldershot: Avebury).

Rogers, A. and S. Vertovec (eds) (1995) *The Urban Context: Ethnicity, Social Networks and Situational Analysis* (Oxford: Berg).

Rutherford, J. (1990) 'A Place called Home: Identity and the Cultural Politics of Difference', in J. Rutherford (ed.), *Identity: Community, Culture, Difference* (London: Lawrence & Wishart) pp. 9–27.

Ruthven, M. (1990) *A Satanic Affair: Salman Rushdie and the Wrath of Islam* (London: The Hogarth Press).

Said, E. (1978) *Orientalism* (London: Routledge & Kegan Paul).

Said, E. (1981) *Covering Islam: How the Media and the Experts Determine How We See the Rest of the World* (London: Routledge & Kegan Paul).

Samad, Y. (1992) 'Book-burning and Race-relations: Political Mobilisation of Bradford Muslims', *New Community*, 18, pp. 507–19.

Sardar, Z. (1991) 'Islam and the Future', *Futures*, 23, pp. 223–30.

Sardar, Z. (1995) 'Racism, Identity and Muslims in the West', in S. Z. Abedin and Z. Sardar (eds), *Muslim Minorities in the West* (London: Grey Seal) pp. 1–17.

Sardar, Z. and M. W. Davies (1990) *Distorted Imagination: Lessons from the Rushdie Affair* (London: Grey Seal).

Schmuck, P. (1982) *Der Islam und seine Bedeutung für türkische Familien in der Bundesrepublik Deutschland* (Munich: Deutsches Jugendinstitut (DJI)).

Shadid, W. A. R. and P. S. van Koningsveld (1995) *Religious Freedom and the Position of Islam in Western Europe* (Kampen, The Netherlands: Kok Pharos).

SOPEMI (1990) *Trends in International Migration: Continuous Reporting System on Migration* (Paris: Organization for Economic Co-operation and Development).

SOPEMI (1992) *Trends in International Migration: Continuous Reporting System on Migration* (Paris: Organization for Economic Co-operation and Development).

SOPEMI (1995) *Trends in International Migration: Continuous Reporting System on Migration* (Paris: Organization for Economic Co-operation and Development).

Szajkowski, B. (1988) 'Muslim People in Eastern Europe: Ethnicity and Religion', *Journal of the Institute of Muslim Minority Affairs*, 9, pp. 103–18.

Taylor, C. (1992) *Multiculturalism and 'The Politics of Recognition'* (Princeton, NJ: Princeton University Press). [With commentary by A. Gutman, S. C. Rockefeller, M. Walzer and S. Wolf.]

Teheri, A. (1989) *Crescent in a Red Sky: The Future of Islam in the Soviet Union* (London: Hutchinson).

van Oijen, H. (1992) 'Religion and Emancipation: A Study of the Development of Moroccan Islamic Organizations in a Dutch Town', in W. A. R. Shadid and P. S. van Koningsveld (eds), *Islam in Dutch Society: Current Developments and Future Prospects* (Kampen, The Netherlands: Kok Pharos) pp. 163–80.

Vertovec, S. (1994) 'Multicultural, Multi-Asian, Multi-Muslim Leicester: Dimensions of Social Complexity, Ethnic Organization, and Local Government Interface', *Innovation*, 7, pp. 259–76.

Vertovec, S. (1996) 'Multiculturalism, Culturalism and Public Incorporation', *Ethnic and Racial Studies*, 19, pp. 49–69.

Waardenburg, J. (1988) 'Institutionalisation of Islam in the Netherlands (1961–1986)', in T. Gerholm and Y. G. Lithman (eds), *The New Islamic Presence in Western Europe* (London: Mansell) pp. 8–31.

Waardenburg, J. (1991) 'Muslim Associations and Official Bodies in some European Countries', in W. A. R. Shadid and P. S. van Koningsveld (eds), *The Integration of Islam and Hinduism in Western Europe* (Kampen, The Netherlands: Kok Pharos) pp. 24–42.

Watt, W. M. (1972) *The Influence of Islam on Medieval Europe* (Edinburgh: Edinburgh University Press).

West, C. (1993) 'The New Cultural Politics of Difference', in S. During (ed.), *The Cultural Studies Reader* (London: Routledge) pp. 203–17.

2 Islamic Groups in Europe: Between Community Affirmation and Social Crisis

Gilles Kepel

Until the middle of the 1980s, the social sciences took little interest in the presence in Europe of populations of Muslim origin. The people in question were generally classified according to categories which, depending on the country, counted them as 'immigrants', as '*Gastarbeiter*', '*extracommunitari*' or 'Blacks'. Each state followed the tradition established by its particular juridical and political norms in the ways it conceived of, and chose to describe, the overseas labour which came to work in its factories at the height of the 'thirty glorious years'– of economic boom unleashed by post-war reconstruction.

Up to the middle of the 1970s, these populations were mainly thought of in the context of the sociology of work or of immigration. Their profiles were relatively atypical compared to those of the host population on account of the over-representation of adult, economically active, working males and of the persistence among many of the wish to return to their country of origin once their 'migration scheme' had yielded enough capital.

The economic crisis, precipitated by the Arab–Israeli war of October 1973, increased the social visibility of these groups. At the same time, the groups began to experience the problems of integration both as prime victims of unemployment and because many of them abandoned the myth of return and began to consider settling in the host country instead.

THE SETTLEMENT PROCESS

This settlement has taken place in difficult conditions which are compounded by family reunion. This, in turn, has transformed the profile of the groups in question. The former 'migrant workers' have been succeeded by populations who can no longer be defined as 'workers' (for many are unemployed and they include growing numbers of children and women who are economically inactive) nor as 'immigrants' (for the younger generations were born in Europe). This sensitive period, which I have called a period of 'transitional settlement' is conducive to various forms of redefinition of identity arising out of both the newness of settlement and of the related phenomena of social exclusion which many members of the groups in question claim to suffer.

In each European country, differences in political tradition, in the organisation of workers' movements and in cultural contours were reflected in differences in the 'transitional settlement': yet everywhere these manifested themselves as contingent identities. Often these identities were first and foremost heavily 'reconstructed' from a synthesis of acquired and inherent elements. Whether one thinks of the significance of the term 'Black' in Britain or '*Beur*' in France, they conjure up, for better or worse, a hybrid identity half way between settlement and exclusion. These transitional – and unstable – identities are not universally accepted by those to whom they are applied and are still strongly contested among them.

PROBLEMS OF IDENTITY

It is in the context of the redefinitions brought about by the 'transitional settlement' that the affirmation of Islamic identities developed in Europe. It is important to underline that these do not consist in a straightforward return to the forms of self-definition which obtained in the country of origin, but are shaped by a process of selection and adaptation of a certain number of features which have proved appropriate to the organisation and structuring of the groups in the host country. Thus, some Islamic modes of expression have fallen into disuse in Europe while others, by contrast, have been given greater prominence in a complex relationship of imitation and differentiation with European societies. The many and varied forms of expression of Islam in territo-

ries which are not part of the *dar al Islam*, and where, politically, alle-
giances are much freer than in the countries of origin (which are more
profoundly characterised by constraints of tradition and of prohibitions)
are, therefore, the result of a number of choices made by individuals or
by those who aspire to represent them and to bargain in their name with
both the public and the private sector in the countries of Europe.

In this sense, the overt expression of Islam does not subsume the
totality of groups of Muslim origin (who may reconstruct whatever
mixture they choose of political, social and cultural identity and who
may accord Islam only a minor, folksy, exclusively private or totally
non-existent place in their lives); more often, like any form of
affirmative identity, they operate as a system of differentiations in
direct competition with other possible constructions. Moreover, there is
nothing monolithic about this: there are intense conflicts among
Muslim associations themselves, among leaders, imams, mullahs,
hocas, the laity, all of whom have their own ideas about how this heterogeneous population should be brought together to form a single
community behind one or other leader or 'spokesman'.

These considerations certainly make for relativity in the expression
of an Islamic identity among those populations of Muslim origin
settled in Europe at the end of the twentieth century. But they cannot
disguise the fact that, on the broad canvas of definitions of Self and the
Other which were born out of 'transitional settlement', modes of
affirmation of Islam have been ceaselessly generated for two decades.
To the point where, in common perception, the term 'Islamic' is
increasingly marked after 1989, the year which, while Communism
and the partition of Europe were swept away with the fall of the Berlin
wall, saw the expression of Islam on the continent take dramatic shape
with the 'Rushdie affair' in Great Britain and the 'headscarf affair' in
France.

Both cases witnessed the tension between 'the community' on the
one hand and 'society' on the other. 'The community' in these circumstances refers not to an atavistic community but to a reconstituted identity which groups people on the basis of an accentuation of certain
characteristics which are thought of as distinctive and irreconcilable
with the norms of the majority society (which are stigmatised as
'assimilationist'). 'Society', on the other hand, refers to a collection of
individuals defined, at least in theory, by what they do rather than by
who they are.

The classic opposition of these two terms is defined thus by F. Tönnies (1944):

> According to the theory of society, this is a group of men who, living and residing, as in the community, peaceably side by side, are not organically linked but organically separated; while, in the community, they remain linked despite the depth of their separation, in society they remain separate despite the strength of their links. It follows that there is no scope here for actions based on an a priori unity and on some sort of necessity; which therefore, inasmuch as they are produced by the individual, express his wish for and sense of that unity, and thus take on the same reality for those associated with him as they do for himself. Here, it is everyone for himself in a constant state of tension *vis-à-vis* everyone else.

It is this 'constant state of tension *vis-à-vis* everyone else' which is reaching breaking point among the members of certain social groups since the dissolution of the mutual ties associated with industrial society and the sense of purpose which flowed from these. This is the context in which new forms of solidarity appear to be establishing themselves and to be evoking community organisation by taking as their point of reference an 'organic tie' capable of surmounting and resolving the tensions inherent in situations where the slackening of social ties occurs in conjunction with a loss of points of reference more widely, with the disappearance of a sense of purpose, and with a general muddying of the *Weltanschauung*. This phenomenon is experienced as anomie and a sense of the system being in dysfunction, but also as a threat to destroy the individual's sense of their identity. Now, this is occurring in societies constituted as such which are also extremely differentiated internally. The collective identities shaped by this process are not – or are not entirely – inherited but largely reconstructed. Weber (1968), in his classic definition of the ethnic group, notes that its members 'entertain a subjective belief in their common descent because of their similarities of physical type or of custom or both, or because of memories of colonisation or migration ... it does not matter whether or not an objective blood relation exists'.

So, behind phenomena which have hit the headlines such as the Rushdie affair or that of the headscarf, new social, cultural, political and religious forces have been established with Islam as a point of reference at the very heart of post-industrial modernity. They are significant at many levels. Certainly, they play an important rôle in the general changes which are taking place in contemporary Islam. In rooting itself outside the areas where this religion was traditionally present, in utilising the universal languages of the West – English above all – and with easy access to the audio-visual media and developing within democratic political systems, the movements concerned with re-Islamicisation in Europe and America are in the vanguard of the expansion of this belief system throughout the world.

LESSONS FOR THE WEST

This phenomenon is also rich in significance and lessons for the Western societies in which it has occurred – and in quite unexpected ways. The claims made for communities in the name of Islam are a prism through which to observe the constructions of identity around which our post-industrial societies are structuring themselves. In this last decade of the twentieth century, declining workers' movement and trade unions have become incapable of taking up the demands and the social destiny of this new proletariat of young as 'black-white-*beurs*' at the margins of the job market, living on rundown peripheral council estates or in the inner cities. In reclaiming Islam for themselves – albeit investing it with very diverse meanings – some young people of Muslim origin (as well as some converts of European 'stock') are effectively choosing to break away culturally, on the basis of a communal identity, from the dominant values of the nations of which they are citizens in principle but from which, according to them, they are excluded in practice.

This communal breaking away is as much a form of defence against a dehumanised or hostile social environment as a way of mobilising the 'brothers' and bargaining collectively in their name with the authorities. They are struggling against drug addiction, violence and all forms of delinquency, but at the same time building an alternative identity thanks to specific teachings, modes of behaviour and attitudes which exacerbate otherness and difference – among which strict respect for all the religious prohibitions and duties plays a fundamental rôle.

[handwritten annotations: "platform for Islam", "Globally created", "Bradford resenie"]

THE BRITISH SITUATION

Starting with the United Kingdom, the Rushdie affair took on a universal dimension thanks to the impact of television which brought the image of the *auto-da-fé* of the *Satanic Verses* in Bradford to the four corners of the earth (Modood, 1990). But before the Ayatollah Khomeini had co-opted the issue to his own political ends, the affair had brought to a point of crisis the contradictions in the system of 'multiculturalism' set up at both the social and the political level in the United Kingdom. It was able to mix these with Islamic traditions from the British Empire in India – the first time in history that Islam was faced at one and the same time with finding themselves in a minority situation and with the loss of power. That was where, in the face of this unprecedented threat, Islamic modes of resistance to a foreign form of modernity were developed, modes of resistance which were transposed in almost identical form, decades later, to Muslim neighbourhoods of English industrial cities. It was possible to adapt this model of retreat into the community – for fear of adulteration of religious identity in an open society – both to Mrs Thatcher's Conservative government, whose philosophy was to minimise the involvement of the state in the area of social policy, and to the electoralism of the Labour party, some of whose MPs saw the imams as effectively delivering the votes of their congregations. This cohabitation between Islamic communities and post-industrial society did not hold with the publication of Rushdie's novel. Many Muslims saw this as an insult to their beliefs, leading to demands for the book to be condemned. Religious leaders saw this as an opportunity to unite the Islamic flocks under their leadership on a radical platform. The extreme consequence of this was the symbolic proclamation of a 'Muslim Parliament', intended to mirror that at Westminster. This initiative (whose supporters were not representative) was designed to be provocative, but it succeeded in pressing to the point of absurdity the inherent contradictions in a political system which favours 'multicultural' coexistence as opposed to individual integration.

THE SITUATION IN FRANCE

Starting from principles radically opposite to those of multiculturalism and which favour the fusion of all external contributions within a lay

form of citizenship, France found herself, none the less, in the very year
of the bicentenary of the Revolution, faced with a phenomenon of community-based affirmation of an Islamic identity. Symbolised by female
Muslim pupils who wanted to wear their traditional headscarf to school
or college, this demand was asserted at the same time as the Islamic
associations of the 1970s and 1980s were beginning to make contact
with that section of Muslim youth born and educated in France which
was becoming disenchanted with the anti-racist and '*beur*' movements
of the previous decade. In parallel, after the loss of power of the FLN
(National Liberation Front) in Algeria, the significant gains of the FIS
(National Salvation Front), founded in 1989, suddenly gave birth not
far from the French mainland to a mass Islamic party on the verge of
political power and shaped by an ideology of virulent opposition to
core French values. These values, according to Ali Benhadj, the FIS
tribune, were nothing less than 'poisoned milk' on which the 'sons of
France' were suckled to excess.

This major transformation in both the internal and external context of
Islam in France at the beginning of the 1990s led the socialist government to encourage centralised management of this religion in order to
free it from Algerian influence – a 'Jacobin' initiative without equivalent
in any other Western country, and one which was not successful. Rather,
as in England, in the most disadvantaged neighbourhoods, movements
dedicated to re-Islamicisation have begun to make up for the failures of
the public services (in the fight against drug taking and the drug trade, in
educational support, etc.) and are trying to bargain support for candidates in local elections against the latter meeting the demands of the
community. Given the French political tradition – which, in contrast
with its counterpart across the Channel, is hostile to communalism – the
turn of events in Algeria, over a million of whose natives and citizens
are currently living in France, any electoral expression of religious identity will be fraught with difficulty. Yet these institutional barriers should
not obscure, in France or in other Western countries, the ways in which
these community-based demands highlight the unprecedented extent of
dislocation at the level of society at large.

CONCLUSION

Thus, the forms taken by the plural and complex expression of Islam in
Europe in this last decade of the twentieth century offer a unique per-

spective on the development of two phenomena which will, without doubt, play a major rôle in the political and social reconstruction of tomorrow's world: the place of Islam among the planet's main points of orientation and the capacity of national societies to maintain the integratory functions which have been theirs since the industrial revolution.

BIBLIOGRAPHY

Kepel, G. (1987) *Les Banlieues de l'Islam: Naissance d'une Religion en France* (Paris: Editions du Seuil).
Kepel, G. (1994) *À l'ouest d'Allah* (Paris: Editions du Seuil).
Modood, T. (1990) 'British Asian Muslims and the Rushdie Affair', *Political Quarterly*, 61, pp. 143–60.
Tönnies, F. (1944) *Communauté et Société* (Paris: PUF).
Weber, M. (1968) *Economy and Society: An Outline of Interpretive Sociology* (Berkeley, CA: University of California Press).

Part II
Long-Standing Presence

3 The Balkan Muslim Communities in the Post-Communist Period

Alexandre Popovic

The question which this chapter addresses is whether the collapse (partial or total, depending on the region) in the Eastern European countries of 'Marxism–Leninism' had any impact at all on the situation of the Muslim communities in the Balkans. Even if the answer to this question seems incontestably to be 'yes', it is still very difficult to gauge the extent of this phenomenon (except, of course, in the case of the disaster which has befallen the Muslims of Bosnia-Herzegovina) let alone to try to describe it. None the less, it appears worthwhile to make some analysis along these lines following on from my study of Balkan Islam (Popovic, 1986). Even so, a sketch of the situation is likely to be overtaken by events by the time this chapter appears, since this part of the world is currently evolving very fast.

That said, and before embarking on a country-by-country overview (in which I shall also include Greece,which is clearly not one of the formerly Communist Eastern European states but is part of the Balkans; similarly this will include Hungary where the 'Muslim question' is inextricably linked to Ottoman and post-Ottoman Islam in South-east Europe), I feel that two preliminary, if rather obvious, comments are required to enhance understanding of what follows.

The first is that I am concerned with 'volatile' religious minorities in a part of Europe which, with the single exception of those in Greece, belonged in the immediate past to states run by tyrants of the worst sort and by dictatorships who gave the appearance of having a coherent ideology and of following a pseudo-science which ravaged large parts of the world. A few intellectuals tried to point out that this pseudo-

science was nonsense, but such efforts were in vain, for it was impossible to make ourselves heard. Now today's situation in this part of the
world proves that we were not entirely right: in fact, things were a
hundred times worse than we ourselves had thought. So we need to re-
examine the repercussions of the collapse of this global chimera on the
situation of these 'volatile' minorities in the Balkans, from one country
to another and from one group to another.

The second comment is that the 'sources' available to us for this brief
analysis are very diverse and not always scholarly. In essence they
consist, on the one hand, of the local press from which, from time to
time, one can pick up 'scraps' of information (which need to be care-
fully unpacked and gone over with a fine-tooth comb, since 45 years of
institutionalised lying at every level of national life have left a profound
mark); and, on the other hand, they consist of what I have been able to
observe or to hear for myself here and there, or of what others have
written to me. It is, of course, a pity that I have not been able to produce
something of greater substance – but all of this, supplemented by the
further information which will come our way in future years, will build
up gradually in our files and in our heads and afford us a better view of
the situation 'on the ground' and a more accurate analysis. For the
moment, therefore, let us be satisfied with what we are able to say today.

I shall begin with the situation in the six South Eastern European
countries: Albania, Bulgaria, Greece, Hungary, Romania and
Yugoslavia, beginning with the smallest groups.

HUNGARY

Contrary to what one reads in the Arab papers and the Muslim press in
general, there is at present no Hungarian Muslim community of the sort
which existed sixty or eighty years ago. All the same, in the sphere of
Islam we are witnessing an interesting phenomenon in this country.
Experts in these matters know that between the two world wars
Hungary was the most significant site in South-east and Central East
Europe of attempts by two of the largest Muslim 'sects' to establish
themselves (that is to say, the Ahmadiyya of India and the Bahais who
disappeared from the region at the beginning of the Second World
War). Now it would appear that immediately following the collapse of
the Hungarian communist regime, the two 'sects' in question have

returned to this country from which they hope to extend again their influence (in an organised and systematic way?) throughout this part of the world. Obviously it is still too soon to gauge the significance of this phenomenon and the likely outcome of this initiative (which can, of course, only expect to achieve its goals over the long term), but it is clearly worth following closely. As for the other Muslims in the country (who do not in any organised sense constitute a 'unified religious community') we are talking, on the one hand, about several hundreds or possibly some thousands, Arabs, Turks, Pakistanis and others who are (supposedly temporary) immigrants to Hungary; and on the other hand, about a handful of local converts whose number appears at the present time to be insignificant.

ROMANIA

The Romanian Muslim community must currently number about 50 000, comprised of Turks and Tatars living, for the most part, in Dobroudja; one also finds a handful in Bucharest and others dispersed throughout the country. Since the communist regime was installed – that is, since the end of the Second World War – this small community has found itself in a precarious position. It has witnessed the closure of Turkish and Tatar schools (in 1957); closure (in 1967) of the 'Muslim seminary' in Medjidiya (the only institution of this kind in the country, responsible for the renewal of the religious leadership); total absence of religious publications; and the impossibility of pilgrimage to Mecca. Then, since 1972, the international situation and the country's economic difficulties ended up forcing the Romanian authorities of the time into some concessions (limited as these inevitably were) to the local Muslim community, clearly aimed at improving the image of the regime in the eyes of certain Arab and Muslim countries.

We know little of the consequences of the fall of the Ceausescu regime for the present situation of this small community. All we know for now is that the former Mufti (a very old man accused of having collaborated with the old order) has been replaced; that a well-known historian, Mustafa Mehmet (possibly in the name of the local community) has made a number of contacts with the Muslim authorities in neighbouring countries and notably those in former Yugoslavia; that a new Muslim magazine called *Kara Deniz* ('The Black Sea') has begun to appear locally, that various other representatives of this community have – on a more or less official basis – visited Muslims in the former Yugoslavia, in particular at Skopje, Prichtina and Sarajevo; and that several young Romanian Muslims were sent during the course of 1991 to study at the famous *madrassa* Gazi Husrevleg at Sarajevo. We know far less about the links which must also have been forged with the various Muslim organisations in the Arab countries, in Turkey and other Muslim countries, and about the likely consequences of these for this small community.

GREECE

The Muslims of Greece must now number between 130 000 and 150 000 (approximately 2 per cent of the total population of the country). They belong to three quite distinct communities which are not united in a common organisation. They are the Turks (and the Gypsies) of Western Thrace, the Bulgarian-speaking Pomaks of the Rhodopea (whose urban fringe is also dissolving little by little into the Turkish communities of Western Thrace who are far more numerous and infinitely better organised; see Frangopoulos in this volume) and lastly a handful of Turks living on the islands of Rhodes and Kos.

The main group, that in Western Thrace, is a vital community, but is kept tightly in check by the local authorities and largely dependent on day-to-day relations between Greece and Turkey on which, in turn, it has a bearing. Recently, we have witnessed a fairly curious phenomenon in respect of this religious minority. While few publications on this little community had appeared in Greece for 50 years (only one book and a pamphlet to my knowledge since the end of the Second World War), recently Athens bookshop windows have displayed four new books on Greek Muslims, three of which appeared in 1990. The reason for this flurry of activity is quite simply because in the last general election in Greece (in June 1989) the majority party had only won by a whisker and, to all intents and purposes, this put the two Muslim representatives from Western Thrace in a position to determine the government.

Of course, this is an exceptional state of affairs, but one which cannot be repeated in the future because a new law has since been passed under which a party cannot be represented in the National

Assembly unless it wins at least 3 per cent of the votes. Meanwhile, we should note that one of the four books is precisely a detailed analysis of the Muslim vote in Greece in all the elections of the recent past (Anastassiadou, 1991–2).

ALBANIA

Seventy per cent Islamicised during the Ottoman domination of the Balkans, in 1945 – that is just after the seizure of power by the Communists – Albania numbered 816 677 Muslims (the rest of the population then comprised 20 per cent Orthodox and 10 per cent Catholics). Twenty years later, in 1967, the same local authorities suppressed all religious organisations in the country at the stroke of a pen and closed all places of worship without exception.

The very recent fall from power of Communism has led – as was to be expected – to the re-opening of places of worship. We are currently witnessing what seems to be a period of large-scale religious revival in Albania, not only among the Muslims but also the Catholic and Orthodox Christians. That said, we should not forget that the country is presently in a state of indescribable chaos (intensified by extreme economic hardship) and that the information we have is likely to be incomplete and unreliable. It would, however, be safe to assume that this religious revival among the Muslims is probably very strong at the individual level, but we know nothing of the likely reorganisation of the local Sunni Muslim community. It would also be very interesting to know what is happening on this front among the Bektachis, whose community has always been very numerous in Albania (to the point of being effectively the fourth of the country's recognised 'churches' at the beginning of the Communist era, along with the Catholic and Orthodox churches and the Sunni Muslim community). We only know that their mother house, the 'Kryegjshata' in Tirana, was recently reopened and that the Bektachi authorities in the former Yugoslavia (those in the town of Djakovica in Kosovo) were invited to attend the ceremony. But we know nothing at all of what has happened to the large numbers of monasteries (*tekke*) of the order which were formerly distributed throughout the whole country, or whether the present government intends to restore them (where they have not actually been destroyed) to their previous owners. As for the other Albanian Muslim mystic orders (Halvetis, Kadiris, Rifais, and others), we are now witnessing an extremely interesting phenomenon (recently confirmed in April 1991 among the Albanian dervishes of Kosovo in the former Yugoslavia; cf. Clayer, 1992). For over a year now, a large number of sheikhs have been making visits of varying duration to Albania in order to provide crash courses for the future local leaders of these orders whose tradition was interrupted in 1967.

To this we should add that the religious revival among Muslims in Albania is likely to be followed with particular interest by the Arab (and non-Arab) countries of the Near and Middle East, as witnessed by the funding offered towards the reopening of the Tirana Mosque by Turkey (albeit a secular, Kemalist state) during the visit of the Turkish Prime Minister Süleyman Demirel, in May 1992; and also by the official accession of Albania in December 1992 to the Islamic Conference Organisation (HICO) through the intermediary of its President, Sali Berisha, who made a trip to Saudi Arabia specially for this purpose.

BULGARIA

According to the 1946 Census (the last official census to ask about religion), the Muslim population in Bulgaria was then 938 418 out of a total population of 7 029 349: that is, 13 per cent of all residents. Taking natural increase into account as well as considerable emigration to Turkey (155 000 in the winter of 1950–1, about 300 000 in summer/autumn 1989) this would rise by now to above 600 000–800 000 persons, perhaps more. This comprises four groups who in ethnic terms are very different from each other.

One such group comprises the Islamised Bulgarians (about 150 000), called Pomaci, or Pomak in the singular. They speak Bulgarian, know no Turkish and live in the Rhodopean mountains and the region of Razlog. Mostly illiterate, until relatively recently they have almost never had an intelligentsia. It would be safe to assume that their assimilation (which was strongly sought after by the Bulgarian authorities following the country's independence and promoted with even greater vigour by the Communists over the last decades) took place with increasing momentum and that, since 1878 (the date of the founding of the Bulgarian state) – and especially since 1945 – their religiosity has succumbed to the onslaught of time.

The largest group by far is the Turks. Their number has fluctuated considerably since 1878 and is likely to continue to do so depending on political changes which remain unforeseeable. It is estimated that there are currently around 550 000 Turks dispersed across the different regions of Bulgaria (Deli, Ornam, Dobroudja, the length of the Danube, eastern Rhodopea) – but we do not know how many of these are practising Muslims.

Also in Bulgaria there are several thousand Tatars of whom some (though it is impossible to put a figure to this) are practising Muslims. They speak Tatar and live mainly in the region of Dobroudja, but one also finds small pockets dotted about elsewhere. Finally we should mention the existence of the Muslim Gypsies whose precise number is unknown but whose religiosity is for the most part not very strong.

The religious position of the Bulgarian Muslim community was, until the fall of Communism, very bad. Officially (as throughout the countries of Eastern Europe) there was freedom of religion, but the Bulgarian state followed a determined policy of secularisation and Bulgarianisation. From 1945 onwards, it used every means to restrict the practice of religion among the faithful (Christians as well as Muslims) such that today the religiosity of the population is in decline throughout the country. With regard to the Muslim community in particular, until very recently this manifested in the following: the enfeoffment of the most senior religious leaders, the suppression of religious festivals, the absence of a Muslim press, the impossibility of Bulgarian Muslims making the pilgrimage to Mecca or establishing contact with Muslim communities elsewhere, the proliferation of clubs for the promotion of 'scientific atheism', and so forth. The recent campaign of 'Bulgarianisation' of Turkish names prompted a massive exodus in 1989 of some 300 000 Muslims, possibly half of whom have returned since.

What has been happening with the Bulgarian Muslims since the 'delayed collapse' of the communist regime? We are witnessing above all a phenomenon which may appear odd but which has its own logic. The long death-throes of yesterday's power (which, obviously, are by no means over) and the weakening of its 'strike force' have been accompanied by a massive return of Muslim Turks (about 150 000) who emigrated to Turkey in 1989. On its return, this population – embittered and at the end of its tether – appears in certain regions to have indulged in acts of brutality against the Bulgarian Christian population. These, in turn, believing themselves to be threatened and abandoned by the Bulgarian authorities, organised in readiness to defend themselves into a 'Republic of Razgrad', taking the name from a place in the north east of the country. For some time now this 'Republic' has had a more or less effective existence. One consequence has been that the development of the situation has tended to favour the Bulgarian Muslims such that in the last elections the democratic party only won a slight majority over the (former) Communists, thanks in particular to an alliance forged with the 'Turkish Party'. This is the 'Movement for Law and Liberty' led by A. Dogan, which is a non-religious movement linked to the Turkish official circles, and should certainly not be confused with the 'party' of the religious Muslims (with which it is in opposition and open conflict) who surround the Grand Mufti who, in turn, maintains excellent relations with representatives of the Muslim religious organisations in the Arab countries (above all with those in Saudi Arabia, Kuwait and the Gulf Emirates).

One may reasonably suppose therefore that the Turkish Party (which had already dreamed for decades of wielding some degree of power) will prove well able to bargain with their votes. The more so since on the horizon (and for Bulgaria the horizon is not far off) looms the rise of a fairly strong religious party in Turkey itself, the Refah party which in the last Turkish elections (in 1991) won between 17 and 18 per cent of the votes. One may imagine therefore that if a Turkish Muslim religious party has such a hold in Turkey itself, we may expect that Muslims in Bulgaria (who are themselves Turks for the most part) will take strength from the future of this party. And one might add that a new Turkish language magazine, *Yeni Išik* ('New Light'), has now been appearing in Bulgaria for some time.

FORMER YUGOSLAVIA

No one knew just how many Muslims there were in Yugoslavia before the lid blew off of that state and the beginning of the civil war which has been raging ever since, given that the censuses of recent decades took no account of the people's religion. Their number, however, must have exceeded 3 million of a total of 22 418 331 (1981 Census).

They were divided into three main groups; these were: (1) in Bosnia-Herzegovina, Slav Muslims with 'Muslim nationality' (that is, whose existence was officially recognised by the Communist authorities for political reasons in 1969), Muslims with Serbian nationality and Muslims with Croatian nationality, in all about 2 million people; (2) in Serbia, in the region of Kosovo, Albanian Muslims above all, number a little over a million, plus some tens of thousands of Turkish Muslims; and (3) in Macedonia, Macedonian Muslims whose precise number is not known but is probably between 100 000 and 200 000; but above all, several hundreds of thousands of Albanian Muslims, plus around 100 000 Turkish Muslims. To these three groups must be added several tens of thousands of Muslims in Montenegro (some few Montenegran Muslims and many Albanian Muslims); also some tens of thousands of Gypsy Muslims and tens of thousands of other Muslims, belonging to all the nationalities referred to but dispersed throughout the country.

As we can see, then, the Yugoslav Muslim community presents in effect as several regional communities whose official (and unofficial) relations with the authorities, as well as their actual situation on the ground, displayed notable differences. That is why, if we are seeking to understand the exact situation of this complex puzzle, we need to look at each of the communities in turn. Let us start by very rapidly examining the totality of the situation before the outbreak of the civil war in Bosnia-Herzegovina in the spring of 1992.

A convenient and detailed analysis of the real position of the Yugoslavian Muslims during the whole of the Communist period (1945/89) may be found in a small book which I published a few years ago (Popovic, 1990). However, the situation has developed considerably since then, for after 45 years of a factitious stability being imposed on them, things started to move very fast indeed and we are, as I write (in 1993), far from the situation which existed only a few months ago. Moreover, there is now a large amount of material on this period but it is difficult to follow because it consists mainly of a large number of articles and all sorts of other bits of information which have appeared in the local press in the far corners of the country (papers which are, of course, almost impossible to find in Paris, where I write). However, a number of researchers – both indigenous and foreign – are currently working on these difficult and sensitive topics, to which at one point the flare-up in the Gulf added further confusion. Let us none the less try to say a few words here about the different Muslim groups in the former Yugoslavia, beginning with the lesser in numerical terms.

As we might have expected, we have absolutely no information at present about the outcome of the situation over this brief period for the Gypsy Muslims of the former Yugoslavia or those of Montenegro. It is also difficult to say anything specific (in terms of religion) about the Muslim Turks of former Yugoslavia whose news media remained determinedly secular and still committed to the 'progressive' 'revolutionary' and pseudo-Marxist style of the preceding decades. However, it is possible to pinpoint the recent creation of a Turkish 'independent' party which aimed to attract the whole of the country's Turkish population, although I am still unaware of its programme or its position on questions of religion (if indeed this has actually been made explicit).

Meanwhile, one heard more and more about the Macedonian Muslims who were seeking desperately to organise themselves in such a way as to be recognised and clearly distinguished on the one hand from their non-Muslim Macedonian compatriots and, on the other (even more so, it seems to me) from other groups of Yugoslavian Muslims (determined above all to escape from the strangle-hold of the Albanian Muslims of Kosovo who had over recent years infiltrated Western Macedonia in large numbers). But this looked as though it would be difficult to achieve, in view of the very small number of 'intellectuals' available to this restricted group.

It was (and still is) practically impossible to say anything specific about the current *religious* situation of the Albanian Muslims from Kosovo and from Yugoslavia in general because the outbreak of Albanian nationalism (which was certainly supported – albeit in an underhand way – by the former Communist regime over several decades) is so pervasive that it muddies the likely chances of analysing the real influence of the Muslim religion, in terms of both the mosques and the religious orders, on these populations.

But it is the situation of the muslims (with a small 'm', that is the more religious Muslims) and the Muslims (with a capital 'M' who tend to be more 'secular', according to current official terminology) of Bosnia-Herzegovina which has clearly been the most complex and the most illuminating. Of course it is the *combination* of these two groups, which are not distinguished for administrative or any other purposes (which provided scope for all sorts of manipulation in the Tito period), which constitutes the 'Muslim community' of Bosnia-Herzegovina in the strict sense of the term. We should also add that the religious Muslims (those with a small 'm') obviously form part of the 'ethnic' Muslims (those with a capital 'M') while the opposite is not the case.

Let us try as briefly as possible to describe the key elements of this brief two year period. The first free elections in Bosnia-Herzegovina since the Second World War saw the total 'déroute' of the Communist Party and victory for the newly created Muslim political party, which on this occasion brought together a 'holy alliance' of all the existing political factions. Shortly afterwards, and before the main defendant in the famous Sarajevo trial of 1983, Alija Izebegovic (who was condemned to prison for 15 years at the time by the Tito régime) became the new president of the Bosnia-Herzegovina government, the Muslim Political Party split into several factions with three main branches which may broadly be described as 'religious', 'secular' and 'leftist' (the latter embracing the Communists, Marxists and pseudo-Marxists). But the last group quickly withered away completely leaving in place only the 'usual' branches, the secular and religious, which clashed with each other increasingly openly in various meetings of their respective followers and through their media channels. The situation naturally appeared far from clear in respect both of the distribution of key posts and of the short- and long-term choices for the new government of Bosnia-Herzegovina and its true direction, when civil war began to be waged on its territory...

So let us conclude by saying a few words about the Muslims of the former Yugoslavia *since* the outbreak of civil war in Bosnia-Herzegovina. The first thing a historian should remember here is the obvious fact that this has been a complete disaster for all the peoples engaged in the conflict and that, for the present, we lack reliable and specific information on the one hand and sufficient distance on the other, to be able to discuss it coherently, and that we are therefore led to propounding very flimsy hypotheses based on our own preconceptions rather than on solid facts. Nor should we fail to stress from the outset one essential fact (largely glossed over by the great majority of our usual sources, both journalists and non-journalists alike): namely, that this has turned out to be a civil war unleashed on the one hand by the Orthodox (that is, Serbians) and the Catholics (that is, Croatians) of Bosnia-Herzegovina, refusing at any price to accept the prospect of living in what they believed (rightly or wrongly) would become an 'Islamic republic'; and on the other by a 'popular army' (as well as various police forces and militias of the 'ex-East-European' type) plentifully armed and equipped for over 40 years to defend the Tito régime against an expected Soviet attack. When the rest of the Communist world collapsed, it was able to draw along behind it (in several opposing camps) the different local nationalist groups ('à dominance pour ne pas dire à base religieuse' – dominated by, or based on, religion) which the previous Communist régime had effectively exploited over decades for its own ends, bringing them to the boil and thus very quickly transforming the civil war into an ethnic and religious war.

What are the consequences of this general disaster for the different Muslim populations of the country and what is their present situation? We can, I think, say without too much fear of contradiction, that the Muslim population of Bosnia-Herzegovina at large is the major loser in this war on all fronts (unless the region is split into three 'ethnic' zones reflecting the respective religious affiliation of their inhabitants, a split which for the present seems quite hypothetical to me inasmuch as it will be extremely difficult to achieve in practice): there is little prospect of its regaining the privileged status it held during the last decades of Communist power. The situation is similar (although infinitely less painful since these populations have escaped the atrocities of war) for the other Muslim groups in the former Yugoslavia referred to earlier – above all for the Albanian Muslims of Kosovo and Macedonia whose standing in the country (as an ethnic as much as a religious group) is currently at its lowest.

CONCLUSION

To begin to understand the position of Muslims in the Balkans after the fall of the Berlin Wall, we must, above all, bear in mind the three following facts. The first is that we are witnessing in five of the six countries of the region, and in a particularly spectacular fashion, a total collapse of all the structures established during the period of 'sovietisation' and periodically given a face lift since then in the course of innumerable 'reforms' which continually attempted to gloss over the essential fact of the moral and economic failure of the local Communist regimes. What has followed has been a period of chaos, a mixture of anything and everything, a period of massive upheaval which will quite certainly last a long time, for there is no chance of a quick miracle-cure in such a situation.

The second fact is that, as far as I have been able to see so far, the main tendency among the various Balkan Muslims comes down to euphoria at the fall of the former Communist regime – which benefits a nebulous and more or less mythical Islam (with the emphasis on the 'more' rather than the less). This is accompanied by a tendency constantly to paper over the differences in the rest of the Muslim world between the Sunnis and Shias, and also between reformist and traditionalist movements, while still trying to oust any trace of fundamentalism, as well as all the other burning issues at the heart of these multiple communities; and without trying to work out clearly the place of this Balkan *religious minority* in the society and the state in which it needs to live in the future.

Finally, the third fact is that – unless the Balkan Muslim populations are regrouped into separate enclaves to create Muslim states along the lines of what was done in Pakistan, for example – everywhere (except in Albania) the Muslim Balkan communities will, whatever happens, remain religious minorities living within non-Muslim states, and whose leaders will thus be called on, as in the past, to negotiate with the authorities of these 'unbelieving' states. The negotiations will conclude in compromises which will be more or less acceptable to the groups in question, thus sowing the seeds of discontent and likely friction to come, depending on unforeseen developments, oscillating between intransigence and the will to find acceptable forms of 'accommodation'. Meanwhile, young Muslims in the various states will pursue their studies, whether religious or otherwise, in Al-Ahzar, in Saudi Arabia, in Libya, in Iran and elsewhere. What they will reap, and what will they sow on their return, no one knows. What we do know, however, is that the present civil, ethnic and religious war in Bosnia-Herzegovina has for the foreseeable future poisoned relations between the various populations concerned, thus creating profound tensions between Muslims and non-Muslims in the whole of the Balkans. For the present, it is difficult to see when and how this major crisis and its consequences can hope to be resolved.

BIBLIOGRAPHY

Anastassiadou, M. (1991–2) 'La transmission du savoir dans le monde musulman périphérique', *Lettre d'information* 11 (March 1991), pp. 64–6, and 12 (March 1992), pp. 76–9 (Paris, CNRS-EHESS).
Bougarel, X. (1993) 'Discours d'un Ramadan de guerre civile', *L'Autre Europe*, March.
Bougarel, X. (1993) 'Le vote musulman en Yougoslavie', *La Revue Française de Science Politique*, Spring.
Clayer, N. (1992) *L'Albanie pays des derviches. Les ordres mystiques musulmans en Albania à l'époque post-ottomane (1912–1967)*, Balkanologische, Veröffentlichungen, Band 17 (Berlin: Otto Harrassowitz Verlag).
Popovic, A. (1986) *L'Islam balkanique. Les musulmans du sud-est européen dans la période post-ottomane*, Balkanologische Veröffentlichungen, Band 11 (Berlin: Otto Harrassowitz Verlag).
Popovic, A. (1990) *Les musulmans yougoslaves (1945–1989); médiateurs et métaphores* (Lausanne: Editions de l'Age d'Homme).
Popovic, A. (1992) 'L'islam dans les Balkans depuis la chute du mur de Berlin', in P. Michel (ed.), *Les Religions à l'est* (Paris: Editions du Cerf) pp. 161–81.

4 Religion, Identity and Political Conflict in a Pomak Village in Northern Greece

Yannis Frangopoulos

The following study is based on ethnographic fieldwork carried out in 1989 in a Pomak[1] village located in a mountainous area in the prefecture of Xanthi,[2] northeastern Greece. My initial interests in undertaking research concerned the complex changes which appear in a local community when it is confronted with a highly monetarised economy. Yet this particular community is an ethnic group within the Muslim minority in Thrace; hence, my overall research was largely affected by cultural aspects of social change affecting the village, aspects involving a question of identity which is no longer religious, but national.

In this chapter I examine religion and its function in the context of the local community, the elements which attest to a certain modification of its function as a universal social code, as well as the interaction between religion and politics at the local (village), regional (Thrace) and national (Greek) level. The role of religion as a symbolic expression of the villagers themselves clearly reveals the interactions within the village. Tradition is brought face to face with a new reality whose prime characteristic is change. The antithetical poles thus created are a faithful reflection of the changes that are taking place. The political conflict between these antithetical poles (here, between the imam and the mayor) is the best illustration of the conscious logic of the opposing factions and the objective logic of the balance of forces, forces indicating the appearance of new actors (farmers who exercise supplementary economic activities, young villagers) whose role as catalysts in the

73

above-mentioned conflict is not negligeable. The autonomy of the political field clearly demonstrates that all opposition on the level of village society is linked to the peripheral society (Thracian Muslims and Christians) and to the embracing society (the Greek state).

THE VILLAGE, ITS PUBLIC PLACES AND THE CONFIGURATION OF THE SOCIO-POLITICAL CONTEXT

A distance of 30 kilometres separates the village of Havari (a pseudonym) from the city of Xanthi. All along the road leading to the village, which is situated on the side of a mountain, the space is organised in a way that divides the slopes of the mountain into small fields. The fields begin at the outskirts of the village. The configuration of the ground dictates a terraced arrangement, both in the village as well as beyond, in the areas under cultivation. This explains why the village occupies a limited area, is densely built and difficult to reach. This arrangement is imposed by the need for arable land, the sole means of production for a largely agricultural population. Even in the village, the garden attached to each house is used for the first stage in tobacco cultivation. The internal morphology of the village corresponds to the architectural type found in other Thracian villages, built before the arrival of the Greek refugees from Asia Minor in 1923. Narrow lanes around the main street and the village square establish the contacts between inhabitants of different *mahala*.[3] Foot passages and terraces intersect these narrow roads. The main square, with the police station, three shops and two of the village's five cafes, is where most public activities take place.

According to village tradition, married sons continue to live in their father's house, together with their wives and children. This tradition of patrilocal residence is buttressed by the system of patrilineal descent. The home becomes the hub around which is organised the work of the farm, which involves the whole family. The importance of family life, clearly distinguished from public life, should not be ignored. Public life and private life are quite separate, as is made manifest by the walls which surround the houses (cf. Vernier, 1981).

The main street passing through the central square divides the village in two, separating the upper *mahala* from the lower *mahala*. On this street are found Havari's two mosques, town hall and primary school. From here one can just see, at the very edge of the village, a tiny

Christian church, practically lost in this wholly Muslim environment. The main square's cafes, the cafes in the side street and the mosques are the venues of a social life which, in its reference points and its collective signalisation, faithfully reflects the economic, cultural and political reality of the village.

I am particularly interested in spatial signification, which reveals the transactions constituting the social life of the village and the attitudes expressed towards a single reality. How do village spatial arrangements become a foundation for human activity and a constituent of the inter-action among the villagers? The various appropriations of space by the actors, morphology in support of group identity, indicate the structure of position in the village, demonstrate the existence of opposing groups, and illustrate the distinctive perceptions of reality and ways of acting (cf. Remy, 1975).

Oppositions, interaction between groups and a state of conflict con-stitute the reality I encountered on my arrival in the village. My initial contact with the village took place in the common area of the coffee houses on the main square. Spending time in public places, in fact, con-stituted the bulk of my on-site activity. My first contacts were made in a cafe on the main square, the one patronised by the imam of the new mosque. Later I went to the cafe on the other side of the square, the one frequented by the supporters of the incumbent mayor. Finally, I discov-ered the three cafes in the side street, patronised by the youth and the adult population of the village. It was indeed a 'discovery', in the sense that this area is removed from the main square, that it plays host to dis-tinct attitudes, and that from it stems whatever is new and different, in comparison with the standard, institutionalised views of the main square.

It was not until the end of my stay that I was able to go beyond the limits of these public places and enter the daily family life of the vil-lagers. For this reason my information on private space is limited, which severely circumscribed my overall work since I was obliged to content myself with the talk of the men. In other words, frequenting public places was my only means of collecting information, particu-larly since the haunts of men are the best place to learn about the political realities of village life.

The cafes are extremely important places in the social life of the village. They constitute the official forum of village life; it is there that public affairs are conducted. As in all of rural Greece, taking part in social life and in everything of significance to the community is a sort of obligation, a means of affirming one's adherence to a collective identity. The poles thus created may be compatible or they may be opposed. They are frequently marked by the political life of the country, and thus present both the reality lived in the microcosm of the village on the one hand, and on the other, the reality which goes beyond the village boundaries. In these communal places, political stands are taken in collective debate and collective memories are constituted and expressed, with the result that these places are socially labelled.

The exclusively masculine participation in public affairs reflects the marked distinction between private and public life. Public life is the privilege of the men, while private life is the domain of the women. Feminine activity can nevertheless have a considerable influence on the definition and constitution of roles in public life.

In the village cafes I frequented, I had so to speak to win a place for myself; and there were many questions on the purpose of my journey and on my installation in the village. What is interesting to note is that people's reaction to me exhibited a certain homogeneity according to the place where it was expressed. In the main square cafe patronised by the imam, suspicion was expressed by the maintenance of a distant attitude prohibiting any contact. It was only after I made the acquaintance of the imam and explained to him the purpose of my journey that I was accepted by the people in the cafe. My participation in the prayers held at the new mosque was seen as respect for their religion and recognition of the Muslim tradition to which they were so deeply attached.

In the cafe across the way – that frequented by the supporters of the mayor – my presence was not accorded any great importance. The mayor maintained towards me an attitude at once distant and friendly: he gave me the use of an apartment, free of charge (just above the cafe, it had formerly housed policemen), but I was not able to have more than a few minutes conversation with him.

The cafes in the side street were where I spent the latter part of my sojourn in Havari. There, personal relations gave rise to encounters and discussions which swept away all trace of suspicion. It was in these cafes that I felt best accepted and most at home, and able to go beyond my condition of observer.

My arrival in the village corresponded to an eventful period for the Muslim minority in Thrace. When the Greek authorities ordered the name of a teachers' association to be changed from 'Turkish Association' to 'Muslim Association', the demonstrations of the

Muslim minority produced an atmosphere of tension. At the same time, at an economic forum in Switzerland, discussions between the Prime Ministers of Greece and of Turkey on the state of relations between the two countries served as a general framework for these events (it was not long ago that Turkish diplomats were raising the question of oppression practised against the Muslim minority in Greece). The demonstration quickly took on a political character, namely one against the Greek state. A number of the villagers took part in the action, and of these the most highly involved were the supporters of the imam of the new mosque. This faction expressed militantly pro-Turkish sentiments, a state of affairs which reflects the trend expressed by a section of the Muslim minority in Thrace. These sentiments were not shared by the rest of the villagers.

Those on the side of the incumbent mayor of the commune cannot be defined in relation to a Turkish national identity. Their political positions follow the political structure of the Greek state. Given that political power in the village has been in the hands of the mayor for forty years, they are seen by the imam's party as belonging to the forces of the oppressor (the Greek state). But at the same time, their religiousness coincides with the devotion to tradition of the imam's people. The coupling of shared cultural values and political divergence only intensifies the conflict between these two poles.

The patrons of the cafes in the side street are generally not involved in such rifts dividing the village. Their manner of participating in Greek reality indicates their distance from the established antagonisms within the village. Nevertheless, the growing political power of this segment of the population within the internal structure of the village is catalysing the rift between the two opposing poles.

In this situation, my coming to the village spotlighted existing tensions. My scrutiny focused them. With me perceived to be on one side and the villagers on the other, we found ourselves caught up in a game where conformity to role delineated positions already existing within the village.

TRADITION IN THE FACE OF CHANGE: THE IMAM OF THE NEW MOSQUE AND THE TRADITIONALIST FACTION

The imam of the new mosque in the hamlet of Havari is an authoritative personality in the social life of the village. Recognised by friend and foe alike as *Imam effendi*, he is often a focal point of cafe discussion. Like the other men, he wears western dress, with a black jacket for religious festivals. His white-bordered garment is the badge of his religious function. The imam, laughing, often advised me to tell the villagers I knew him in order to facilitate contact with them. He was well aware of his power in the village.

Master of sacred things, focus of religious expression, capable of reciting lengthy passages of the Qur'an, he stands out as a scholar. His command of Greek at a superior level was of great assistance to his fellow-villagers in the past, especially in administrative dealings with the state. Since the arrival of a municipal secretary in the village, and with the raising of the average general level of education among the villagers, his role as go-between with the administration is steadily declining. The imam, however, is still the principal spokesman for the Muslim community of the village with the religious administration of the Muslim minority. All matters relating to the *Sharia*, or Muslim law must be settled by the central religious authority in the prefecture, the *mufti*, in Xanthi (Sefertzis, 1985).

The role of the imam in village life is thus still an essential one. Besides his religious duties at the mosque, he gives the Pomak children lessons in reading and understanding the Qur'an. He set up this school himself to supplement the state school and to provide religious training for Pomak children every day after school. The imam's insistence on preserving religious tradition can be clearly seen in the children who, when primary school is over, attend the Qur'anic school for a further two hours. The socialisation of the Pomak youth by the imam occupies a second level, for basic religious instruction is also given at the state school by the *hoca* (priest) of the old mosque.

Believers turn to the imam for guidance in all matters of ethics: this is a fact of extraordinary importance. Questions of theodicy and people's obsession with a life led according to divine will (represented by the imam) are still very real and very important in the local community. The imam is always ready to answer questions and succour the faithful.

Bound up with village reality, with the lives of his believers and all their problems (he is himself a tobacco farmer), and having thus the most direct of contacts with the reality of village life, he is a personality on the one hand vehemently supported and on the other silently rejected. He could be called a 'charismatic leader', an image which embraces all the ambivalence of acceptance and refusal, fascination and aloofness.

That segment of the population which sees the imam as a man consecrated to the divine, a man endowed with power, is also that which is the most firmly attached to maintaining Muslim tradition. This nucleus is formed of a few *Hadjis* (who have made the pilgrimage to Mecca), the old men of the village and those of the adult population who pray in the new mosque and who frequent the same cafe as the imam.

Members of this religious faction in the village, for whom their leader is also their outward expression, see reality in terms of traditional Muslim morality. They are for the most part tobacco farmers with sufficient land for their needs, and no need to look for other sources of income (such as in forestry, seasonal migration, salaried positions in the city).

The patrilinear and patrilocal system, which is also applied within the agricultural process, defines power relationships within the family and within the community as a function of age. It is the older men who hold authority over the younger as well as over the women and children. It is the older men who organise the various tasks pertaining to tobacco cultivation. The seasonal emigration of the young men, the introduction of salaried incomes, the diminishing importance of agricultural labour, the introduction of a new system of values in the village (especially by way of television, video and alcohol), increased interest in travelling (even for economic reasons), and contacts with urban centres (Xanthi, Piraeus) are seen by traditionalists as threats to the internal stability of the village.

The steady decline in religious observance among the young people is a fact which does not leave the imam and the nucleus of believers in the village indifferent. The perceived progressive de-Islamisation of society produces a changing situation which provokes the opposition of the traditionalists among the villagers. Spokesman of this opposition is the village imam, the coherent expression of the demands of this segment of the village. It would seem that those who hold to cultural conservatism are taking the offensive in the face of a change seen as threatening. At the same time, the fact that the Pomaks are a Muslim minority in a society which is overwhelmingly Christian gives additional impetus to the search for and the affirmation of a cultural identity.

The inside (the village) facing the outside (the foreign) creates a series of structural oppositions which approach the conflict of good and evil, as seen by the people belonging to the imam's faction. For the imam, Islam is the universal frame of reference explaining social reality. Any dissociation between religious matters and political matters is condemned outright. As for the elements necessary for survival, their presence or absence falls within the sphere of Divine Providence and Muslim morality. Allah is omniscient: He knows when the rain will fall, when the fields will be ready for the young tobacco plants, and so forth (yet this does not prevent the imam from insuring his crop against natural disaster).

THE HOCA OF THE OLD MOSQUE AND THE POTENTIAL FOR DEFINITION OUTSIDE THE PURELY RELIGIOUS FIELD

The hoca of the old mosque is a man whose place in the social life of the village is not so obvious. He is rarely seen in the cafes. He is usually to be found either in the village primary school, where he gives religious instruction to the Pomak children, or in the old mosque. His salary as a teacher is paid by the state. The people who go to the old mosque, where he officiates every Friday, do not frequent the same cafe as the imam, but patronise either the cafe across the square or the other cafes in the village.

This structural dichotomy of public places demonstrates the opposition between the two factions, that of the imam and that of those who pray at the old mosque. The divergent appropriation of the religious message depending on locality spotlights the conflict reigning between the two poles of expression and becomes an illustration of the village's social structure. The fact that the hoca teaches at the primary school and is paid by the Greek state is frowned upon by the traditionalists. Moreover, the hoca of the old mosque does not follow the orders and the political tendencies of the Islamic clergy of the Muslim minority headed by the mufti, whose attitudes toward the Greek state are frequently negative and thus a source of tension and conflict. Given a substantial segment of the Muslim minority in Thrace is Turkish-speaking (perhaps 70 000; Kettani, 1980), its special legal status, and a number of other political factors (not least the tense state of political relations between Greece and Turkey), the religious authorities tend to express vigorously pro-Turkish opinions. The imam of the new mosque follows this path. The hoca, however, maintains a clear distinction between

Islam and the political choices of his flock; he disapproves of the mufti adopting a political position.

The hoca thus becomes the pole of attraction of those villagers who are opposed to the imam but who are not overtly against the Greek state. The marked opposition between the Muslim village and the Greek state, seen by the traditionalists as a force of oppression, creates a state of conflict within the village and a reality which confronted me from the time I arrived in Havari.

The hoca appears to promote a more secular religion. This means that people can be left free to define their positions outside the narrow frame of religion. (At the same time, he is one of those old-fashioned Muslims who have never accepted Kemal Ataturk's laicisms!) In fact, those who attend his mosque support the mayor of the village or belong to other political factions. The hoca's stimulation of a certain political consciousness is a vital factor. He also dwells on the importance of the Muslim faith as a fundamental value for Pomak society. He frequently uses the term 'Pomak', whereas the imam finds it completely unacceptable and unrepresentative of the ethnic origin of this society. It should be noted that the question of ethnic origin is an issue promoted principally by the traditionalists.

RELIGION: LOCUS OF CULTURAL AFFINITIES, EXPRESSION OF A NATIONAL IDENTITY

The question of ethnic origin and the affirmation of a national identity arises from among the traditionalist segment, even though the reference position (piety, conformity to tradition, rhythm of life according to the religious time frame) of the adherents of the incumbent mayor is entirely compatible with that of the traditionalists. There is a very deep rift between these two factions, and the basis of differentiation resides in the affirmation by the traditionalists of a Turkish national identity.

The point of incompatibility within a model (the model of a Muslim culture) appears to me as an indication of dissociation and as a frame of illustration, within the village, of positions within the process of change. A second point, which should be analysed primarily from the political point of view, is that which attests the emergence of new principles for the perception of reality and the differentiation of these principles from the 'classic' opposition of the two factions we have been talking about. By this we mean the political consciousness of those farmers (tending to the socialist), who also exercise other economic activities, and of the youth of the village. Here I should like to remark that in this part of my analysis the role of external factors is critical. The ethnic origin of the Pomaks has frequently been called into question, and this is very significant. Many books on the history of this population have been written, by Greek (Foteas, 1978; Hidiroglou, 1989), Bulgarian (Karpat, 1985) and Turkish (Aydinli, 1973) historians. This situation can result in social destabilisation and acculturation, whose effects on the individual and the collective psyche may be considerable.

Within the village of Havari, the mayor's party finds it convenient to assert the cultural (Muslim) character of the Pomak population. The hoca of the old mosque calls for a distinction between religion and political position. While belonging to the world of tradition and having a perception of reality in moral terms, these people see 'the outside' – the powers that be, the state – as a reality with which it is in their interest to conform. To this extent, the dichotomous manner in which the traditionalists perceive reality (weakness/force, good/evil) is outmoded: the adherents of the mayor do not see the power of the state as a great injustice which must be put right (obviously within the measure with which they themselves assume its power within the village).

The position of the village on cultural identity does not prevent acceptance of outside political power. The appropriation of political power in the village (in office for forty years) enables the mayor's party to assume a sort of equilibrium and accomodation. The dichotomous universe which paints reality as black and white is here seen in shades of grey. This is the essential difference between the imam's faction and the mayor's party, the latter for whom neither the village's cultural particularity nor the classic antithesis between town and country is a source of conflict with the external political power – the Greek state.

The cafe patronised by the incumbent mayor is a place of contact between the villagers and the outside world. The post-box is here, and here mail is distributed and pensions paid. This cafe is also frequented by the village police chief and his men and by several of the municipal councillors: in fact, the owner is also the deputy mayor of the village.

The political consciousness of those farmers who exercise supplementary economic activities and that of the youth of the village ignores the issues in which the conflict between the two factions (imam–mayor) is rooted. The common denominator between these two sub-groups is economic activity outside the village. The farmers' affirmation of a Muslim cultural identity (although they keep religion and politics separate) and the young peoples' new system of references (the Greek model, the desire to leave the village) leave a space in which individual autonomy is the principal factor. On the level of social relations, these groups' direct contact with urban economic life and their search for alternatives within the village shatter the dichotomic universe of the traditionalists.

For the traditionalists, the situation is perceived quite differently. Structural oppositions accumulate and turn into intersecting semantic axes: economic weakness, the lack of control of information and the lack of political power are associated with moral quality and characterise the inside, the village. Political and economic power and control of information are equated with moral perversion and characterise the outside, the city and the state. For these people, the Greek state is an outsider with a direct ascendancy over the life of the village: this is therefore a tremendous injustice which must be remedied. The imam sees this as a betrayal of village tradition on the part of the mayor, for the mayor, although belonging to the village, has joined forces with the oppressor.

This antithetical view of the relationship between the urban and the rural is important: generally speaking, throughout the Greek countryside the state is seen as the source of the village's difficulties. In the case of the Pomaks, this differentiation (us/them, rural/urban) is transposed to the symbolic level (national identity). The cultural model (as Muslim Turk) is the best possible answer to the search for the 'good times' of the past, where the dominant element is religious expression.

The questions which arise at this point refer to the meaning of the symbolic expression (national identity) and the process which mobilises it. The process of change is a relatively recent phenomenon in the village. It constitutes the general framework for interaction within the community. The various segments of the population express their different attitudes according to their position in the structure of social relationships. Nevertheless, their attitudes do not always adhere to a strictly intentional logic. This is where the role of symbolic expression comes into its own.

The religious reading of reality on the part of the traditionalists is a fact. The threat experienced by these people in their reality (including the ultimate fear, evoked at critical moments in the relations between minority and state: Christianisation!) is expressed in symbolical language. Since it is associated with power, with the external, with the Greek state, this menace fuels the search for an imaginary, but not therefore necessarily fictitious, place of well-being. The assertion of their difference from the 'outside' world (cultural identity) and the subsequent placing of this model in a 'real' setting where it may exist (Turkey) are the two steps in a process which leads to their affirmation of a Turkish national identity.

Here the role of the leader of this faction (the imam) is very important. It is he who gives coherence to the expression of the traditionalists, and it is he who brings information to his supporters, the privileged agent. He has ties with the religious administration of the Muslim minority in Thrace (muftia), and he shares their pro-Turkish sentiments. In this way he is the expression of the measure in which the tendencies of the Muslim minority constitute the global framework for interactions within the village.

SOCIAL CHANGES IN THE URBAN MILIEU AND ITS ECHOES IN RURAL SOCIETY

At the moment, part of the broader Muslim minority in Thrace is caught up in a process paralleling that described in the case of the village of Havari.[4] Although this minority was, until the 1960s, largely agricultural, recent urbanisation has given rise to an urban middle class whose increasing influence in Greek society cannot be ignored (Sefertzis, 1985). Open to socio-economic types of transactions, it affirms an autonomous presence on the public scene. This urban elite is gathered around poles of expression both symbolical (muftia) and political (Muslim candidates on the lists of political parties represented in the parliament).

The transactions and liaisons on the economic level (urban middle class), on the symbolic level (re-affirmation of a Muslim cultural identity represented by the muftia) and on the political level (Muslim members of parliament) are all factors conducive to violent confrontations (such as the demonstrations in Komotini in February 1988).

The echoes of these changes taking place in the urban centres (Xanthi, Komotini) reach the village via privileged agents, who to this extent structure the villagers' perception of reality. The emotional mobilisation of the imam's faction during the events in Komotini is a reality. Demonstrations by the Muslim minority in Komotini on the one hand, and on the other the brutal declarations in the cafe frequented by the imam on the subject of Turkish national identity (during the reading of a review asserting state oppression of the minority), constitute the two faces of the current reality.

THE POLITICAL DOMAIN: ATTITUDES, OPPOSITIONS AND CONNECTION

The commune of Havari, numbering some 2000 inhabitants (according to a 1951 census) belongs to the prefecture of Xanthi. The political leader of the village is the mayor, who is elected for a period of four years by the entire adult population. He represents the village before the administrative authorities of the country; he lays the requests and the needs of the village before the state for its intervention. Within the agricultural production marketing cycle, the state – and particularly the Minister of Agriculture – plays the role of intermediary between the village farmers and the tobacco dealers. Here the mayor's role is obvious: each problem which arises and which comes under the umbrella of the state requires his intervention.

All public works projects in the commune and in the surrounding area must be promoted and managed by the mayor. For all special status problems arising in the village (that is, affecting the Muslim minority under special legal jurisdiction: questions of freedom of religious observance, education of the minority, and so forth), the mayor has a particular ascendancy. His role as intermediary puts him in direct contact with the prefect in Xanthi.

Communal elections are held one year after the national parliamentary elections. As is to be expected, they become an occasion for the expression of the oppositions existing within the village. The social structure of the village is evident when one takes into account the political attitudes and the manifest tendencies which aggregate around the roles of expression (candidates).

Three parties contested the last local elections in the village. These three parties all exist at the national level and are represented in parliament. When I was first in the village (March 1988) the third party, a religious party supported by the village imam, had no equivalent on the national scene. It was not until the parliamentary elections of June 1989 that two lists of 'independent' Muslim candidates appeared in Thrace. The first list (prefecture of Xanthi) was called *Gûven* (confidence) and the second (prefecture of Rhodopi) *Kismet* (destiny). One Muslim 'independent' (A. Sadik) was elected in the prefecture of Rhodopi (see Thanopoulos, 1990).

The New Democracy (ND) party won the parliamentary elections of April 1990 with the bare minimum of 150 seats, and the role of the 'independent' candidates was crucial. The voters elected an 'independent' in the prefecture of Xanthi (A. Faikoglou, an ex-socialist deputy) and another in the prefecture of Rhodopi (A. Sadik), which meant the loss of a seat for both the New Democracy party and the Panhellenic Socialist Movement (Pa So K). The seat lost by New Democracy would have given an absolute majority (150+1 seats in a chamber of 300) to this party, which did in the event form a government with the support (one seat) of the Democratic Renewal party (DiAna). At this time, the eyes of Greece were turned to Thrace, and what the Greek political world watched was the emergence of a political group marked solely by the Muslim faith and boasting an extraordinary unanimity.

In the village, each of these three parties fielded a candidate: a candidate supported by the imam of the village, a candidate (now mayor) supported by the right-wing party (ND) and a candidate backed by the socialist party (PaSoK). In the last elections the out-going mayor was re-elected.

The imam, having set himself up as the champion of village identity and the interests of the oppressed Muslim minority, is opposed to the mayor who is seen as belonging to the Greek state, the foreigner, the oppressor. This antithesis reflects the two poles of opposition – Muslim village/Greek state – and is manipulated by the imam. It is also shared by the traditionalists who attend the imam's mosque and frequent the cafe he patronises. Further, this opposition reaches dangerous levels when the imam's faction starts to assert an identity that is no longer cultural but national (Turkish).

The polarisation becomes extreme when it is expressed in moral terms: there is a notion of 'the mayor, that traitor', which displays the homogeneity of the imam's faction and expresses its rage. For his part, the mayor maintains a more diplomatic position with regard to the other groupings: he no longer lives in the village, but is there every day; he does not use the imam's cafe, but I have seen him praying in the new mosque. He is definitely a threat to the imam; and he is capable of penetrating his circle, either to affirm his respect for his religion and for traditional standards, or to endeavour to soothe the rage of the traditionalists in order to garner votes in the next elections.

The dualism of the traditionalists means that anyone who is paid by, or has contacts with, the state is regarded with suspicion. The secretary of the commune, the rural policeman, the teacher in the Pomak primary school (himself a villager), and above all the hoca of the old mosque, are all viewed in this way.

The trend expressed by the socialists is new to the village. The people who constitute this faction do not patronise either the imam's cafe or the mayor's, but frequent the three cafes located in a side street near the main square. Generally speaking, I would say that these people who call themselves socialists are those whose economic positions are among the weakest in the village: the afore-mentioned young people whose common denominator is seasonal migration, and farmers still living in the village who also exercise other supplementary activities (salaried positions in the city, work in the forest, public works in the area, etc). Their contact with the reality of Greece means that they are part of it and have adopted a different position with respect to it. They thus turn to a political life which goes beyond the limits of the village. The political consciousness thus affirmed moves away from the traditional rifts characteristic of political life in the village. Alongside the classic opposition between state and village, Christian and Muslim, new structural principles modifying the political scene are now emerging. The ever harsher confrontation between the Pomaks and a reality no longer corresponding to their traditional world has produced a new reading of the balance of powers and of interests in the political arena, thus shattering the traditional model of a strictly religious reading of reality.

CONCLUSION

The spatial definition of human activity assumes an important explanatory autonomy and becomes a method offering a framework for the global analysis of the society being studied. The socio-economic groups identified – that is, those farmers who grow nothing but tobacco, those farmers who exercise other supplementary economic activities and the seasonal migrants – correspond to the current of cultural traditionalism (the elderly, some of the adults), the 'modernist' current (adults, married men) and the 'migratory' tendency (most likely young people). The first group is divided into the pro-Turkish faction, supporters of the Muslim independent member of parliament, and the pro-Greek faction, supporters of the right: this is the fundamental dichotomy dividing both this village and the entire Muslim minority in Thrace, as we have seen. The other two groups seem to hold themselves apart from this opposition, and include both socialists and rightists.

What is noteworthy with respect to the emergence of these new reality-structuring principles and balance of forces created on the political scene is that these (socialist) tendencies – expressed after 1980 in the social structure of the village as well as throughout the entire Muslim minority – have not been able to mature and take root. Rather, they appear to have been subsumed in another reality-structuring principle, that of militant Islam politicised against the Christian state. This structuration has been conducive to the creation of a politicised Islam embracing all the symbolic messages of redemption and of the renaissance of the Muslim population. It is as if the traditionalist analysis of reality in terms of morality has been supplemented by another rational vision which takes careful account of the play of forces in the surroundings. This is the work of the intellectual avant-garde of the Thracian Muslim minority: could it not also be the work of the imam in the microcosm of the village?

Bearing in mind the results of the briefly-mentioned parliamentary elections in June 1989 and April 1990, it is clear that the creation of Muslim political parties can only indicate that the minority has fallen back on the model of activist Islam, thus reinforcing the link between religion and politics. Might this not be a specificity of Greek Islam?

Yet what is Greek Islam? Does the close link between religion and politics justify its description as traditionalist, when the present religious situation displays the influence of a spirit of reform (evidenced in a Qur'an written in Latin characters, western dress)? Is it an Islam marked by the secular pronouncements of the reformer Kemal Ataturk? Or is it an Islam which embraces all these elements (traditionalism, reformation, secularisation) but which superposes its own special character and follows its fortune on the basis of the socio-political interactions within the Greek state, a situation which echoes its status of a Muslim minority within a Christian majority? In this case, its behaviour would be marked by the selective exploitation of those elements necessary for the creation of a unanimous social movement, despite the oppositions remaining within its ranks.

ACKNOWLEDGEMENTS

I would like to thank Professors Stathis Damianakos, Felice Dasseto, Robert Deliege, Maurice Godelier, Jean Remy, Fotini Tsimbiridou and Bernard Vernier for their helpful comments on an earlier draft of this paper. This project would not have been continued, toward a PhD in sociology at the Catholic University of Louvain, without the financial and moral support which was so generously offered to me by the Administrative Council of the Museum of the Macedonian Struggle, the 'A. S. Onassis Foundation' and the Service 'Task-Force, Human Resources' of the Commission of the European Communities.

NOTES

1. The Pomaks are a people dwelling in the mountainous areas of the prefectures of Xanthi and Rhodopi; there are also a few Pomak villages in the prefecture of Evros. The same name also refers to another population living beyond the Greek border, in Bulgaria (see Popovic, Chapter 3 in this volume). The homogeneity of the Pomak people is due to their geographical distribution (hamlets and villages in the mountains, far from urban centres), their Muslim faith (different from that of the majority of Greeks, who are Orthodox Christians), and their language, which is purely a spoken tongue descended from an ancient Slav language. This group of some 35 000 people forms a part of the Muslim minority in Thrace (approximately 110 000), which also includes the Turkish-speaking Muslims (about 70 000) living on the plain and the semi-nomadic Muslim Gypsies (*Yifti*).

2. The prefecture of Xanthi, with that of Rhodopi (capital Komotini) and that of Evros (capital Alexandroupolis), together make up the province (Diamerisma) of Thrace.

3. *Mahala* is a Turkish word indicating a part of the village that is often set apart by some physical obstacle; frequently, however, the specificity of the *mahala* is expressed in terms of linguistic differentiation (e.g. Turkish-speaking *mahala*) – see Tentokali (1989).

4.   There are, however, important differences. In the village the effects of economic change which are seen as destructive (at least by the traditionalists) provoke a 'symbolic' reaction, while for that segment of the broader Muslim minority which holds the same positions, it is a re-affirmation of its existence within the Greek social structure (the urban middle class). Its role as intellectual avant-garde for the rural areas is here quite clear.

REFERENCES

Aydinli, A. (1971) *Bati Trakya faciasinin iç yûsû* (Istanbul: Akin). [Summary translated into Greek by K. Andreadis in *Valkaniki Vivliografia (Balkan Bibliography)*, 1 (Suppl.), pp. 311–456.

Foteas, P. (1978) *The Pomaks of Western Thrace* (Komotini: Morfotikos Omilos Komotinis) (in Greek).

Hidiroglou, P. (1989) *The Greek Pomaks and their Relations with Turkey* (Athens: Herodotos) (in Greek).

Karpat, K. (1985) *Ottman Population, 1830–1914: Demographic and Social Characteristics* (Madison: University of Wisconsin Press).

Kettani, M. A. (1980) 'Muslims in Southern Europe', *Journal of the Institute of Muslim Minority Affairs*, 2, pp. 145–57.

Remy, J. (1975) 'Space and Sociological Theory: Research Methods', *Recherches Sociologiques*, 3, pp. 279–93.

Sefertzis, G. (1985) 'The Muslims of Western Thrace: The History of a Multifold Drama', *Tetradia dialogou, erevnas ke kritikis (Dialogue, Research and Criticism)*, 11 (spring–summer), pp. 59–66.

Tentokali, V. (1989) *The Organisation of Inhabited Space as an Expression of Family Structure: The Case of Organi* (Thessaloniki: University Studio Press) (in Greek).

Thanopoulos, K. (1990) 'The Muslims in Thrace and the Greek State', *Eleftherotypia*, 16 (August) (in Greek).

Vernier, B. (1981) 'Mythical Representation of the World and Male Domination among the Pomaks in Greece', *Greek Review of Social Research*, special issue, pp. 122–42.

5 The Muslim Minority in Poland

Bogdan Szajkowski

Muslims account for one of the smallest religious groups in Poland. They are comprised of three groups, each with a distinctive history, set of traditions, and place in Polish society. The first group, the Tatars – or more precisely, Poles of Tatar origins – have been part of Polish history, cultural tradition and religious landscape since the fourteenth century. The second group are the newcomers from Arab countries, who arrived in Poland predominantly as students since the early 1970s, married in Poland and subsequently settled. The third group is comprised of very recent refugees from war-torn Bosnia-Herzegovina.

There are no accurate figures concerning the Muslim minority in Poland. Estimates of practising believers (excluding several thousand students and other temporary visitors to the country) given in Polish sources vary from about 1800 (Tokarczyk, 1987) to over 3000 (Konopacki, 1977). Non-Polish sources give much larger figures of 15 000 (Ramet, 1984) and 22 000 (Kettani, 1986). Both of the non-Polish figures are clearly exaggerated, even if taking into account expatriate Muslims residing temporarily in Poland. The lack of accurate data on the Polish Muslims reflects a general dearth of reliable information on religious affiliation in Poland. In censuses carried out during the Communist period, no questions pertaining to religious affiliation were allowed; consequently, all religious denominations have based their membership on learned guesses. However, in the case of small groups such as the Muslims, one can gain a reasonably convincing estimate of their numbers from attendance of religious ceremonies and membership of relevant religious, cultural and social organisations. On the basis of the available data, one should conclude that the most accurate figure for the number of practising Polish Muslims is probably around 3000, the majority of whom belong to the Sunni tradition of Islam.

The majority by far of Polish Muslims are of Tatar origins, although the denomination also includes a very small number of recent Polish converts to Islam. Some of the converts brought the Islamic faith back to Poland after their extended working visits to the Middle East and Arab Gulf states. However, since the recent converts constitute a minuscule group, and since there is no reliable sociological or ethnographic material on the other main Muslim populations of Poland, this essay focuses on the long established group of Tatars.

THE TATAR PRESENCE THROUGH HISTORY

The term 'Tatar' means 'archer.' The name has come to be applied to several related, but spatially disparate peoples. Today's Tatars cannot be regarded as direct descendants of the Tatar Mongols of Manchuria who overran much of Eurasia in the thirteenth century. Instead, contemporary Tatars are to be recognised as distant scions of the Turkic-speaking Volga-Kama Bulgars, to whom they owe their Islamic heritage.

The Tatars arrived in the Lithuanian part of the Kingdom of Poland and Lithuania in the fourteenth century. The first mention of the Tatars in Lithuanian–Polish lands comes from the Franciscan Chronicle of Lukasz Waddiga in 1324. Later, according to the fifteenth century Polish historian Jan Dlugosz, 'many thousands' of Tatars were taken prisoner by the Lithuanian Grand Duke Witold in 1397 during his expedition on the Volga river, and were subsequently relocated with their entire families to his lands. Tatar regiments fought on the side of the Polish and Lithuanian armies at the decisive battle of Grunwald (Eastern Prussia) against the Teutonic Order in 1410. By 1412, Grand Duke Witold had begun to build a chain of forts on the right bank of the Dnepr river and garrison them with Tatar mercenaries known as Kazaks or 'free adventurers'. These frontier communities attracted a growing number of people, including Slav peasants and outlaws who adopted the lifestyle of the Tatars (Davies, 1981). The chain of garrisons served as a shell against the incursion of the Teutonic Order into Lithuania. Over the next three centuries, many more Tatars followed the earlier arrivals. Most of these came from the area of the Crimea.

Following a succession of famines, epidemics, internal clashes and feuds in their native Khanates, a considerable number of Tatar nobles left their houses and resettled in Polish lands, mostly around the Lithuanian capital Vilnius, but also in the foothills of the Tatar Mountains in southern Poland (Podlasie) and in the Lublin regions. They were given equal rights to those of Poles and Lithuanians, except for the right to engage in political activities. Renowned and experienced warriors, they served mostly in special Tatar units with either the royal forces or the local magnates' own private armies. Tatar noblemen legally enjoyed the same privileges as the Polish nobility. In return for their services to the crown, they acquired large estates and land-titles. Those of more humble origin established themselves in villages and small cities, becoming known as excellent horse breeders, horse traders, gardeners, horticulturists and artisans.

By the end of the sixteenth century, the Tatar presence in Poland was firmly established. In 1569 the parliament (*sejm*) of nobility which gathered in Lublin gave formal permission for the construction of mosques and Tatar schools. In 1591 the number of Tatars in Poland was estimated at between 60 000 and 70 000, among whom there were some 400 mosques (Podhorodecki, 1971). A census ordered in 1631 by King Sigismund III listed more than 100 000 Tatar resettlers in Poland. The Turkish historian Ibrahim Pasha Pachevi, who died in 1640, gave details of some 60 Tatar settlements in Poland (Tokarczyk, 1987). While the Tatars themselves flourished by way of religious tolerance and the maintainance of contacts with Islamic centres abroad, many Tatar customs became part of Polish tradition, especially among the Polish nobility: these included their traditional long robe (*Kontusz*), fur cap (*Kolpak*), and curved sword (*Karabela*) – elements of costume which were themselves imitations of the garb worn by Crimean Tatars. Further, the traditional Polish light cavalry, the Ulany, is named after a famed Tatar captain (Adam Ulan, who was raised to the nobility in 1681 and founded a long succession of Tatar officers commanding these formations named after him).

The last important colonisation scheme involving Tatars was started in the late seventeenth century by King John Sobieski. However, as a result of constant and long-drawn-out wars, Sobieski found himself unable to pay his Tatar officers' overdue salaries. In 1679 the king decided to give the Tatar soldiers, in lieu of their earnings, nine villages from the state-owned estates (these were: Bohoniki, Drahle, Kruszyniany, Luzany,

Nietupa, part of the settlement of Pniantowicz in the Grodzien district, Studzianka, Lebiediew and Malaszewicze in the Brzesc district).

The Tatars lost their language, most likely sometime in the seventeenth century, and began using the local Polish or Byelorussian vernacular. Although most Tatars had lived in their ethnic enclaves, they became Polonized through inter-marriage and the slow adoption of values of the Polish majority. This process was undoubtedly accelerated by the increasing religious intolerance towards the end of the seventeenth century and a prohibition on the construction of mosques. The pressure to forego their identity became that much stronger when, towards the end of that century, inter-marriage for Tatars was forbidden under the threat of capital punishment. The prohibition, however, did not apply should they renounce their heritage.

After the third division of Poland in 1795, when the Polish state ceased to exist, the Tatars joined the Poles in the fight for the country's independence. The Tatar fighters swore their allegiance to Poland on the Qur'an in the presence of their imams. Their leader at that time, Stefan Mochorski, urged them to fight for Polish independence, stressing that the Tatars were equal to Poles and that they had a duty to defend their homeland (Metwali, 1993). The restrictions on Tatars imposed earlier were rescinded in 1807 during the short existence of the remnants of the Polish state, the Duchy of Warsaw (1807–15). The cancellation of restrictions came largely as a recognition of the Tatars' patriotism for Poland. They also played an important part in Napoleon Bonaparte's Russian campaign in 1812, and in the two national uprisings (1830 and 1863) against the Russians. For these reasons, Polish Tatars were bitterly persecuted by the Tsarist regime.

Although some civil functions had been carried out by imams from at least the sixteenth century (for example, the oldest surviving birth certificate issued by an imam is dated 1556), by the eighteenth century imams were recognised as having both religious and civil or state responsibilities. Imams led prayers, registered marriages and births and issued appropriate certificates, and were generally responsible for the welfare of the community. The first Polish translation of the Qur'an was made in 1858 by Marza Tareq Potszatski.

Before the First World War, the number of Tatars on the territories which subsequently became part of the newly independent Poland was estimated by one source at 15 000 (Podhorodecki, 1971). Another source gives the membership of the Union of Tatars of Poland, Lithuania and

Byelorussia, established in 1917, at 13 000. (This figure refers to Tatars in the Kingdom of Poland, Lithuania and Volhynia.) It is also worth recalling that after the 1905 revolution in Russia, an underground Circle of Polish Muslim Academics was founded in St Petersburg, although this functioned for only four years. In 1917 many Tatars from Volhynia (Wolyn), Lithuania and the Kingdom of Poland (which in 1918 became part of Poland) emigrated to the Crimea and Azerbaijan, presumably attracted by the Bolshevik promises of self-determination for ethnic minorities. (One should remember that the Crimean Tatars were later deported *en masse* in 1944 on Stalin's orders.)

During the First World War, the Tatars fought in the Polish Legions. Their fervent patriotism was acknowledged and admired by Poles and non-Poles alike. When, in 1918, Poland regained its independence and statehood, only a small number of Tatar enclaves in the north-eastern provinces remined within the Polish borders. The Tatar total population of these areas was 5425 (Stanislaw Kryczynski, 1938, cited in Tomaszewski, 1985). In 1925 the first nation-wide congress of Muslims took place in Vilnius, electing Jakub Szynkiewicz (a PhD in oriental studies) as the Chief Mufti of Poland. Also in 1925, the Socio-Cultural Association of Tatars was formed with headquarters in Warsaw. The Association published *Tatar Annals* (*Rocznik Tatarski*) and a periodical called *Tatar Life* (*Zycie Tatarskie*). In 1936, a special legal act permitted the formation of the Muslim Religious Union in the Republic of Poland, which published its own periodical entitled the *Islamic Review* (*Przeglad Islamski*). According to its provisions, the nineteen Muslim congregations and seventeen mosques were under the religious supervision of the Chief Mufti. Each community was built around a parish council with its imam and had, as a rule, its own mosque and an appropriate religious cemetery.

Between 1936 and 1939, a Tatar cavalry squadron existed in the Polish Army. During the Second World War, most of the Tatar intelligentsia was exterminated by the Nazis in retaliation for the gallant fight of the Tatar detachment against the invading German armies in September 1939.

After the war, only two Tatar villages named Bohoniki and Kruszyniany, originally given to the Tatars by King Sobieski in 1679, remained within the borders of Poland. As a result of the redrawing of the Polish boundaries some 500 km westwards, most of the Tatar settlements became part of the Soviet Union. Some Tatars from these former

Polish territories were resettled in the recovered lands in western and north-western Poland. This of course meant that a vital part of their religious and cultural heritage, mosques, cemeteries, and schools were left behind. Only the two communities in Bohoniki and Kruszyniany (both in north-eastern Poland) had mosques and traditional burial grounds. Other Tatars, dispersed in several localities in various parts of the country, had no designated places of worship and lacked organisational structures. This had a substantially negative impact on the preservation of religious and ethnic values, and accelerated further the Polonisation of the Tatars.

CONTEMPORARY CHARACTERISTICS

It was only in 1969 that steps were taken toward rebuilding the organisational structure of the Muslims in Poland. In that year, the Polish government permitted the holding of the first post-war Congress of Polish Muslims, which created the Muslim Religious Union of Poland. Led by a five-man body called the Muslim Board (and headed by a non-imam), the Union became the collective 'spokesman' on behalf of this proud but dwindling minority. By 1971, the government's Office for Religious Denominations created a new legal basis for religious work among the Muslims.

Since then, the mosques in the two oldest Tatar settlements, Bohoniki and Kruszyniany, have been restored with grants from the Arab Gulf states. In September 1984 a foundation stone was laid for the construction of a new mosque in Gdansk-Oliwa, the first to be erected in Poland for 192 years. The funds for the construction of this mosque were donated by Turkey and the Arab Gulf states. The project was organised by the Arab industrialist Ali Abd Turki, and the mosque is named after Jamal-ad-din Al-Afghani, the founder of pan-Islamic philosophy. The complex has a library and facilities for the teaching of Arabic in addition to its normal religious functions. The mosque is located in close proximity to a Roman Catholic church. The sound of the imam's call to prayer often mixes with the ringing of church bells calling the faithful to the celebration of the mass.

Also during the 1980s, Polish Muslims began to establish closer contacts with the wider Islamic world. In 1984 the Chief Mufti of Lebanon, Hasan Khaled, visited Poland for the first time. His visit was followed by a delegation from the Organisation of Islamic States (OIS), headed by the OIS Deputy Secretary General Sheikh Mohammed Naser Al-Abudi. The delegation visited all the Muslim communities in Poland and apparently was most impressed by the mosque in Bohoniki. As a result of the visit, the first group of Polish Muslims was able to take part in the annual *Hajj* pilgrimage to Mecca. Some scholarships for Islamic Studies in Saudi Arabia were also made available. In August 1988, Polish Muslims were visited by the Secretary General of the OIS, Dr Abdulah Omar Nasif. Overall, however, Polish Muslims have treated attempts by foreign Muslims to court them with polite reserve. There has always been a healthy theological relationship with the nearest Muslim Academy in Sarajevo, but visits by Middle Eastern leaders have had only symbolic rather than real cultural significance (Miles, 1993).

In 1992 the Union of Polish Tatars was re-established. Its programmatic declaration speaks of the long tradition of the Tatar communities in Poland. It also gives an interesting insight into the ideology of the Polish Tatars and their ties to Poland. According to one of their documents, the Union has been re-constituted as a

> commemoration and continuation of the history of our Tatar and Muslim ancestors who settled in the Republic six centuries ago. She gave them land and nobility and assured them freedom of profession and all civil rights ... she became our motherland. For ever loyal to her, the Polish Tatars, dedicated their services to the augmentation of her splendour not only in military craft but in all spheres of national life, including science, diplomatic service, agriculture and the arts. Loyal to the memory of our fathers, their deeds of love for this land we restore the Union of Polish Tatars.   (in Warminska, 1993)

Today, most Polish Muslims live within six congregations (parishes). The oldest are Bohoniki, Kruszyniany and Warsaw. New parishes, formed by Polish Muslims who in 1945 found themselves in the former Soviet Union and subsequently were repatriated to Poland, are in Gdansk-Oliwa (comprising a community of some 300 members), Szczecin and Bialystok. The largest is the Bialystok parish with an estimated 800 members. There, work began in 1990 on a new Islamic Centre, designed by the Polish Muslim architect Krystyna Kakarinko (who worked as an architect for many years in Algeria). The Centre will consist of a mosque, Qur'anic school and a guest house, part of which will accommodate elderly people. In addition to these small concentrations, separate Muslim families live throughout a dozen cities in Poland. The six administrative parish units control four Islamic cemetaries, two of which are located in Warsaw. In cities with no Islamic cemetaries, the municipal authorities have designated special sectors in the local cemetaries to be reserved for Islamic burials.

Following from the fact that there have long been no Qur'anic schools in Poland, for religious purposes the Muslims use a dialect which is a mixture of the Polish and Byelorussian languages, with some vocabulary taken from Turkish and Arabic. Many of the Muslims, especially among the younger generations, have migrated from the countryside parishes to towns. However, they usually maintain some sense of their traditions and links with their communities by returning to their villages at times of Islamic festivals.

Currently, the Polish Muslims have four separate organisations. The oldest is the Muslim Religious Union of Poland with its headquarters in Bialystok. The majority of its members are Polish Muslims of Tatar origins. It was the sole organisation representing Muslims' interests during the Communist rule. From 1969, the Union held a national congress every five years, attended by delegates from each of the parishes who elected the Highest Collegiate (the governing body) of the Union.

The Mahdists, who belong to the Shia tradition of Islam and who maintain the Association of Muslim Unity with its headquarters in Warsaw, first established themselves in Poland in 1936 and founded their organisation in 1937. It has some 100 members and is currently headed by a Chief Imam. In 1993 this post was held by Imam Mahmud Taha Zuk (who, it is interesting to note, first studied as a Muslim at the Catholic Academy of Theology in Warsaw and later at the Department of Comparative Religion at Warsaw University).The Association has its own Islamic Institute, which in 1992 began publishing *The Islamic Yearbook* (*Rocznik Muzulmanski*). The Institute is presently preparing its own critical translation of the Koran. The Association of Muslim Unity has taken a prominent part in various inter-religious and ecumenical activities, including meeting Pope John Paul II during his visits to Poland.

Since the demise of Communism, two other organisations have been created. The Association of Muslims AHMADIYA, with its headquarters in Warsaw, is connected with the teaching and philosophy of Imam Gulam Ahmady and his ideas on 'Islamic reformation'. Headed in 1993 by Hamid Karim Mahmud, it had 53 members and some 100 sympathisers, with one mosque in Warsaw and another in Bydgoszcz. Another new body is the Association of Muslim Brotherhood, which has its headquarters in Pruszkow (near Warsaw) and is headed by the Chief Imam and Ayatollah of Poland, Ryszard Rusnak (note the very typical Polish name).

Little is known about the social or occupational structure of Polish Muslims. Preliminary research suggests that some 20 per cent are peasants and tanners, around 55 per cent belong to blue and white-collar occupations, and some 25 per cent are intellectuals and artists (Konopacki, 1969).

CONCLUSION: MAINTAINING POLISH MUSLIM IDENTITY

The Polish Muslims consider their position as very special within the wider context of Muslim minorities in East Central Europe. They contend that by combining certain elements of Eastern and Western culture they can contribute to the moral revival of Europe and Islam. They hope to become the mediators between Poland and the Islamic countries. According to them, history shows that Polish relations with Turkey and other Muslim nations have always been good. Some of the Tatars emphasised that Poland 'is the greatest European country not to be blemished by colonisation', a country that has 'the glorious tradition of religious tolerance'. Some Polish Muslims feel neglected by the state, however, and are therefore even more irritated by what they perceive as academic voyeurism. 'We are not an anthropological curiousity', suggested a Muslim activist in Bialystok, 'We are Poles who happened to be Muslims and who could sometimes do with a bit of help' (in Warminska, 1993).

The Polish Muslims have historically made a substantial contribution to the Polish/Lithuanian state, and indeed have helped to establish and buttress the independence of the Polish nation. For much of this period they retained a strong awareness of their own cultural and religious distinctness (Szajkowski and Niblock, 1993). The case of the Polish Muslims provides a useful model of how Muslim communities can relate to the wider national communities of which they form a part in Europe: retaining their own identity and contributing positively to the wider community.

REFERENCES

Davies, N. (1981) *God's Playground: A History of Poland*, vol. 1 (Oxford: Clarendon Press).
Kettani, A. (1986) *Muslim Minorities in the World Today* (London: Mansell).
Konopacki, M. (1969) 'Spolecznosc Tatarska w Polsce wczoraj i dzis (Tatar society in Poland in the past and at present)', *Przeglad Orientalistyczny* (The Oriental Review) 2, pp. 171–4.
Konopacki, M. (1977) *Bialostocki szlak Tatarski (The Bialystok Trail of the Tatars)* (Warsaw: Krajowa Agencja Wydawnicza).
Metwali, D. (1993) 'The Muslims in Poland', *Al-Arabi*, February.
Miles, S. (1993) 'Diminishing Tatars', *The Guardian*, 29 October.
Podhorodecki, L. (1971) *Tatarzy (The Tatars)* (Warsaw: Ksiazka i Wiedza).
Ramet, Pedro (ed.) (1984) *Religion and Nationalism in Soviet and East European Politics* (Durham, NC: Duke University Press).
Szajkowski, B. and T. Niblock (1993) 'Islam and Ethnicity in Eastern Europe', paper presented at the International Conference on Muslim Minorities in Post-Bipolar Europe, Skopje, Macedonia.
Tokarczyk, A. (1987) *Trzydziesci wyznan (Thirty Confessions)* (Warsaw: Krajowa Agencja Wydawnicza).
Tomaszewski, J. (1985) *Rzeczpospolita wielu narodow (Republic of Many Nations)* (Warsaw: Czytelnik).
Warminska, K. (1993) 'Ethnic Identity and Ethnic Equality in the Ideology of the Polish Tatars', paper presented at the Conference on 'The Anthropology of Ethnicity', Amsterdam.

Part III
New Formations

6 The Bradford Council for Mosques and the Search for Muslim Unity

Philip Lewis

'Settlement by tiptoe' was the striking phrase used in a 1981 Bradford Council report to characterise the history of migration into the inner city over the previous twenty years. It described a parallel society whose members looked outward to mainstream British society for jobs, schools and services, but who still looked inward in their desire to preserve their traditional culture, religion and language. While the city had been free of the racial and inter-communal unrest which had marked other cities in that year, the authors of the report worried that,

> we have no direct knowledge of Asian needs and requirement, and we have no automatic way of knowing the issues they feel important ... (we need) some new channel of communication between the Council and the communities – something to compensate for the lack of political representation.   (City of Bradford Metropolitan Council (CBMC), 1981, p. 49)

Ten years later a national newspaper discussing the opening of the controversial 'Muslim Parliament' in London cited with evident approval the remarks of the President of the Bradford Council for Mosques, for whom this new initiative was a 'cruel joke for the Muslim community' threatening both to raise unrealistic expectations and fix in the public mind 'the image of every Muslim being a warlike separatist, ready to fight jihads at every opportunity', Mihir Bose, who wrote the piece, contrasted the unelected 'Muslim Parliament' with the Bradford Council for Mosques 'an elected body ... probably the most representative voice of Islam in the land' (*The Sunday Telegraph*, 5 January 1992).

This chapter explores the significance, locally and nationally, of the Bradford Council for Mosques, formally constituted in September 1981. The Council for Mosques was an institution whose time had come. Bradford Council had found that 'new channel of communication' it had sought – at least for Muslims – and other public bodies welcomed the creation of an organisation which they could consult on a range of issues. Many Muslims in the city supported its creation as an advocate and pressure group for their concerns.

The chapter is divided into three sections which, cumulatively, will enable an assessment of the large claims made for the Council for Mosques' significance by Mihir Bose. The first section provides a brief history of migration, settlement and consolidation of Muslim communities in Bradford. The second section reviews the Council's early history and some of its activities from its creation until the publication of the *The Satanic Verses* in September 1988. During this period the Council for Mosques was essentially a local body with a modest remit to address issues of concern, especially in the area of education. However, it was to gain in confidence and to develop its campaign skills as it became embroiled in a number of public controversies. The final section unravels some of the important issues interwoven in *The Satanic Verses* affair. This convulsion in inter-communal relations catapulted the Council for Mosques onto the national stage; its personnel were active both in seeking to translate anger and outrage at the novel into institutional unity at a national level, and to begin a debate on a range of issues exercising Muslims in Britain.

MIGRATION, SETTLEMENT AND MOSQUE FORMATION

Undivided, pre-partition India had long provided recruits for Britain's merchant navy. The tradition became established that,

> firemen ... for Bombay crews were Pathans and Mirpuris and for Calcutta crews the majority of engine-room hands were from Sylhet. ... The other parts of the crew were also recruited on a regional basis ... [thus] in Bombay the deck crews came from Gujarat. (Adams, 1987, pp. 22–3)

The first group of Muslims in Bradford were a group of seamen, who in 1941 were 'directed from such seaports such as Liverpool, Middlesborough and Hull to munitions factories and essential wartime industries in the Bradford and Leeds areas' (Dahya, 1974, p. 84). The early history of migration and settlement into Bradford, the push and pull factors operating, have been well documented (Dahya, 1974; Khan, 1977; Barton, 1986). There is no need here to do more than identify some key features. The 1961 census indicated that there were some 3376 'Pakistanis' in Bradford – which included West and East Pakistanis, the latter would be described as Bangladeshis as from 1971. The majority were unskilled, male workers, sustained by a 'myth of return' – only 81 women were enumerated in the census.

This pattern of migration changed as immigration procedures were gradually tightened throughout the 1960s and the automatic right of entry for Commonwealth citizens was progressively circumscribed. However, the phenomenon of chain migration of single men did not end until the Immigration Act of 1971, which none the less did permit the entry of dependants. Local authority figures suggest that by 1981 there were some 32 100 residents whose family origins were in Pakistan and Bangladesh, with possibly an extra thousand Muslims from India. By 1991 this figure had increased to 53 250.[1]

Tariq Modood (1990, p. 145) has characterised South Asian Muslims in Britain generally as 'a semi-industrialised, newly urbanised working class community that is only one generation away from rural peasantry'. This is certainly true of Bradford, where most of the first settlers had little formal education. This is hardly surprising since many came from the least developed areas of Indo-Pakistan. A majority came from Azad Kashmir, an area, pre-partition, under the control of Maharajahs by whom it was 'shamefully neglected' and which 'contained hardly any schools' (Rose, 1969, p. 59). Even today, for Pakistan as a whole, according to a recent Federal Minister for Education, 'educational statistics are appalling: 8 per cent of its population are educated up to primary, 2 per cent secondary and 0.02 per cent university level ... (official statistics are "padded" and inflated)' (Ahmed, 1988, p. 201).

There are two main exceptions to this socio-educational profile. The few hundred South Asians who were 'twice migrants' and fled or were expelled from East Africa in the late 1960s and early 1970s. They represent a distinct category, in that they collapsed the four-phase pattern of migration – pioneers, chain migration of unskilled workers, consolidation of settlement and the emergence of a British-born generation (Ballard and Ballard, 1977, pp. 28–43) – into one movement and enjoyed a higher educational and social status, not least since they were mostly English-speakers. Secondly, a group of largely foreign students attending the local university. Their numbers were only large enough to organise and sustain a separate mosque – a converted terraced house – from 1980.

Dahya's (1974) seminal article on Bradford's Pakistani communities, based on research done in the early 1970s, outlined a two-stage process of community formation whereby an initial tendency towards fusion – in which pioneer settlers associated together regardless of their regional, caste,[2] or sectarian origins – gradually gave way, as numbers grew, to fission and segmentation; in this second stage of fragmentation, ties of village-kinship and sectarian affiliation grew steadily more significant as the basis of communal. This process, which Dahya illustrated with reference to housing settlement in the 1960s, can also be seen in the proliferation of mosques and supplementary schools, the latter being centres used for teaching Muslim youngsters the Qur'an, the basics of Islamic faith and community languages.

In 1959 the city's first mosque was opened in a terraced house in Howard Street. It was run by the Pakistani Muslim Association, and initially its trustees included both East and West Pakistanis from a variety of different sectarian traditions (see Robinson, 1988). Fusion gave way to fission over the next few years as Howard Street came to be dominated by settlers from the Chhachh, a district on the borders of the Punjab in the North West Frontier Province of Pakistan. The appointment of a Pathan trained in the Deobandi tradition as its first full-time imam, in 1968, also gave it a clear sectarian character.

Fission became increasingly evident with different regional groups, albeit in the same sectarian tradition, forming their own mosques. Thus, in 1961 the Bradford Muslim Welfare Society – most of whose members were from villages around Surat in Gujarat, India – established their own Deobandi mosque, in Thorncliffe Place. A second group of Gujarati Muslims, also from Surat, arrived from Kenya in the late 1960s. While they initially, worshipped with Gujaratis from India, they soon sought to give institutional expression to their different histories and caste identities.[3] In 1971 and 1978 they established two community centres, which included supplementary schools.

In 1966 Pir Maroof Hussain Shah opened the first mosque in the Barelwi tradition, the first of many within his Jamiyat Tabligh ul Islam, Association for Preaching Islam. Table 6.1 classifies by sectarian allegiance the number of mosques and supplementary schools in existence in 1989. These include the mosque open for all students and not aligned to any one sect and an Ahmadiyya mosque, a heterodox sect whose right to belong to the Muslim community is hotly contested.

The creation of mosques and supplementary schools also yields information on the growth and differential settlement patterns of distinct regional and linguistic communities. Table 6.2 makes this clear by enumerating both the number of mosques and supplementary schools formed each decade and the number each regional group controls.

These data of mosque formation enable us to hazard some broad generalisations about community formation. The Indian Gujarati community did not delay settlement and had already established its two mosques by 1962. The Bangladeshi community was slower to shift from male settlement to family consolidation: it had no separate mosque until 1970 and its three other mosques had to await the 1980s. Family consolidation for the Mirpuris has also been an extended process. While their first mosque was functioning in 1966, the bulk of their centres – 14 out of 18 – did not open until the 1980s. The bulk of the Punjabi and Chhachhi centres were complete in the 1970s.

However, while Muslims in Bradford are divided along caste, ethnicity and sectarian lines, the same data make clear that these divisions are

Table 6.1 Sectarian affiliation of mosques and supplementary schools in 1989

Sect	Mosque	Supplementary school
Barelwi	11	7
Deobandi	12	2
Jamaat-i-Islam	2	
Ahl-i-Hadith	1	
Shi'a	2	
Ahmadiyya	1	
Non-aligned student	1	

Table 6.2   The number of mosques and supplementary schools
established in each decade and the regional groups controlling them

	Mosque	*Supplementary school*
1960–9*	5	
1970–9†	11	2
1980–9‡	14	7

* Mirpur, Punjab, Chhachh, Gujarat (2).
† Mirpur (3), Punjab (3), Chhachh (4), (East African) Gujarat (2) Bangladesh.
‡ Mirpur (14), Punjab, Chhachh (2), Bangladesh (3), student mosque.

not absolute. Sectarian allegiance does not simply correspond to ethnic
difference. Further, once we focus on a shared Muslim identity we can
also identify commonalties of interest. Such solidarities and aspirations
to unity were given institutional expression with the creation of the
Bradford Council for Mosques in 1981.

THE COUNCIL FOR MOSQUES: A VEHICLE FOR LOCAL UNITY

The six founding members of the Bradford Council for Mosques
represented all traditions of Islam present in the city.[4] Three were local
businessmen – the most successful was Mr Sher Azam, whose name
was to become almost synonymous with the Council for Mosques in
the late 1980s, at the height of the Rushdie affair. Mr Azam was to be
President of the Council for almost half of its first decade, which speaks
both of the importance of the Deobandi presence in the city –
Mr. Azam was President or vice-President of the Howard Street
mosque for the previous six years – and the trust and respect he commanded across the different traditions. Pir Maroof,[5] another of the
founding fathers, was never an elected officer of the Council. However,
his Barelwi organisation, Jamiyat Tabligh ul Islam, always provided
the President or one of its two General-Secretaries throughout this
period, except during its first year.

The first President of the Council for Mosques was Mr Umar Warraich, a public health inspector, and member of one of the two mosques in the Jamaat-i-Islami tradition in the city. He was the only President who did not belong to either of the large Barelwi or Deobandi groupings in the city and his presidency testifies to his role as the prime mover behind this initiative. Mr Warraich identified three interrelated concerns which led him to propose the creation of such a Council: Muslims required a common platform from which to negotiate with the local authority in the vexed arena of educational provision, the focus of widely shared anxieties; a Council for Mosques could manage and reduce sectarianism and create a forum for members of different mosques to meet; finally, such an organisation would be in a strong position to elicit financial help from local and central government.

It is no accident that, with the exception of Pir Maroof, none of the prime movers behind the Council were *'ulama* (trained theologians). Indeed, the Council has never had an *'alim* as President. The role of the *'ulama* within the Council was severely circumscribed from its inception. The Council was, in part, intended to relate to public bodies in the city and most *'ulama* possessed neither the language, skills, nor experience to fulfil such a task. Further, the Council was intended to minimise sectarian differences, another reason for limiting their active involvement. Umar Warraich and others of the founding fathers, however, were used to co-operating in a variety of local political and social arenas – community centres and South Asian political parties with branches in Bradford – which included men with different sectarian, regional and caste loyalties. As employees of mosque committees the *'ulama* were effectively excluded from the Council by its constitution which declared ineligible for membership anyone who 'held a paid position in the Council or with any member organisation'. They served a consultancy role when required.

The Council for Mosques' constitution was framed to maximise co-operation. Thus, the Council was committed to non-interference in the internal affairs of its member organisations and could only support the views of one of its members when these were not at variance with those held by other constituent bodies. The only group excluded from the Council was the Ahmadiyya sect, since the constitution included the clause that the Prophet Mohammed is 'the last prophet and there can be no new prophet till the Day of Judgement'. The constitution also declared that one of its objectives was 'to promote understanding, unity and Islamic Brotherhood'. In this regard it has been more successful than a similar initiative in Birmingham which fragmented into rival mosque councils (Joly, 1987). The President and Secretary-General had to belong to different organisations. This constitutional coda has meant that in Bradford whenever the President belonged to the Barelwi group – invariably Jamiyat Tabligh ul Islam – the Secretary-General was a Deobandi and vice-versa, thus preventing any rupture between the two most numerous groupings in the city.

Mr Warraich's hopes for the Council for Mosques were to prove realistic. The city council supported the Council for Mosques with a Community Programme grant of £13 000 enabling it to purchase a large semi-detached house to serve as its headquarters. From 1983 until the autumn of 1988, when the ground rules for Manpower Services Commission (MSC) projects were redefined, the Council for Mosques was the centre for an ambitious MSC scheme providing at its height some fifty workers servicing a range of projects: two centres for the elderly, a variety of advice workers, male and female, for the various mosques and Islamic centres, and a service for women in hospitals and clinics.

The success the Council for Mosques enjoyed in the 1980s in getting the local education authority to be responsive in the curriculum and ethos of local schools to their religious and cultural traditions turned on two main factors. The first was the education authority's willingness to respond under the new educational banner of 'multi-culturalism'. The second factor was the political and the institutional support they could muster locally to implement anti-racist initiatives.

Education had long been a source of friction between the Muslim communities and the local authority. A geographer mapping the social and ethnic geography of Bradford in the 1970s, reflecting on the 'cultural self-sufficiency' of the Muslim communities, noted that 'education ... constitutes the principal "leak" in an otherwise fairly closed system' (Richardson, 1976, pp. 175–6). Muslim anxieties about aspects of the educational system were evident as early as 1973. In that year Mr Riaz Shahid, standing as an independent candidate in a local election, was pressing the local authority to provide more single-sex, girls' schools. He defeated the labour candidate in the ward election, and just failed to pip the Conservative candidate (Le Lohe, 1979, p. 197).

What is important to notice is that the local authority did adopt a series of educational measures to honour the all-party twelve-point race

relations initiative in 1981, which, *inter alia*, sought to reassure all
minority communities in the city that they had 'an equal right to maintain [their] own identity, culture, language, religion and customs'.
Local educational memoranda sought to respond to Muslim concerns
about dress codes for girls, single-sex swimming and physical education; they showed flexibility over extended visits to South Asia; they
provided *halal* meat for Muslim school children and capitalised on gen-
erous subventions from the Home Office to meet 'special needs' of
ethnic minority children, e.g. community language teachers were
employed in upper schools, a supplementary schools' officer was
appointed to bridge the gap between the state school and the
supplementary schools.

Without a willingness by the local authority to implement 'multicultural' and 'anti-racist' initiatives the Council for Mosques would
have made little headway. However, this existed locally and nationally
in the 1980s since there was a desire to identify and ameliorate the
deprivation underlying explosions of urban violence across the country
(Hiro, 1992, pp. 80–96; Scarman, 1983, pp. 18–36). However, the
Council for Mosques also had to engage in energetic advocacy of its
agenda and mobilise support, especially when confronted by local
opposition to particular measures, such as provision of *halal* meat and
to 'multi-culturalism' itself, in the person of a local headmaster,
Mr Ray Honeyford.

The political influence of the Council for Mosques was strengthened
because of the overlapping membership and co-operation between
Muslim councillors and Muslims active in the Council for Mosques and
the Community Relations Council (CRC). When an issue fell clearly
within an anti-racist framework, the Council for Mosques was able to
capitalise on tactical alliances with other minority groups, involved in
the CRC, and mobilise political support through Muslim councillors.

It is worth stressing the significance of the CRC as an organisation
where Muslim councillors and Muslims active in the Council for
Mosques could meet. The CRC has functioned as a nursery for Muslim
politicians, where the necessary skills, confidence and contacts were
developed. Five Muslim councillors were active in the CRC in the
1980s. The cross-cutting membership is clearly seen with Councillor
Ajeeb. Ajeeb was to be the first South Asian chairman of the CRC from
1976 to 1983 and held other positions in the organisation throughout
the 1980s. He was elected a councillor in 1979 and for two years was

senior supervisor of the MSC project located at the Council for Mosques, a position from which he resigned when he became the first 'Asian' Lord Mayor in 1985. In 1984, a crucial year which saw the resolution of the *halal* meat crisis and the beginning of the Honeyford affair, the CRC executive included two councillors – Ajeeb and Hameed – and the President of the Council for Mosques, Mr Sher Azam, and Mr C. M. Khan, the President for the following two years. Thus the CRC was the main forum where officers of the Council for mosques and Muslim councillors met and where support for Muslim concerns in the wider community could be tested.

Three major educational controversies in the early 1980s highlight both the influence the Council for mosques enjoyed and its limits. In 1982 Bradford education authority had issued guidelines to schools intended to accommodate Muslim cultural and religious needs 'within one educational system and within the framework of a common school curriculum'. As part of this package of measures the authority stated that it was 'considering the provision of Halal meat in schools and ... actively investigating ways in which this can be done' (CBMC, 1982). The wild card in the pack was the Muslim Parents Association (MPA), which in January 1983 submitted a request to convert five schools, with a largely Muslim intake, into Muslim voluntary-aided schools, two first schools, two middle schools and one upper school. The education authority clearly wanted to maximise concessions to Muslims so as to preserve the integrity of the local education system by undercutting support for the MPA.

On 17 July 1983, the Council for Mosques and members of the education authority met. The Council for Mosques was frank that there was no consensus on the MPA proposals since Muslims in Bradford comprised 'different ethnic, national and sectarian strands'. However, they had rejected, for practical reasons, by a margin of thirteen to eight, with four abstentions, the particular MPA proposal. They were not convinced that 'this organisation would be able to run and administer (let alone finance) the five schools'. There was a sting in the tale for the education authority: the Council stressed that they had *not* taken a decision on the principle of separate Muslim schools and that it would become increasingly hard to convince its members that 'what was good for Catholics was not good for Muslims unless the Authority did all in its power to honour its new found commitment to multi-cultural education in both spirit and letter' (cyclostyled report of the meeting provided by the Council for Mosques).

The Council for Mosques, by rejecting the MPA proposal – a spectre which continues to haunt the education authority – won the gratitude of the authority, which did not delay in providing *halal* meat to fourteen hundred Muslim children in September 1983. The intention was to extend the service across the metropolitan area and within two years to provide such meals to all of the authority's fifteen thousand Muslim pupils.

Far from being the end of the matter, the publicity surrounding the provision of *halal* food triggered an angry campaign led by animal rights activists, who objected to the fact that the prescribed method of slaughter precluded the pre-stunning of animals. In December an editorial in the local press, entitled *Prejudice*, worried that 'behind the veil of respectability offered by the animal rights people, racists have relished the chance to criticise Muslims in our community' (*Telegraph & Argus*, 12 December 1983). One animal rights campaigner refused to pay her rates and courted imprisonment. In February 1984 the Bradford Council conceded to requests for a full debate on *halal* meat in full council.

The Muslim community was angered by this decision which seemed to threaten their recently won right, as tax payers, to have school meals which their children could eat. The Council for Mosques began to mobilise. It circulated an appeal, in Urdu, *Historic Decision on Halal Meat*, to Muslim parents asking them to boycott school on 6 March – the day on which Bradford Council would debate the issue – and, with their children, to demonstrate outside City Hall. A large majority of Muslim parents heeded this appeal, with an estimated ten thousand children taken out of school and many participating in the demonstration.

The Council for Mosques could rely on a broad-based alliance of groups to support them. The CRC was incensed that a racist backlash threatened to reverse a decision to meet the 'special needs' of minority community. Muslim councillors spoke eloquently in the crucial debate on 6 March in the Town Hall. Councillor Iftikhar Qureshi warned the City Council that if 'it went back on its decision it would be regarded as unworthy and biased by the Muslim community' (*Telegraph & Argus*, 7 March 1984). In the event, the Bradford Council voted by fifty-nine votes to fifteen to retain *halal* meat. The local press dubbed

the furore over *halal* meat as 'the issue of the year' (*Telegraph &
Argus*, 30 December 1983). A public boycott of schools and thousands
of Muslims demonstrating outside City Hall guaranteed the national
media, too, were beginning to take an interest in the city's Muslim
presence.

No sooner had the *halal* debate been resolved when another controversy erupted. This time it turned on articles written by a local headmaster critical of the city's multi-cultural and anti-racist policies.
Mr Ray Honeyford, the head of Drummond Road Middle School, was
to signal his misgivings about such issues as early as November 1982
in an article in the *Times Educational Supplement* (*TES*) under the
heading 'Multi-racial Myths'. However, it was only in early March
1984 that his opinions entered the public domain when his article in
the January edition of a small circulation, right-wing journal, *The
Salisbury Review*, entitled 'Education and Race – An Alternative View'
was summarised in the *Yorkshire Post* (see Halstead, 1988).

Press coverage of Mr Honeyford's opinions triggered a conflict
which was not to be resolved until December 1985, when he agreed to
take early retirement and accept a cash settlement of £71 000. In
between these two dates an astonishing saga unfolded: a Drummond
Parent's Action Committee (DPAC) came into being, pressing for the
head's dismissal; an alternative school was set up in the local Pakistan
Community Centre; Mr Honeyford was first dismissed and then his
reinstatement was upheld by the High Court; an adjournment debate in
the House of Commons was granted to a local Conservative MP,
Marcus Fox; a boycott of the city's schools by Muslim pupils proved
abortive; the Prime Minister, Mrs Thatcher, invited the head to attend a
discussion of educationalists, and finally the Appeal Court overturned
the High Court decision and thus allowed the local authority to resolve
the affair.

One irony of the affair was that Mr Honeyford was by no means
unsympathetic to many Muslim attitudes; the writer Hanif Kureishi, in
an essay on Bradford, was able to identify several overlapping concerns
between Mr Honeyford and Mr C. M. Khan, the President of the
Council for Mosques during much of the crisis (Kureishi, 1986).
However, such commonalties were obscured by the head teacher's
intemperate asides and innumerable *non sequiturs* in both the
September 1983 *TES* article and that in the January 1984 *Salisbury
Review*. Pragmatic concessions to Muslim sensibilities, such as allow-

ing girls to wear tracksuits in PE, were variously described as capitulating to 'Moslem extremists' and 'religious fanaticism' by those intent on subverting sexual equality by a 'purdah mentality'. The term 'fundamentalist Moslem', as imprecise as it is sinister in connotation, was bandied about (*Telegraph & Argus*, 26 November 1985).

Mr Honeyford compounded his folly by rehearsing stereotypes about West Indians and Indians and thus ensured the CRC's support for the DPAC campaign to remove him from the school (Annual Report, CRC, 1984/5, p. 2). Since in 1984 the CRC included on its executive committee two Muslims Councillors and two members of the Council for Mosques, the campaign against Mr Honeyford was assured of wide support.

The Council for Mosques was involved throughout the campaign, often as a moderating voice, increasingly worried at the escalation of tension. On 21 June 1985 there was a demonstration numbering some four hundred and twenty marchers.

> There were eleven speakers: six Pakistanis, two Bangladeshis, one Hindu, one Sikh and one white. ... Mr C. M. Khan (President of the Council for Mosques) was effective to the extent that he curbed the would-be rabble-rousers. Despite their efforts, and the high percentage of Angry Young ... men in the audience, everyone dispersed quietly.   (Murphy, 1987, p. 124)

With Mr Honeyford's return to the school in September 1985, picketing intensified and the children were given stickers to wear in their class-rooms on which was written, 'Honeyford Out' and 'Ray-CIST', as well as bearing leaflets insisting that the head teacher had 'insulted your religion, and your culture' (Murphy, 1987, p. 127). On 15 October the DPAC declared a Day of Action and the Council for Mosques issued a leaflet in Urdu urging Muslim parents to boycott the city's schools on that day in protest against the head who had 'displayed defamatory opinions against Asian and African parents' – a clause indicating that the Council never presented the issue as simply one involving Muslims.

If the Council for mosques were hoping for a boycott as successful as that against the threat to *halal* meat in 1984, they were disappointed. This time only one in four children was withdrawn (Halstead, 1988, p. 107). After this debacle the Council for Mosques decided to support a cooling off period. Mr Sher Azam explained to the CRC that after consulting with the parents and assessing the situation in the city as a whole, they realised that they could 'not fight a campaign when the majority of the population was not on their side' (CRC Minutes of Executive Meeting, 22 October 1985).

The Council for Mosques was understandably anxious. One mosque had withdrawn in 1985, objecting to the politicisation of the Council under the Presidency of C. M. Khan, a member of the Labour party – Mr Khan was to be the first and last President who was a member of any political party. Mr Warraich, a founder member of the Council, had tried to set up an alternative mosque council in 1985, the Council of Masajid and Islamic Centres. Mr Warraich's initiative, which included little more than the two Jamaat-i-Islami centres, was to prove abortive, but it does indicate disquiet with the direction the Council for Mosques was taking under C. M. Khan. Anxiety was evidenced by the poor response to the Council for Mosques' request to Muslim parents to withdraw their children from school on 15 October in support of the DPAC Day of Action.

The Council for Mosques' reputation and standing had been diminished by its involvement in the Honeyford affair, both within the Muslim community and in the city at large. Mr Honeyford's opinions on three important inter-related issues – racism, free speech and accountability, the nature and limits of multi-culturalism – were never exposed to open debate, but merely shouted down. Both right and left of the political spectrum were responsible for this: the right for lionising Mr Honeyford as a doughty defender of freedom of speech and the left for demonising him as a racist. Neither perspective allowed for any real debate on such issues as:

> how to resolve the tensions between the preservation of the distinct cultural identity of minority communities on the one hand and the encouragement of social integration on the other.   (Halstead, 1988, p. 64)

In a campaign the Council for Mosques did not even control locally and which soon moved out of a local into a national political arena, Muslims found themselves tarred with the excesses committed by opponents of Mr Rushdie. The Honeyford affair was misconstrued as simply a 'Muslim' issue with negative terminology – fundamentalism, extremism and fanaticism – and disturbing images of 'Muslims' fixed in the public mind; pictures of angry parents and children baying for the head's blood outside the gates of the school were flashed across the nation's television screens. Marcus Fox's 'Authorised Version' of the affair even presented Muslims, with others, as a threat to democracy with their supposed attack on freedom of speech – an accusation anticipating those made against Muslims in the Rushdie affair. The often moderate and pragmatic stance of the Council for Mosques' leadership remained invisible. Thus the resolution of the issue in December 1985 with the headmaster's early retirement and financial settlement was a pyrrhic victory for the Council.

THE SATANIC VERSES AND AN ELUSIVE NATIONAL UNITY

The Council of Mosques and Local Protests

On the 28 May 1985 a civic service was held for the new Lord Mayor, Councillor Ajeeb. Since he was the first Muslim to hold the office the service was held in a mosque – the central mosque of Pir Maroof Hussain Shah's association in Southfield Square. Civic dignitaries attended the service which included selections from the Barelwi devotional poem 'Salaam', translated into English. The verses chosen included the following in praise of the Prophet:

Blessed be my strength in misery,
My hope and wealth in poverty.
Blessed be that rose of nature,
Glorious symbol of Creator.
Blessed be the look affectionate
Caring, kind and compassionate.
Blessed be that magnanimous mind,
Whit sought God's mercy for mankind.
Blessed be the Prophet's family members,
Who are all like heavenly flowers
(Service sheet, p. 3)

Much has been written about *The Satanic Verses* affair. If the sense of outrage which galvanised the Muslim communities in Bradford, when news of the 'contents' of the novel began to circulate, is to be understood, two factors have to be kept in mind. Firstly, although the book was published in Britain, news of its 'contents' and the shape of the indictment against it were formulated and mediated to Bradford's Muslims by their co-religionists in India (Appignanesi and Maitland, 1989; Ruthven, 1990). In that country marked by troubled and deteriorating inter-communal relations, it is hardly surprising that the distinguished Sikh writer Kushwant Singh, an editorial adviser to Penguin Books in India, on reading a novel in which 'the Prophet had been made to be a small-time impostor' advised against publication (*Impact International*, 28 October–10 November 1988, p. 14). Secondly, the city's Muslims shared with their South Asian co-religionists a deep devotion to the Prophet. It is hard to exaggerate the veneration of the Prophet which informs Islamic piety and practice in South Asia in all traditions, but especially amongst the Barelwis as evident in the 'Salaam'.

Any work which can be construed as insulting the Prophet can be guaranteed to unite the most diverse groupings of Muslims in South Asia and throughout the South Asian Muslim diaspora. In 1924 a Hindu in Lahore published a work in Urdu with the deliberately provocative title, *Rangila Rasul* (*The Pleasure-Loving Prophet*), portraying the Prophet as a libertine. This book so enraged Muslim sensibilities that its author was murdered by two Muslims. They themselves were considered martyrs when they were sentenced to death and executed by the British. The British, to forestall a repeat of this episode, introduced Article 295A to the Indian penal code making it an offence to 'insult or outrage the religious feelings of any class' (Ruthven, 1990, p. 87). The sentiments underlying such an enactment have been given a sharpened focus recently in Pakistan. In July 1986 the National Assembly of Pakistan adopted the Criminal Law (Amendment) Bill which,

> provides that whoever by words, either spoken or written, or by visible representation or by any imputation, innuendo or insinuation, directly or indirectly, defiles the sacred name of the Holy Prophet ... shall be punished with death or imprisonment. (*Dawn Overseas Weekly*, 17 July 1986)

The Bradford Council for Mosques kept a documentary record of the letters they sent, the replies they received and the coverage given to their protests in the local and national media between October 1988 and the end of March 1989. From this record it was clear that their response to the publication of the novel in Britain on 26 September 1988 was initially shaped by expectations informed by a South Asian legal and cultural context, which gradually yielded to the painful realisation that the British situation was markedly different. The Council's decision to burn a copy of the novel on 14 January 1989 – which ironically emphasised how little the Muslim elders understood of their new legal, political and cultural context – was part of an attempt to draw attention to their continued anguish and anger when confronted by continued incomprehension, by politicians and media alike.

The first letters in their file are those in Urdu and English from the Deobandi organisation in Blackburn, Hizb ul 'ulama, The Society of Muslim Scholars in the UK. This largely Gujarati association sent the Bradford Council for Mosques an account of the novel summarised by two editors of Urdu newspapers published in Delhi and in Surat, Gujarat – summaries of the novel, drawn, in all probability from interviews with Mr Rushdie in the Indian press – with the recommendation that Muslims should petition 'either Her Majesty the Queen, the Prime Minister or the Home Office Minister' to ban the book.

Mr Sher Azam, President of the Council for Mosques throughout the period 1988–90, then wrote to the Prime Minister on 12 November, rehearsing much of the contents of the Blackburn letter. Mr Azam, making no claim to have read the work itself, urged the Prime Minister to follow the example of the Indian government and ban it. His letter focused on the 'distress' the work had caused Muslims. There were no threats to the author and, unlike the Blackburn letter, he did not refer to Mr Rushie as an apostate, *murtadd*, a serious accusation in Islamic law.[6]

This was the first of a series of letters the Council sent to the publishers, local MPs and councillors, the UN, and Bradford's chief executive. They urged Bradford Local Authority to refuse to provide the book to libraries, schools and other educational institutions. The response from Viking publishers was predictable: they insisted that as 'a serious publisher' they were committed to 'freedom of expression'; they disavowed any intention to offend by publishing the novel; they quote Mr Rushdie's comment that the offending sections of the work occur 'in a dream, the fictional dream of an individual movie star and one who is losing his mind, at that' and finally pointed out that the work had been acclaimed in certain sections of the Indian press, had been shortlisted for the 1988 Booker Prize and had just won the fictional category of the Whitbread Award.

The responses of two of the local MPs are instructive. Pat Wall reminded the Council for Mosques of his advocacy for Muslims when victims of racism, but reminded them that the government had recently made a fool of themselves in trying to ban 'Spycatcher' which proved counterproductive and 'resulted in a colossal increase in the sales internationally'. Another MP who proved sympathetic to Muslim sensibilities was Max Madden. His constituency included a large proportion of Muslims from whom he was able to gauge directly the depth of anger and outrage, still invisible to the majority of the local community. Mr Madden suggested to the publishers that they might insert a statement by Muslims as to why they found the work offensive and urged a television debate between Mr Rushdie and his Muslim critics. In this letter to the publishers, Mr Madden drew attention to 'the extraordinary anomaly in modern multi-faith Britain' of a blasphemy law which only protected the established Christian faith.

It was the Council for Mosques' misfortune that they invariably misread the situation in Britain. Their initial letters fuelled the suspicion that they wanted to ban a novel by a distinguished author on the basis of little more than hearsay. Only later did they co-opt on to the Council, as an individual member, Shabbir Akhtar, a Cambridge graduate in philosophy, who was able to forcibly *argue* a Muslim case in the national media and in his book, *Be Careful with Mohammed* (1989). The Council's appeal to the Bishop of Bradford for 'justice' and a 'change in the law of blasphemy' was only made after the book-burning episode, at a regional rally the Council organised on 14 January 1989, had alienated would-be sympathisers.[7] In an editorial in the *Yorkshire Post* (19 January 1989) under the heading 'Satanic Fires', Muslims were excoriated as 'intellectual hooligans' manipulated by demagogues into burning a book most had not read and they were likened to the Nazis.

For the national media, Bradford had become the epicentre of the shock waves convulsing the Muslim communities across Britain. Ayatollah Khomeini's intervention a month later was to prove disastrous for the Muslim campaign in Bradford and in Britain. Two members of the Bradford Council for Mosques' executive exacerbated the situation by allegedly supporting the *fatwa*, the legal decision sentencing to death the author and publishers responsible. A public outcry ensued and the West Yorkshire Police passed on these comments to the Crown Prosecution service. The local press reported that 'the world's press converges on Bradford' as the Council for Mosques held an emergency meeting distancing themselves from these comments. The Secretary-General insisted that they had been misquoted and that 'we do not support the Ayatollah ... he is not our leader ... we are living in England ... and do not take directives from him' (*Telegraph & Argus*,17 February 1989).

The Council for Mosques was now centre stage but no more in control of presentation of the issues than it had been in the Honeyford affair. A process of demonisation of Muslims already begun in this earlier episode now accelerated (Parekh, 1990). Sometimes local Muslims themselves colluded in this process. Shabbir Akhtar penned a defence of 'religious fundamentalism' in a national daily, arguing that 'any faith which compromises its internal temper of militant wrath is destined for the dustbin of history' (*Guardian*, 27 February 1989). Since the article introduced him as a member of Bradford Council for Mosques, the impression was left that the Council was full of passionate 'fundamentalists'.

As with the Honeyford saga, media images of angry demonstrations and inflammatory placards projected and fixed in the public imagination a fearsome and negative picture of Muslims and served to alienate rather than enlist support. In June 1989, a rally organised by the Council erupted into sporadic violence engineered by a small group of Muslim youngsters. This appeared on the front page of the local press with a coloured picture of an effigy of Mr Rushdie daubed with red paint and slogans such as 'Kill the Pig' (*Telegraph & Argus*, 17 June 1989). The Bradford Council for Mosques was to suspend public demonstrations locally, when violence flared again at what had been a peaceful Muslim youth rally. The Council concluded that 'open-air rallies were too vulnerable to provocateurs and others looking for trouble' (*Guardian*, 28 May 1990). By then the damage had been done, not least by the media's 'remorseless tendency to trivialise, or where feelings are running high, to polarise' (Ruthven, 1990, p. 118).

The Council for Mosques found that on this issue the Muslim communities were increasingly isolated with few allies, with the exception of the MP Max Madden and the established church (Lee and Stanford, 1990, pp. 85–96). The CRC was caught in a dilemma:

Mr Rushdie was respected for his views on anti-racism and his written and video materials were widely used. Moreover, *The Satanic Verses* included much material congenial to the left and accessible to an anti-racist constituency. Therefore, the CRC decided to 'adopt no position on the book ... [since] the specific issues relating to the concerns of the Muslim community ... are of a religious nature ... the best people to represent [their] concerns ... are the properly constituted religious organisations in the city' (CBMC/CRC Annual Report, 1988/9, p. 6).

The National and International Dimensions of the Campaign

It was clear to the Council for Mosques that concerted national action was required both to direct the anger the book generated into constructive channels and to bring pressure to bear on the government. The difficulty was to create a national body which could transcend the main Barelwi/Wahhabi sectarian division.[8] Here the Bradford Council for Mosques had a vital role to play in that it included both groupings and was supported by two personalities who enjoyed a national following in both traditions, Pir Maroof and Sher Azam. Mr Azam's role in lending credibility to any such national initiative was crucial. He was President of a respected local Council for Mosques which had several significant gains to its credit, and whose campaign experience had been honed in lengthy, local campaigns. Moreover, Mr Azam was already known outside Bradford through his involvement with the Council of Mosques UK and Eire. This organisation, created in 1984, was sponsored by the Muslim World League, based in Mecca, and chaired by the Director of the London branch of that organisation. Its policy was to have a British Muslim as vice-chairman and Mr Azam held that position from 1986 to 1988.

Thus, when in October 1988 the UK Action Committee on Islamic Affairs (UKACIA) was formed in London to oppose the book, its convenor was a Saudi diplomat, Dr Mughram Al Ghamdi, Director of Regent's Park Mosque, and Mr Azam was one of its twelve-strong steering committee. The presence of Mr Azam and Mr Maan of the Islamic Council of Scotland, who both belonged to groupings comprising various sects, meant that there were always some Barelwis affiliated to UKACIA, including Pir Maroof's World Islamic Mission. The UKACIA was a useful mechanism for bringing pressure to bear on the government through Muslim ambassadors in London and lobbying the Organisation of the Islamic Conference (OIC).

Mr Azam was one of a UKACIA delegation attending the OIC meeting from 13 to16 March 1989, in Riyadh, Saudi Arabia. The UKACIA lobbying of the OIC met with qualified success when the OIC adopted a declaration against blasphemy which, while not endorsing the Iranian *fatwa*, urged member states 'to ban the book ... to prevent the entry of its author in all Islamic countries and [to call] upon publishing houses to immediately withdraw the book from circulation and ... to boycott any publishing house that does not comply' (Ahsan and Kidwai, 1991, p. 334).

The UKACIA newsletter in July 1989 offered a realistic assessment of the difficulties confronting their campaign, reminding its readers that the Muslim community in Britain was:

> not a homogenous community ... not yet a united community ... an inexperienced community ... [with] a lot to learn. Compared to other communities it has as yet no effective clout in the seats of power, in the media or in economic circles.... [However, for the first time] people whose work was localised or limited to members of their own particular school of thought have now got to know, meet and appreciate others.... . Muslims as a result of this campaign are beginning to learn more about the political ... and legal processes of the country ... it is heartening to note the support ... from some MPs, leading members of the Church, the Jewish and other religious communities. (*Bulletin UKACIA*, July 1989)

The UKACIA was not the only group seeking to mobilise Muslim anger. On 1 April 1989, Dr Kalim Siddiqui, Director of the pro-Iranian Muslim Institute in London, in his presidential address to a conference convened to consider the implications of the Rushdie affair, suggested 'symbolic breaking of the law' might be necessary. This suggestion was quickly repudiated by the UKACIA. However, many British Muslims were growing restive with the UKACIA's apparent lack of success and Barelwis, particularly, were inclined to put it down to a want of resolve and commitment to defend the Prophet's honour on behalf of the Saudis and their surrogate organisations.

An individual member of the Bradford Council for Mosques voiced such impatience. He noted that many Muslims 'applauded Khomeini as a hero' since he had 'stood up for the honour of the Prophet' in contrast to 'the deafening silence' from the Arab heartlands. The vigour of the Saudi response to the prospective showing in Britain of the film 'Death of a Princess' – deemed an insult to the Saudi royal family – which triggered a withdrawal of ambassadors and a hint of economic sanctions, was contrasted with their 'unduly soft approach' when confronted with an insult to the Prophet. This was put down to their being Wahhabi and thus having 'no adequate appreciation of the greatness of Mohammed' (Akhtar, 1989, pp. 64, 83).

It is to the credit of the Bradford Council for Mosques, under Mr Azam's presidency, that they deftly negotiated these difficult crosscurrents without fragmenting. They continued to explore all avenues to influence public opinion, taking local initiatives and co-operating with the UKACIA when the situation required a national response. In April 1989 they sent questionnaires to all MPs to gauge the level of support for their campaign. Only fifty replied, but an analysis of these made it clear that in all the furore 'Muslims have never really presented their case clearly, for example, to explain that they have no fear of intellectual ... criticisms ... [but] what is untenable is a slur on the integrity of the Prophet' (*The Muslim News*, October 1989).

When the Minister of State at the Home Office, John Patten, set out the government's thinking on the issues raised by the Rushdie affair in an open letter to 'influential British Muslims' on 4 July 1989, The Council for Mosques chose to be part of a considered national response written under the aegis of the UKACIA. Mr Patten argued that the government had been 'guided by two principles: the freedom of speech, thought and expression; and the notion of the rule of law'. The only principle the government and law could 'realistically protect' was that 'individuals should be free to choose their own faith and to worship without interference, in an atmosphere of mutual respect and toleration'. The UKACIA rejoinder pressed for amendments to the law of blasphemy to include within its purview non-Christian works clearly antipathetic to 'mutual respect' (UKACIA, 1989, pp. 5–9).

On 17 July, the Bradford Council for Mosques launched a ten-point charter during a public demonstration. The charter included lobbying local and national politicians, making future electoral support conditional on a positive response and the establishment of a Muslim thinktank to combat anti-Muslim propaganda in the media. They continued to participate in and to organise regional meetings. From 8 to 12

January 1990, they organised with the UKACIA a five-day vigil outside the headquarters of Viking Penguin in London.

Although Muslims did not succeed in banning the book, the Bradford Council for Mosques' campaign, as it unfolded, indicated that certain lessons had been learned. Nothing shows this more clearly than the shift from book-burning to vigil as a way of winning a more sympathetic hearing for their grievances. The Council also organised a national conference of Muslims in Bradford on 29 April 1990. Under the title of 'Fair Laws for All' they sought to 'begin a nationwide debate on the future of Muslims in this country'. They structured the day to include input on Muslim aspirations and anxieties in the areas of education, social and economic life, political participation and the responsibilities of mosques and '*ulama*. Realising how isolated Muslims had become, the conference invited the Bishop of Bradford and leaders of the Hindu and Sikh communities in the city, as well as local politicians. According to Sher Azam, the conference was an attempt to begin a new phase in the campaign to enlist the support of key institutions by convincing them 'through discussion of the rights of our cause' (*Yorkshire Post*, 30 April 1990).

What was impressive about the conference was the range of speakers enlisted, locally and nationally. These included: Yusuf Islam (the onetime pop star Cat Stevens) who is a leading British Muslim convert; Maulana Rabbani, who is the President of the Jamiat-e-Ulama Britannia (the umbrella organisation for Deobandi '*ulama*); Pir Wahhab Siddiqui, a distinguished Barelwi from Coventry; Dr Asif Hussain, a sociologist and the Director of Muslim Community Studies Institute in Leicester; and Mr Akram Khan-Cheema, a Bradford educationalist who was the chairman of the education sub-committee of The Council of Mosques, UK and Eire. It is hard to imagine any other Muslim organisation in the country enjoying the trust of all the sects and able to host such a gathering of professionals and religious leaders alike.

The emphasis of the conference was on the need for a constructive engagement with the nation's institutions, political, social and educational. Muslim concerns were articulated in an idiom accessible to the non-Muslim majority: Akram Khan-Cheema coined the slogan of 'special but not separate' to encapsulate Muslim demands on the educational system. There was a readiness to be self-critical. Yusuf Islam upbraided the '*ulama* for being slow to engage with contemporary issues, whether genetic engineering, abortion or ecology. Such a conference was

a tribute to the realism of the Bradford Council for Mosques and a refusal
to allow Muslims to withdraw into sullen resentment.

NOTES

1.   This figure is made up of 3500 Sylhetis from Bangladesh; Indians and
     East Africans from Surat district in Gujarat numbering 2300 and 900
     respectively; and the rest from different regions of Pakistan: 30 250 from
     District Mirpur in Azad Kashmir; 5500 Punjabis, mostly from Jhelum,
     Gujar Khan and Rawalpindi; 10 000 from Attock district of Chhachh;
     1800 Pathans from Bannu, Chhachh, Hazara, Kohat, Mardan and
     Peshawar. This breakdown is based on such local authority figures as are
     available and discussions with community leaders who run associations
     for the various regional and linguistic groups.
2.   The issue of what counts as caste or *zat* in a South Asian Muslim context
     is an issue of continuing debate amongst social scientists. One recent
     study of Muslims in Manchester helpfully mapped the points of conver-
     gence and divergence with Hindu caste: Muslim castes, like those of
     Hindus, are: (1) heredity; (2) ideally endogamous; (3) recruited from
     occupational categeories and ethnic groups; (4) comprehensive and
     ranked hierarchically. Yet they differ from Hindu castes in that '(1) the
     muslim *zat* system is not based, except at its extremes, on notions of
     ritual purity and pollution ... [thus] commensality between members of
     all *zats* is permitted ... (2) ritual services are not necessarily provided by
     a "pure" caste but by lay specialists ... (3) all Muslims are equal in
     matters of law, worship and religious conduct' (Werbner, 1990, p. 85).
3.   The Gujaratis from east Africa – Khalifa – largely belong to artisan
     castes, while the majority of those from India belong to a landowning
     caste, the *vohra jat*. Those from East Africa are usually professional,
     urban and bi-lingual – including English – while the majority of those
     migrating from India are rural with little English. It is the Khalifa com-
     munity which provided Bradford's first Muslim woman councillor in
     1992.
4.   Along with Mr Sher Azman and Pir Maroof Hussain Shah was Mr
     Nazim Naqvi, President and founder of Anjuman-e-Haideria, the earliest
     of the city's two Shia centres, Mr Abdul Haq Pandor, President of the
     Gujarati-controlled Deobandi mosque at St Margaret's Road, Mr
     Muhammad Ansari, President of the city's only Ahl-i-Hadith mosque
     and Mr Umar Warraich, President of the UK Islamic Mission mosque.
5.   The term *Pir* is the Persian word for elder and is an honorific title used
     within the Barelwi tradition for a Sufi leader, who takes responsibility
     for the guidence of his devotees.
6.   Apostasy carries the dealth penalty for men in Islamic law (Gill, 953,
     p. 413). Mr Rushdie was also seen as guilty of *sabb al nabi* or *shatm al*

rasul, insulting the Prophet, which involves a similar draconian punishment (Ahsan and Kidwai, 1991, pp. 52–3)

7. Ironically, the visual media did not attend the book-burning and the only record of the incident was the video made by the Council for Mosques itself. Thus, whoever wanted to show it on television contributed to campaign funds!

8. The Barelwis scornfully dismiss such groups as the Deobandis, Ahl-i-Hadith and Jamaat-i-Islami, collectively, as 'Wahhabi'. The term is used for those who look for inspiration to the reform movement initiated by Muhammad ibn 'Abd al Wahhab (1703–87) and the tradition he generated. This eighteenth-century reformer from the Hijaz sought to return to the fundamental principles of the Qur'an which he felt had been obscured and compromised by medieval accretions. To this end he sought to undercut the veneration for Islam's holy men. With Ibn Saud's conversion to it in 1745 'Wahhabism became the religious ideology of tribal unification … in central Arabia' (Lapidus, 1988, p. 673).

REFERENCES

Adams, C. (1987) *Across the Seven Seas and Thirteen Rivers* (London: THAP Books).

Ahmed, A. S. (1988) *Discovering Islam* (Lahore: Vanguard Books).

Ahsan, M. M. and Kidwai, A. R. (eds) (1991) *Sacrilege versus Civility* (Leicester: The Islamic Foundation).

Akhtar, S. (1989) *Be Careful with Muhammad!* (London: Bellew).

Appignanesi, L. and Maitland, S. (eds) (1989) *The Rushdie File* (London: Fourth Estate).

Ballard, R. and Ballard, R. (1977) 'The Sikhs: The Development of South Asian Settlement in Britain', in J. L. Watson (ed.), *Between Two Cultures* (Oxford: Basil Blackwell).

Barton, S. W. (1986) *The Bengali Muslims of Bradford*, Monograph Series, Community Religions Project (Leeds: Department of Theology and Religious Studies, University of Leeds).

City of Bradford Metropolitan Council (CBMC) (1981) *Turning Points: A Review of Race Relations in Bradford*.

CBMC (1982) *Local Administrative Memorandum: Education for a Multicultural Society: Provison for Pupils of Ethnic Minority Communities*.

Dahya, B. (1974) 'The Nature of Pakistani Ethnicity in Industrial Cities in Britain', in A. Cohen (ed.), *Urban Ethnicity* (London: Tavistock).

Halstead, M. (1988) *Education, Justice and Cultural Diversity: An Examination of the Honeyford Affair, 1984–85* (Sussex: Falmer Press).

Hiro, D. (1992) *Black British, White British: A History of Race Relations in Britain* (London: Paladin).

Joly, D. (1987) *Making a Place for Islam in British Society: Muslims in Birmingham*, Research Papers in Ethnic Relations 4 (Coventry: Centre for Research in Ethnic Relations, University of Warwick).

Khan, V. S. (1977) 'The Pakistanis: Mirpuri Villagers at Home and in Bradford', in J. L. Watson (ed.), *Between Two Cultures* (Oxford: Basil Blackwell).

Kureishi, H. (1986) 'Bradford', in *In Trouble Again*, Granta 20 (Middlesex: Granta Publications).

Lapidus, I. I. (1988) *A History of Islamic Societies* (Cambridge: Cambridge University Press).

Lee, S. and Stanford, P. (eds) (1990) *Believing Bishops* (London: Faber & Faber).

Le Lohe, M. (1979) 'The Effects of the Presence of Immigrants upon the Local Political System in Bradford, 1945–77', in R. Miles and A. Phizacklea (eds), *Racism and Political Action* (London: Routledge & Kegan Paul).

Modood, T. (1990) 'British Asians Muslims and the Rushdie Affair', *Political Quarterly*, 61, pp. 143–60.

Murphy, D. (1987) *Tales from Two Cities: Travels of Another Sort* (London: John Murray).

Parekh, B. (1990) 'The Rushdie Affair and the British Press' in D. Cohn-Sherbok (ed.), *The Salman Rushdie Controversy in Interreligious Perspective* (Lampeter: The Edwin Mellen Press).

Richardson, C. (1976) *A Geography of Bradford* (Bradford: Bradford University Press).

Robinson, F. (1988) *Varieties of South Asian Islam*, Research Papers in Ethnic Relations 8 (Coventry: Centre for Research in Ethnic Relations, University of Warwick).

Rose, E. (1969) *Colour and Citizenship: A Report on British Race Relations* (London: Oxford University Press).

Ruthven, M. (1990) *A Satanic Affair: Salman Rushdie and the Rage of Islam* (London: Chatto & Windus).

Scarman, Lord (1983) *The Scarman Report: The Brixton Disorders, 10–12 April 1981* (London: Penguin Books).

Shorter Encyclopaedia of Islam (1953), ed. Gibb, H. A. R (Leiden: E. J. Brill).

UK Action Committee on Islamic Affairs (UKACIA) (1989) *The British Muslim Response to Mr Patten*.

Werbner, P. (1990) *The Migration Process: Capital, Gifts and Offerings among British Pakistanis* (Oxford: Berg).

7 Tablighi Jamaat and the Deobandi Mosques in Britain

John King

Tablighi Jamaat is an internationally proselytising and preaching movement, dedicated to reaffirming the basic principles of Islam and to drawing back into the fold of the religion Muslims who may have strayed. At the same time, the preaching is intended to confirm and to strengthen the faith of the Tablighi missionaries themselves. Tabligh is professedly a non-political organisation, and because it operates entirely within the Muslim community, it is relatively invisible to outsiders.

Tabligh is influential, but within the South Asian context of its origin, its influence is limited to certain sections of the Muslim community. As this chapter demonstrates, it is especially linked with the Deobandi school of Islam. Nevertheless, Tabligh appears to have discovered a mission to the wider world where its influence is not so constricted, and it is attracting increasing attention among Muslims throughout Europe.

Tabligh's founder, Muhammad Ilyas, lived in India from 1885 to 1944. He studied at the Islamic university at Deoband, with which his family had been connected, and was a Deobandi *'alim* (religious scholar). He also became a Sheikh of the Sabiriyah branch of the Chishtiyah Sufi order, and the practices of Tabligh draw to some extent on Sufi ideas. Ilyas's own preferred title for his movement was Tahrik-i-Iman, in Urdu 'The Faith Movement'.

In this Chapter I describe the origins of Tablighi Jamaat and its relationship with the Deobandi expression of the Muslim faith. I make some conjectures about the nature of its vitality as a world movement

129

and as a means by which Islam is transmitted both geographically and from one generation to another. I will also describe the reasons for the limitation of Tabligh to the Deobandi community in the context of South Asian Islam, in India and Pakistan, as well as in Britain and round the world. Tabligh's apparent success among another population, Maghrebi Muslims of North African origin, will also be explored.

Global scope is of the essence of Tabligh. According to the most comprehensive study of Tabligh in English (Haq, 1972), by the early 1970s the movement had spread from India to thirty-four countries throughout the Indian subcontinent, in Arab territories, as well as across Africa and in South-east Asia. Toward the end of the 1980s, it was estimated to have reached ninety countries (Kepel, 1987), including Muslim minorities in the United States, Canada and Trinidad.

The British presence of Tabligh is now very well established, with a national structure whose centre is at the Markazi Mosque and its associated *madrasa* (school) at Dewsbury, sometimes known as the Dar ul-Uloum, whose official title is Jamiat Talimul Islam. Tabligh is also well represented today in other European countries, especially France (cf. Kepel, 1987) and Belgium (Dassetto, 1988a, b). In these francophone countries Tabligh is often called '*Foi et Pratique*'. British Tabligh members have mentioned to me the presence of Tabligh in Spain and the Netherlands. It appears that the spread of Tabligh in Europe follows the spread of Moroccan communities across Europe while Jørgen Nielsen (1992, p. 19) remarks that it is particularly strong in Algeria.

Tablighis are of course nothing if not adventurous, and on an anecdotal level I should record that I have met or been told about British-based Tabligh members who have undertaken the preaching missions, known as *gush* in Urdu or *khuruj* in Arabic, as far afield in Europe as the former East Germany, the former Czechoslovakia and Hungary. These more far-flung excursions involve personal intrepidity on the part of those who undertake them, as they are well aware that they will appear exotic to customs and immigration officials in the countries they visit, and that their mission to contact and visit with Muslims they may encounter in the countries through which they pass may well not be successful.

The fact that such missions are undertaken at all indicates two underlying and, to some extent, contradictory features of the Tabligh movement. The first is that the motivation of the members of Tablighi Jamaat is powerful and they are driven by a profoundly serious faith, so that they are more than willing to encounter the difficulties inherent in missionary work in unfamiliar countries in order to fulfil the obligations they have willingly undertaken. The second is that to Muslims who are in any case part of a world-wide network of contacts and influences, such excursions appear more parochial and easier to undertake than might be supposed by Western observers.

The core theme of my research regarded the manifestation of Tabligh in Britain and its relationship to the world movement, including the surprising connection between Tabligh in Britain and in Morocco – a connection which reflects much about the movement's flexibility and adaptability. There are continuing contacts between British Tabligh and Morocco, with senior students from Morocco among the students and visitors at the *madrasa* and also younger Moroccan pupils at the *madrasa*, mainly from Moroccan families living in France. The implication is that the version of Muslim solidarity expressed through and engendered by Tabligh is capable of transcending not only profound cultural and linguistic differences but also internal divisions within the learned tradition of the Muslim community, since North Africans follow the Maliki madhhab of Islamic law while the Indian tradition is Hanafi. I describe below ways in which this transmission of the Tablighi idea takes place across cultural divides within the Islamic world.

Whatever the reason for the appeal of Tabligh, a vital feature of the movement is that it is in a very real sense a cosmopolitan phenomenon. To take the case of a Moroccan pupil in Dewsbury, whose mother tongue may be French or Moroccan Arabic or both: he will be coping with classical Arabic and Urdu, the language of instruction at Dewsbury, while he will hear both Gujarati and English spoken around him. According to informants, English is not infrequently the language adopted for international communication by meetings of Tablighi Muslims of varying national, linguistic and ethnic origins. Meanwhile, informants encountered during the course of my own research into the Tabligh movement included Gujarati Muslims from Cape Town in South Africa and from Zambia, as well as Keralese Muslims from Southern India, resident now in Birmingham, Leeds and Dewsbury. All have travelled outside the country since their migration to Britain.

One Tabligh activist of my acquaintance comes originally from Trivandrum, the capital of Kerala in Southern India, where the Muslim community is proud of its ancient origins, which predate the arrival of the Mughals in Northern India and are traceable to the sea trade between Arabia and the Indian coast. He came to Britain as a young man by way of an upbringing in Rangoon, the capital of Burma, where he was sent to live with an uncle after the untimely death of his father. His mother tongue was Malayalam, and he also acquired Burmese, Urdu and English while in Burma, in addition to his reading knowledge of Qur'anic Arabic. In Rangoon he studied for British educational qualifications and came into contact with Tablighi preachers. His commitment to Tabligh flowered after his arrival in Britain, when Pakistani students took him to Tabligh meetings in Dewsbury. In a sense, this man's polycultural and multilinguistic background, and his casual awareness of the wider world, make him a typical and emblematic Tabligh figure.

I should also remark at this stage on the impact made on the researcher by the intense and very real piety and enthusiasm of Tablighis. Activists insist that there is no qualification to become a member of Tabligh and no compulsion on any Muslim to join. But it is their quietly joyful contemplation of God and of the good Muslim life, as well as the opportunity of a context in which to achieve the fulfilment of the Muslim's active duties towards society which draws Muslims into the movement to become members and activists.

Perhaps the movement's strength lies in its concentric structure, with an inner core of full-time workers, and an outer group of enthusiasts who may come and go (Dassetto and Bastenier, 1988), an arrangement which is conducive to the mobilisation of activists.

Tablighis often speak of the quiet satisfaction inherent in a preaching mission, when a group of ten or so Muslims will go to another town, another region, or even another country to preach their faith to their fellow Muslims. Away from familiar surroundings and everyday cares, the talk is all of religious and ethical subjects, with the more experienced leading the discussion of the neophytes, and the preachers themselves will return home refreshed, renewed and gratified.

There is no doubt that as a global movement Tabligh is a success. In these pages I examine some reasons as to why this may be the case. But first I shall look at the origins and nature of the Deobandi Muslim movement in India, which was the soil in which the seed of Tabligh first germinated, and in which it flourishes today, to the exclusion of other areas of South Indian Islam.

THE DEOBANDI DIMENSION OF TABLIGH

Jørgen Nielsen refers to Tabligh as 'the active pietism of the Deobandi movement' (1992, p. 133). The link between Tabligh and the Deobandi interpretation of Islam is historical and arises directly out of the circumstances of Tabligh's establishment. It is still a close and intimate relationship in Britain, as well as in other places where the Muslim population is of South Asian origin. In other countries where the movement has gained a foothold, but where the Muslim population is not of South Asian origin or descent, the link between Tabligh and the Deobandi interpretation of Islam is not of central significance.

Within the context of South Asian populations, however, the connection is of considerable importance and limits the way Tabligh spreads and operates, because of the basic division within South Asian Islam between the Deobandi school and the Barelvi schools, to one or other of which most (but by no means all) South Asian Muslims belong. Asked by non-Muslims about the distinction between them, both Deobandis and Barelvis will play down the differences and stress that the most important fact is that both are Muslims. There is much justification for this attitude, especially as the purpose of inquiries by outsiders may be precisely to discern lines of separation in a Muslim community which would rather regard itself as unified.

Nevertheless, it must be admitted that there is a very real intellectual and emotional distinction between Deobandis and Barelvis. Though both are Sunni, and both interpret Islamic law following the Hanafi school of Islamic jurisprudence, Deobandi and Barelvi populations differ markedly in their approach to Islam, and their difference is sometimes expressed as mutual distaste which can sometimes take a strong form (Alavi, 1988).

This potential or real antagonism gives rise to the paradox that within the South Asian community, inside which Tabligh originated, the movement is limited to the Deobandi section, while outside, in the Muslim world as a whole, its appeal is more universal and less limited to a particular segment of the Muslim population.

The division between Deobandi and Barelvi communities is familiar to those who have studied Islam in its South Asian or British context, but is less well known to those whose contact with Muslims lies more with populations of North African or Turkish origins. Francis Robinson (1988) has described the situation in Britain in the context of its South

Asian background. The historical circumstances of the development of the Deobandi school help to throw some light on the way Tabligh is structured today.

The Deobandi movement came into existence in India in the mid-nineteenth century, and takes its name from the site of the movement's great Islamic university, the Dar ul-Uloum at Deoband in Uttar Pradesh, in India, now widely viewed as the Islamic world's second great university after Al-Azhar in Cairo. The university at Deoband was founded in 1867. In its origins, the movement was linked with the resistance against the British colonial domination of India which began to gather pace during the 1840s.

Khurshid Aziz has pointed out that most British observers at the time of what was known in Britain as the Indian Mutiny and in India as the First Indian War of Independence, in 1857, believed that Muslims were the prime opponents of the British in India (Aziz, 1962). Muslims certainly took up arms against the British with enthusiasm (Mortimer, 1982). In any case, in the aftermath of the struggle of 1857–8, Muslims in India sought ways to intensify the practise of their faith in a more private way, while a lasting antagonism between the Muslims and the colonial authority took root. The reaction of Deoband was to look for a pure and austere form of Islam suitable for the private practice of the faith, derived from Islam's basic texts and the interpretations of the Hanafi jurists (Metcalf, 1982).

Deoband's great rival, the Barelvi movement, also originated in the latter half of the nineteenth century, and took shape under the leadership of Sheikh Ahmad Raza Khan. It is important to understand the nature of its opposition to Deoband. Though it was similar in its origins, as a movement which sought to organise the popular expression of Islam it drew on a different clientele, and took a different theological direction (Robinson, 1988; Alavi, 1988). Named after the town of Bareilly, also in Uttar Pradesh, the Barelvi school embraced Islam as it was found in the India of its day.

As distinct from the Deobandi school, Barelvi Islam is quite explicitly a popular expression of the faith. It is linked to the cult of *pirs*, or saints who are believed to have the power of intercession with God and to be able to bring about cures and other favourable outcomes. In addition, festivals are celebrated, including the celebration of the birth dates of saints – especially of the great twelfth-century Sufi saint Abd al-Qadir al-Jilani, the eponymous founder of the Qadiriyya Sufi order which in the Indian sub-continent is found particularly in the Punjab and in Sind. Much personal devotion is offered to the Prophet Muhammad, and this of course is an explanation why it was the Barelvi community in particular which took the lead in attacking the British writer Salman Rushdie, whose work was interpreted by them as an assault on the Prophet's private life (see Lewis in this volume).

Barelvi mosques in Britain sometimes refer to themselves as 'Sufi', but though the *ulama* (trained religious scholars) associated with these mosques may well be practising members of Sufi orders, it is perhaps misleading to see this as their principal point of distinction from the Deobandi mosques. Deobandis may also be members of Sufi brother-hoods (Metcalf, 1982, pp. 157–64): indeed, one of the leading founders of the university at Deoband, Maulana Muhammad Qasim Nanautawi, was a leading sheikh of the Chishtiya. But the principal difference between the two schools is in their style of devotion, in which the Deobandis are as plain and austere as the Barelvis are ornate and enthusiastic.

Hamza Alavi's (1988, pp. 81–4) work on ethnicity and ideology in Pakistan underscores the point that the Deobandi/Barelvi distinction is crucial to an understanding of South Asian society; by implication, this point is significant by way of approaching South Asian social patterns as they are transplanted to Britain. 'Deobandis and Barelvis differ in every respect,' Alavi initially observes, ' by virtue of their different doctrinal positions, the different classes (and regions) amongst whom they have influence and their different political stances.' He goes on to stress the doctrinal difference which gives rise to antagonism between the two groups:

> In contrast to the Deobandi ulama. Barelvis profess a populist Islam, more infused with superstition, and also syncretism, that make up the religious beliefs of the peasantry. The Barelvi version of Islam emphasises belief in miracles and powers of saints and pirs, worship at shrines and the dispensing of amulets and charms, all of which are detested by the Deobandis as un-Islamic. Deobandis and Barelvis detest each other and much sectarian conflict consists of fights between the two.

Alavi also underlines the separate origins and loyalties of the two groups:

Historically, Deobandis have tended to be mainly urban and from the middle and upper strata of society, whereas Barelvi influence has been mainly in rural areas, with a populist appeal. This has changed somewhat in recent decades, for Barelvi influence has extended to towns and cities.... Traditionally Barelvi influence has been weaker in the UP [then United Provinces, now Uttar Pradesh] ... than in the Punjab and to some degree in Sind. On the other hand the main base of Deobandis was in UP, especially among urban Muslims, who are the muhajirs (refugees from India) in Pakistan.

To this, Alavi adds that Deoband has made inroads among the rural and urbanised Pathans in Pakistan. In addition, I would like to observe that Deoband has also spread among the Gujarati Muslim community who were early converts to Islam through their trading contacts with Arabia, like the South Indian Muslims of Kerala.

The predominance of Barelvi mosques in Britain is therefore a consequence of the mainly Pakistani origin of the South Asian Muslim population in Britain (see Chapter 1 and Table 1.2). The constituency of Deoband lies largely with the smaller group of Indian Muslims, or those of Indian origin who may have arrived in Britain by way of a family emigration from India to Africa at an earlier stage, who make up some 168 000 of Britain's total South Asian Muslim community.

None the less, the number of Deobandi mosques is significant, with a clientele composed either of these Indian Muslims, many of them from the Gujarati community, which plays a major part in the Deobandi movement in Britain, or of Pakistani *muhajirs*, descended from migrants who left India for Pakistan at or after the partition of India in 1947, or of other Pakistanis who have attached themselves to Deoband by choice, or of Pathans.

As a local phenomenon, Deoband has strong roots within the Gujarati Muslim community in Britain, but it would be wrong to suppose that the Deobandi movement is in essence linked with Gujarati ethnicity. A list of graduates of Deoband in the Dar ul-Uloum's first century from 1867 to 1967 included only 138 Gujaratis among over seven thousand graduates. But in Britain, Gujaratis do seem to play a major part in both Deoband and Tabligh. The British 'Amir' of Tablighi Jamaat, who with his advisory council controls the mosque and school at Dewsbury, is a Gujarati, for example, and Tablighis I have met socially at Dewsbury spoke as if a strong Gujarati presence there was to be taken for granted. One key informant for the present study, who is the head of the mosque committee at a leading Deobandi mosque in Birmingham, is also Gujarati.

The particular nature of the Gujarati community in Britain and its significance in the international context deserves some attention. Gujaratis are prominent among Asians abroad because of their role as a merchant community which has spread round the world from its Indian base. Alavi remarks that the Gujarati trading community adopted Islam at the time of its early contacts with Arab traders. Gujarati merchants have spread throughout India, and then into Asia and Africa, and now into Europe and the Americas. They have taken Islam with them, and their habits as travellers and their international family and business links have naturally led them to be attracted to the similar spreading network represented by Tabligh, and to be ideally able to serve Tabligh's purposes at the same time as their own business interests.

Structurally, then, Deoband and Tabligh coexist, feeding and reinforcing each other. The Deobandi mosques form the static framework of a system which also involves Tablighi Jamaat as a mobile element. The Deobandi mosques provide a haven for Tablighi preachers and other travellers engaged in *khuruj*, while they also encourage their own members to leave their local areas in order to preach, either for short periods, or for spells of months or even years which may involve foreign travel, to India or to other Muslim countries, or to countries with minority Muslim populations. The following section describes some of the attraction of Tabligh, the way it recruits its activists and the way they work.

THE WIDER APPEAL OF TABLIGH

So far, we have looked at the Tablighi Jamaat within the South Asian context and as part of the way the Deobandi community functions. One set of important features which remains to be explained is the movement's wider appeal and the way in which it has spread to be a worldwide phenomenon, the mechanisms of which also relate to its success within the Deobandi community itself. The way in which Tabligh is transmitted internationally is clearly one key to this question.

Tabligh has found four major means of dissemination. These are: the pilgrimage to Mecca; the network of Indian merchants in Asia, Africa and Britain; the immigration of workers to Western countries; and the Deobandi connection (Gaboriau, 1986). The last three of these relate essentially to the Deobandi link and to the development of Tabligh within the Deobandi community. However, the pilgrimage to Mecca, and pious journeys to Mecca by Muslims at other times of the year, seem certain to have been a means of transmission. The founder of Tabligh, Mawlana Muhammad Ilyas, himself made the pilgrimage twice in his lifetime. Contacts between Muslims of different nationalities and ethnic origins in Mecca have always been a fruitful channel for the world-wide dissemination of Muslim ideas. In more modern circumstances Tabligh members take every advantage of travels undertaken either for the specific purpose of preaching or for any other purpose, business, family or social, to pursue their religious aims. But if there have been, and are increasingly in an age of migration and rapid travel, many opportunities for Tablighis to work, the question remains, what is it that has made a success of Tabligh as a missionary movement outside its community of origin?

The answer seems to lie in the style of Tablighi proselytisation, which both motivates activists to spread their faith abroad as far as possible and appeals in different ways to the recipient audience. The activities of Tabligh follow closely the prescription of the movement's founder, Muhammad Ilyas, who was also a Deobandi *'alim.* He began his own personal mission, which in due course developed into Tablighi Jamaat, because he was overcome by the urge to bring the truth of Islam as he saw it to the ignorant nominal Muslims by whom he was surrounded in North India, and to teach them the real nature of the faith. His practice was based on the ways of the Prophet Muhammad himself, as Ilyas understood them.

Ilyas set out principles, which include emphases on: (1) the centrality of the *kalimah*, the statement that there is no God but God and Muhammad is the prophet of God, which must be understood as well as enunciated; (2) the importance of prayer, whose inner purpose is to help the believer to refrain from sinful or base actions; (3) correct behaviour towards fellow Muslims, whoever they may be, in pursuit of which one must be prepared to sacrifice one's own rights; (4) the ideal that every Muslim must undertake each action with the primary aim of pleasing God, and with only the secondary aim of improving himself; and (5) the view that every Muslim must be prepared to take part personally in preaching expeditions, and in the endeavour to spread an understanding of the true faith within the community. To these positive principles is added the negative rule that Muslims should refrain from wasting their time in superfluous talk and action, and should of course refrain from sinful acts. These are all Sufi principles.

Towards the end of his life, Ilyas became more specific about the ways in which preaching, teaching and *khuruj* should be undertaken – including an emphasis on *zikr* 'remembrance', (repetition of divine names or religous formulae) and on learning and knowledge, or *ilm*. Haq (1972, p. 145) point out that:

> Ilyas regarded learning and *zikr* as the two wheels of the carriage of his work, and said that knowledge without *zikr* led people into darkness and gloom, while *zikr* without learning placed temptations before them and caused dissension. He felt that without knowledge and *zikr* his movement would lose its spiritual character and become materialistic.

Why should this movement – begun in India in the 1920s – have such a strong appeal in modern circumstances and in diverse countries and circumstances? Gilles Kepel suggested a mechanism which would explain the appeal of Islam in migrant populations outside their country of origin and beyond the *dar-ul-Islam* or realm of Islam (personal communication; see also Chapter 2 of this volume). This lies in the migrant's search for identity, and applies with perhaps even more force to the children of Muslim migrants who may have the right to, or have acquired, a European citizenship. An Algerian, for example, will find increasingly as his period of residence in France or elsewhere in Europe lengthens, that he is cut off from his own original country whose experience he has not shared. At the same time, his French neighbours make it clear to him that he cannot regard himself as French, whatever the legalities of his situation may be. The attraction of Islam is obvious: it serves as a constant source of identity available to a person who has lost his national orientation.

A parallel but separate attraction applies to some Muslim inhabitants of Islamic countries (that is to say, countries where Islam is the religion of the majority and may be the official religion). Many such countries are in the process of economic transformation which has created new and marked economic distinctions and has imposed materialist criteria of success. In this case, as Majid Tehranian (1992) has suggested, poverty itself becomes identified as deviancy within the society, and the poor will turn to the alternative value system which is at hand – Islam – which seems to belong to them more than the imported standards and criteria do, thereby giving value to their lives.

Tabligh, whose philosophy encourages its adherents to travel ever more widely and to take advantage of all forms of contact to spread the faith of Islam, is ideally suited to satisfy these contexts and developments. The reason is that it is simple and broadly democratic, and offers instant progress for the newly recruited believer. The neophyte is urged from the beginning to take part. From his first profession of the *kalimah* and his embarkation on a programme of prayer and *zikr*, the newcomer is ready to take part in a junior capacity in preaching excursions himself. At the most basic level, the appeal of Tabligh is such that it tells the new recruit there is something he can do immediately to serve the organisation, while more sophisticated understanding may come later.

Like some other organisations, Tabligh uses the concept of service within the group both to bind the loyalty of its members and to give them satisfaction. Short periods away from home in the company of other Tabligh members serve to deepen the loyalty and commitment of members. Because of the 'concentric' organisation, where an inner group of full-time Tabligh personnel is surrounded by an outer ring of more experienced members and an outermost circle of more loosely attached collaborators, there is always both a level within the organisation where a member can feel comfortable and another activist who is known to him to whom he can turn for advice.

Here I would like to return to the question of what Tablighis, following Sufi tradition, call *zikr*, and its significance and its role in Tabligh's activities. The word literally means 'remembrance' in Arabic, or even, as Haq (1972, p. 201) suggests, 'commemoration'. Its adoption from Sufi orders was quite deliberate, Haq (1972, p. 62) suggests: 'Bearing in mind the long sufi tradition among Muslims in India, Ilyas inaugurated a religious movement which aimed at reviving spiritual devotion by emphasising Sufi practices which he adopted for his work with certain changes.'

According to Metcalf (1982), the founders of the university at Deoband were mainly Chishti sheikhs. Muhammad Ilyas himself enrolled some of his more enthusiastic disciples into the Chishtiyah order, but believed that some aspects of Sufism were important for all his followers. Of these *zikr* was central. The actual practice of *zikr* consists of repeating either silently or aloud a prescribed number of times a prayer, or a name of God, or the *kalimah*. This must be done a certain number of times each day, and silent *zikr* can also be performed. In the Sufi context it often involves rhythmic chanting, but Deobandi and Tablighi practice is, I gather, more restrained.

It is this centrality of Sufi practice, the Sufi nature of Ilyas's rules and prohibitions, and *zikr* in particular which has no doubt provided the link between Tablighi and the Muslims of North Africa. Sufi orders (the *tariqat*) are a central part of North African Muslim experience, and particularly in the rural and popular contexts. A proselytising movement which works partially through the Sufi orders, and which relies in any case on some aspects of Sufi practice even for its non-initiated members, is in possession of an important key to influence in North Africa. In addition, the Chishtiyah order, with which Tabligh is linked, takes a very ecumenical view of other orders, and does not shrink from absorbing Qadiri, or Naqshbandi practices, or ideas from other orders.

As to the actual dates of transmission, Tabligh seems to have been limited to the Indian subcontinent during the lifetime of Muhammad Ilyas, but to have begun to expand in the 1950s. According to my own informants, the first Tabligh groups came to Britain in 1956. Tabligh appear to have begun to make its major move into other parts of Europe in the 1960s. For example, although a first Tabligh mission to France in 1962 failed, by 1968 the organisation was effectively established in that country (Kepel, 1987, pp. 190–1). A final conjecture may be made about the way in which the movement spreads, in connection with the reason for its activists efforts in Europe rather than the mechanisms of their success, if we suppose that the urge to travel outside the English-speaking world and to find new fields for conversion may spring from a sense of frustration at the movement's limitation within the English and Urdu speaking sphere.

CONCLUSION: TABLIGHI JAMAAT, MUSLIM MODERNITY AND COSMOPOLITANISM

It is easy for outside observers to see an organisation such as Tabligh as seeking to reimpose the discipline of a mythical past, or leading to communal separatism or seclusion. Indeed, Muslim society is regarded as 'backward' by Western commentators who fail to interpret what they see. Such observers not infrequently order their perceptions in the light of what they refer to as Islamic 'fundamentalism'. But 'fundamentalism' is basically a Western concept, rather than a Muslim one. It is a way in which Western observers of Islam can categorise and link Muslim organisations which may in practice have little in common with each other, an example of what Edward Said (1981) calls a 'coercive label'.

The idea of 'fundamentalism' is connected with the notion that Islamic activists are backward-looking, and that their way of thinking is in some sense medieval and opposed to Western ways of organising society, which are here taken to be axiomatically the most favourable to social and human development. There is much here to argue with, but I will content myself with a critical appraisal of the notion that Islam itself is backward looking, and argue that organisations such as Tabligh are essentially innovative and pioneering rather than retrogressive.

On the one hand, there are some senses in which Tabligh is the kind of organisation which might be described from a Western point of view as 'fundamentalist', or, as the French put it, 'intégriste'. The movement demands that Muslims with whom it comes into contact should reinstate Islam as the central element in their lives, and that Islam should provide the criteria according to which they structure their lives. It also makes it clear that it is impossible for a Muslim to pick and choose about which parts of Islam will fit into his life: it is all or nothing. On the other hand, the notion of 'fundamentalism' is itself controversial from the Muslim perspective. Muslims will explain that they are not adding anything to Islam, or carrying out their observances in any special way. Many Muslims will make the point that what is described, mainly in the West, as 'fundamentalism' is nothing more nor less than wholehearted Islam.

There is a clear sense in which Tabligh is non-'fundamentalist', since it is concerned only with religion in the private sphere; it is non-political. Contemporary organisations in Muslim countries identified by the West as 'fundamentalist' in general tend to have political ambitions – particularly in the present post-Iranian-revolution period. Even within Islamic countries, however, Tabligh does not concern itself with the argument that Islam should provide the framework of political life (although it did, after initial reluctance, support the foundation of the state of Pakistan). Meanwhile, Tablighis adopt the orthodox Muslim

view that outside Islamic countries Muslims are under a political obligation to live as responsible citizens of the society in which they find
themselves.

But whether or not Tabligh can be meaningfully said to be 'fundamentalist', a more important question arises about how 'fundamentalist' movements – that is to say, pious, militant, or political Islamic
movements – are seen by the outside world. A common Western view
of Islamic 'fundamentalists' is that they are harking back to the past,
and want a return to some mythical state of Islamic society, or adherence to some set of rules which has formerly been accepted. Quite to
the contrary, however, I believe phenomena such as Tablighi Jamaat,
whether or not they are seen as 'fundamentalist', should be regarded as
thoroughly modern.

Tablighis do not call for a return to some former version of Islamic
society, but rather attempt to construct something new and in tune with
contemporary needs. It can be argued that no social organisation has
been truly Islamic since the earliest days of the state constructed and
left behind by the Prophet Muhammad in Arabia. Modern 'fundamentalists' do refer to that as an ideal, but realise that their enterprise must
be concerned with the construction of a new and different form of
social organisation.

The body of Islamic tradition and jurisprudence to which they refer
was constructed in the times which followed Muhammad's early
society, and the later polities in Muslim countries were in many senses
not Islamic. Organisations such as Tabligh are responding to changing
circumstances with a flexible approach to the organisation of an Islamic
society, not rejecting anything from the past, but applying it and adapt-
ing it in new ways. The flexibility of Islam is something which many
informants have stressed.

Furthermore, Tabligh is not an inward looking organisation which
sees its aim as the production of an isolated and withdrawn society. It is
often held that notions such as 'the Muslim community' are misleading
and inappropriate when used in the British or other European contexts,
because the Muslim populations of Europe come from diverse sources
and do not constitute a single group. Tabligh's aim, however, is to weld
different groups together, and to produce a Muslim society which is
not only Islamic and modern but also cosmopolitan.

The style of Tabligh, from the days of its founder Muhammad Ilyas,
confirms this view. Initiating neophytes into his Sufi order, Ilyas

claimed to welcome them simultaneously into the four orders locally prevalent in north India: the Qadiriya, the Naqshbandiya and the Suhrawardiya as well as his own Chishtiyah. And in the context of the schools of Islamic law, he tried to reconcile the teaching of his own Hanafi school with the interpretations and judgements of the other schools.

Modern followers of the founder take a similar view. The chairman of a mosque committee in Birmingham deplored and played down the distinction between Deobandi and Barelvi Islam, and emphasised the underlying importance of Islam's basic principles on which everyone agrees. The Amir at Dewsbury disclaimed the idea that the interpretations of any particular religious school took precedence in the teaching at his *madrasa*. Though regretfully admitting that, in the words of one informant, 'we go where we are welcome', Tablighis have a clear vision of a single Islam of mutually supportive and understanding believers, and do not look inward to particular communities.

Tablighis are proud of the international extent of their movement, recall fondly their own travels, and draw attention to the diverse membership of the organisation. My impression is that they see Tabligh's destiny as the framework on which a global Islamic society can be built. The non-political nature of their movement and their stated intention of good relations with the civil and political structures of the non-Muslim societies in which many of them live is also an indication of another aspect of their cosmopolitan ambition. The Islamic society they aim to construct will be an essentially new phenomenon.

BIBLIOGRAPHY

Alavi, H. (1988) 'Pakistan and Islam: Ethnicity and Ideology', in F. Halliday and H. Alvi (eds), *State and Ideology in the Middle East and Pakistan* (Basingstoke: Macmillan).
Aziz, K. K. (1962) *Britain and Muslim India* (London: Heinemann).
Darsh, S. M. (1980) *Muslims in Europe* (London: Ta-Ha Publishers).
Dassetto, F. (1988a) 'Le Tabligh en Belgique', *Sybidi Papers* , No. 2 (Louvain La Neuve: Academia).
Dassetto, F. (1988b) 'The Tabligh Organisation in Belgium', in T. Gerholm and Y. Georg Litman (eds), *The New Islamic Presence in Europe* (London: Mansell).

Dassetto, F. and A. Basenier (1988) *Europa: nuova frontiera dell'Islam* (Roma: Edizioni Lavoro).

Gaboriau, M. (1986) 'What is Tablighi Jamaat? Preliminary Thoughts about a New Strategy of Adaptation to a Minority Situation' (unpublished manuscript).

Gellner, G. (1992) *Postmodernism, Reason and Religion* (London: Routledge).

Haq, M. Anwarul (1972) *The Faith Movement of Mawlana Muhammad Ilyas* (London: Allen & Unwin).

Joly, D. (1987) 'Associations amongst the Pakistani Population in Britain', in J. Rex, D. Joly and C. Wilpert (eds), *Immigrant Associations in Europe* (London: Gower).

Joly, D. (1984) 'Making a Place for Islam in British Society: Muslims in Birmingham', University of Warwick Research Papers No. 4 (Coventry: Centre for Research in Ethnic Relations).

Kepel, G. (1987) *Les banlieues de l'Islam* (Paris: Seuil).

Kepel, G. (1990) 'Les mouvements de "reislamisation"', *Le Monde*, 29 September.

King, J. (1994) *Three Asian Associations in Britain*, University of Warwick Monographs in Ethnic Relations, No. 8 (Coventry: Centre for Research in Ethnic Relations).

Metcalf, B. (1982) *Islamic Revival in British India: Deoband 1860–1900* (Princeton, NJ: Princeton University Press).

Metcalf, B. (1987) 'Islamic Arguments in Contemporary Pakistan', in W. R. Roff (ed.), *Islam and the Political Economy of Meaning* (London: Croom Helm).

Modood, T. (1992) *Not Easy Being British* (London: Runnymede Trust and Trentham Books).

Mortimer, E. (1982) *Faith and Power: The Politics of Islam* (London: Faber).

Nadwi, S. A. H. A. (1983) *Muslims in the West: Message and Mission* (Leicester: The Islamic Foundation).

Naylor, F. (1989) *The School over the Pub* (London: The Claridge Press).

Nielsen, J. (1992) *Muslims in Western Europe* (Edinburgh: Edinburgh Univerity Press).

Owen, D. (1992) 'Ethnic Minorities in Great Britain: Settlement Patterns', University of Warwick Statistical Papers No. 1 (Coventry: Centre for Research in Ethnic Relations).

Raza, M. S. (1991) *Islam in Britain* (Leicester: Volcano Press).

Rex, J. (1991) *Ethnic Identity and Ethnic Mobilisation in Britain*, University of Warwick Monographs in Ethnic Relation No. 5 (Coventry: Centre for Research in Ethnic Relations).

Rex, J. (1992) 'The Integration of Muslim Immigrants in Britain', *Innovation*, 5 (3), pp. 65–74.

Robinson, F. (1988) 'Varieties of South Asian Islam', University of Warwick Research Papers, No. 8 (Coventry: Centre for Research in Ethnic Relations).

Said, E. (1981) *Covering Islam* (London: Routledge).

Tehranian, M. (1992) 'Interview with Malise Ruthven', *Sunday*, BBC Radio 4, 28 March.

Tozy, M. (1984) 'Champ et contre-champ politico-religieux au Maroc', *Faculte de droit et de science politique*, Aix-Marseille (unpublished manuscript).

Tozy, M. (1990) 'Le prince, le clerc et l'Etat: la restructuration du champ religieux au Maroc', in G. Kepel and Y. Richard (eds), *Intellectuels et militants de l'Islam contemporain* (Paris: Seuil).

8   The Political Culture of the '*Beurs*'

Rémy Leveau

The French-born children of immigrants from the Maghreb (Tunisia, Algeria and Morocco) are colloquially referred to in France as '*beurs*'. An analysis of the political culture of the Maghrebian minority which stresses the new generation raises several important issues. First of all it suggests that Islam should be considered as an independent behavioural variable. There is Gérard Noiriel's remark, on previous research on immigration, that 'the issue of origins for French people of foreign origin had no importance' (Noiriel, 1987). If Islam is taken as the central element of a political tradition, does one have to compare that culture with that of other minority groups such as the Jews (Leveau and Schnapper, 1987)?

Today Islam is a factor which cannot be ignored both because of the public debate as well as the works of academic researchers. However, there is a question as to which of the two factors in the construction of this Islamic identity is most important: is it the internal positive forces of tradition, on which a neo-communalism has been built, or is it the negative, exclusionary forces of French society which determine political action? If it is the latter, then the religious discourse is nothing more than an ideological camouflage.

PARENTS' INHERITANCE: A POLITICAL CULTURE OF SETTLEMENT

As long as Maghrebian settlement sees itself and is perceived as being transitory, its Muslim identity appears as a secondary factor. It has neither more nor less importance than those of the North African

147

soldiers who came to fight for France at the time of the two World Wars. But, as soon as Maghrebian workers, whose jobs have been put at risk because of the changes in industrial society, fear that their rights to a domicile might be revoked, Islam appears as a visible mark of identity (Kepel, 1987). The assertion of Islam, in recent years, as France's second religion is really an alternative means of political mobilisation, produced by a social group lacking local references or refusing those which are prescribed for it. One could put forward the paradoxical hypothesis that the manifestation of Islam has little to do with the religion of the countries of origin, but instead constitutes a tradition re-invented for the situation in France.

This approach signifies an implicit break with the countries of origin as it does not recognise nationality as being the major factor of belonging; above all, as it denies the national political authorities the right to speak in their name. By keeping a cultural rather than a national reference point (which is at the heart of the political stance) it preserves a legitimate but deeply ambiguous link with the Maghreb, for the referential community stands above the nation-state. By becoming visible as Muslims, the Maghrebian minority tries to establish a dialogue about the difficulties of integration, for themselves and even more for their children. But, concerning Islam, the long-settled Muslim groups and their élites are going to perceive the provocative characteristic and the breaking of the rules of the game they themselves had established.

This approach, which uses an identity discourse with a religious content, stems from the demand for integration. Muslims in France, most of them of Maghrebian origin, were estimated in the early 1990s to number nearly 3 million – that is to say about 6 per cent of the total population (Peach and Glebe, 1995; Nielsen, 1992; Mission de Réfléxion, 1991; Etienne, 1989). The group is growing quickly. Nearly half have acquired French nationality, about a third of them were born in France and nearly 60 per cent have been residents for more than ten years. Their integration is progressing. However, they do not wish integration to lead to a split from those who, whether by choice or circumstance, or from the sometimes painful memory of the countries of origin (especially in the case of Algeria) have kept their foreign nationality.

In contrast to other immigrant minorities, the Maghrebians negotiated their integration using the religious factor. Poles, the Italians and the Spanish made more use of the trade-unions and political parties, especially the Communist Party. This approach stresses the transitional identity played by Islam in a way which is clearly different from the use of the religious factor by the old, settled minority groups, including the Jewish immigrants at the end of the nineteenth century or between the two World Wars. One should not conclude from this, given the sudden visibility of Islamic identity, that Maghrebian immigration presents a uniform political culture. There are significant cleavages between generation and between places. Lille and Marseilles, for example, are very different situations.

THE NEW DETERMINING FACTORS

Quantitative analyses and local studies are still too few to permit a well-founded approach of the differentiating factors. Starting from the various sources of available data, the continuity with the parents' transplanted Islam seems secured. The determining factors of new generations' political culture are to be found at school and in the media. Differentiation is produced by socio-professional factors or local cultures. As with earlier social groups with immigrant roots, being born in France and length of residence seem decisive. The fact of going to school at an early age plays an important part, in spite of the criticisms addressed to the institution. School helps getting out of the group, mainly by creating a value-system different from those of the family and by preparing the conditions for social mobility. When they are asked the question 'Do you feel closer to the way of life and to the culture of the French people than to that of your parents?', 71 per cent of a sample representing young people between age 18 and 30, born in France, answered 'yes' (Gallup/IFOP/*Le Monde*/RTL, 1989). On the whole, other inquiries conducted during the headscarf crisis (see the Introduction to this volume) or during the Gulf War (Dazi and Leveau, 1988), indicate equal or even higher rates of acceptance of French society. 93 per cent (Gallup/IFOP/*Le Monde*/RTL, 1989) consider that it is perfectly possible to be integrated and at the same time practice Islam in private and 71 per cent think that it is possible to live in France and to practice all the prescriptions of Islam.

Thus political culture seems to establish itself between these two poles, on one side a very strong will to integrate into France, on the other side the feeling of an Islamic identity which in fact goes beyond the borders of private life as they had been defined by the long-settled groups. Evidence of that integration will is plentiful: 64 per cent of these young people say they are ready to defend France militarily, and in the middle of the Gulf War, 70 per cent declared that they wanted to live in France, while fearing that the conflict might engender more problems for them in their daily lives (police controls, racism, difficulties in finding a job) (Gallup/IFOP, 1991).

If one goes deeper in the analysis of individual behaviour affecting acceptance of the wider society, one finds also a bundle of concordant signs. For example, 73 per cent of young people have already had sexual relationships with a non-Maghrebian and 70 per cent would consider marrying such a partner in spite of family reservations. These percentages have remained constant since 1989 at the height of the headscarf affair. Other signs of acceptance may be found in the answer to the question 'If one of your close relatives was going to abandon the Muslim religion, what would be your reaction?' In this case, 72 per cent said they would go on seeing that person, accepting their decision. The principle of freedom of individual conscience is thus widely accepted and, among young people, a nearly equal percentage say they are against the adoption of a special status for Muslims in such issues as marriage, divorce, custody of children and so forth.

Within this group, one can differentiate two sub-groups which can help to sharpen the analysis. The first represents 25–30 per cent of the samples, depending upon the questions. They could be characterised by an attitude of nearly total adhesion to the values of secularity, going as far as wishing not to be visible as Muslims. Their first wish is to be perceived according to professional or social success. Concerning the wearing of the headscarf at school or the building of mosques with minarets or of Muslim private schools, their answers are identical to those of the whole of the society.

Within the group that displays integration values, there is an equal percentage of people who are in favour of a greater visibility of Islam in public places, disregarding the previous low-profile conventions. The building of visible minarets, the celebration of Muslim feasts, observing Ramadan and food prohibitions constitute a sort of definition of the group in which their demands are similar to those of Muslims who make more strictly communitarian choices (Gallup/IFOP/*Le Monde*/ RTL, 1989). However, for this group, becoming French does not constitute a rejection of Islam and these cultural markers are clearly not connected to the nationality issue. Political participation is regarded as a kind of community duty which should take place at the local level. Seventy-three per cent of those questioned were in favour of voting rights in local elections for non-EC foreigners and a nearly equal percentage would willingly consider having a Muslim mayor in charge of their city (Gallup/IFOP/*Le Monde*/RTL, 1989).

It was evident, during the Gulf War, that there was a deep allegiance felt by the Maghrebians towards the French political authorities involved in a war against an Arab and Muslim country (Gallup/IFOP, 1991). François Mitterand headed the list of personalities receiving a favourable opinion (67 per cent), far ahead of Arab heads of state, starting with Saddam Hussein (26 per cent). France's Muslims would have preferred a less violent end to the conflict but they recognised the right of the legally elected President of the Republic to use military means. They considered George Bush, Israel and Saddam Hussein as the main actors responsibe for that conflict. They were willing to recognise the attempts, unsuccessfully made by France, to mediate a settlement. Finally, those who said they were ready to commit violent acts through solidarity with Iraq represented only a tiny minority (2 per cent of the 20 per cent who said they are in favour of Saddam Hussein).

Other factors enable us to understand the Maghrebian relationship to politics. At the end of the 1980s, they were more sensitive to the *Intifada* than to events related to the Maghreb. They identified themselves strongly with the young Palestinians throwing stones at the Israeli army (Dazi and Leveau, 1988; Gallup/IFOP, 1989; Gallup/IFOP 1991). In the Gulf War, their reactions did not reflect the Maghreb's public opinions, which exploded. The dissociation was discreet but nevertheless painful. Never have the suburbs been so quiet, in spite of the anxiety displayed by the authorities and in a certain way relayed by the intermediary élites of the associative movement. It is probably possible today to make the same assumption concerning that group's reactions towards Algeria as it descends into civil war with the growing power of the FIS. This split is even more painful as it does not shelter the group from a suspicion of complicity in external violence and a collective stigmatisation.

This attitude of French authorities does not help the political integration of young *beurs*, a situation which remains problematic for reasons peculiar to the group. In fact, it is clear that the *beurs* have not yet succeeded in using the influence they could exert in a democratic society through their weight of numbers. The problem was discussed by various national and local associative networks in the 1980s. 'France-plus' makes it one of its favourite themes with the access to nationality. Exit polls after voting in 1988 and 1989 indicated strong support for the Socialist party and especially for François Mitterand (Leveau, 1991). From the headscarf crisis to the Gulf War, the support for the left increased from 44 to 47 per cent, but the number refusing to express their opinion remained stable at around 45 per cent. According to a classical pattern, those who are the most politically involved are the most socially integrated. The level of education also plays a positive part in social integration (Kepel, 1993). That route has proved to be more efficient than the use of the vote as source of co-optation of individuals and access to the welfare-state's resources.

The élites from these circles were able to extract a price for their allegiance as intermediaries capable of guaranteeing calm in the suburbs after the 'hot summers' at the beginning of the 1980s, through the headscarf crisis and finally during the Gulf War. On the whole, they presented themselves as the last rampart of secularity in the French manner in the face of communalistic drift. But they also required, as a *quid pro quo*, some recognition of the group and attention to its Muslim culture. Speaking a secular language when they addressed French institutions, they preserved the possibility of using their Muslim identity when they needed to mobilise their supporters.

NEO-COMMUNALISM TENDENCIES?

If all these factors indicate a major tendency in favour of integration among the *beurs*' political culture, it is none the less necessary to pay special attention to a certain number of factors which can be interpreted conversely as leading to a neo-communalism.

At the beginning, it was pointed out that the political culture of the *beurs* could not be treated as homogeneous, while at the same time indicating broad generalisations derived from qualitative studies and polls. Local dimension, the way of speaking, the accent, support of a football club (such as the O.M. in Marseilles) constitute sometimes conflicting forms of integration which ought to be explored. Next to the President of the Republic, the mayor is the most immediate authority in their lives and the one most often blamed for inadequate or hostile policies from which they suffer. It is true that most of the time problems of housing and employment create the conditions for exclusion and that the response to them comes in the form of a neo-communalism.

Traditionally, the analysis of the political culture or the basis strategies of the *beurs* is centred upon the boys, who are the more visible actors of that social change. One hardly says anything about the girls apart from some trivial remarks about the fact that they take better advantage of the school system, that they are less exposed to drugs and delinquency and that they are the focus of family conflicts created by their desire for behavioural freedom. They are already better taken into consideration in Gallup polls and in some studies where they appear to be rather close to the standards of society in general and especially to the behaviour of young girls of the same age. A study conducted in Dreux revealed Muslim girls to be less hostile to society and more open to political participation. Their attitudes about the values of the family, procreation and sexual partners, revealed deep changes compared to the traditional models imported from the Maghreb by their parents, who have re-inforced the models with more rigidity because of their own experience of transplantation.

Now, in a context of exclusion in which girls progress far better than boys, the latter will tend to use the traditional model in order to enforce stricter social control upon their sisters. Their own authoritarianism may be interpreted as a reaction to French society which rejects them and also against those of their own ethnic group who succeed in avoiding exclusion. When re-imposing constraints in the name of tradition, they are putting themselves into the place of their discredited parents who have failed or even, in some cases, may appear as accomplices of their daughters. To assert their authority in front of everyone, they call on the *sharia*.

A block of between 15 and 30 per cent of the samples gave, depending on to the questions, what could be interpreted as neo-communalistic types of answers. For instance, in 1989, 30 per cent were in favour of wearing the headscarf at school; 26 per cent said that they supported Saddam Hussein in 1991 and 15 per cent were in favour of a Gulf conflict which turned into a war between Israel and the Arab countries. A similar percentage (14 per cent) declared in 1993 that it participated in or approved of Muslim separatism. However, one cannot conclude from this that solid identification with the FIS existed because the image of Algeria itself is so degraded and rejected among immigration circles. The real reason for these answers is in relation to French society and relates to a demand for integration. Neo-communalism comes about because neighbourhood organisation around Islam is the only recognition available to excluded youths. Religion is the totem capable of attracting the interest of global society.

CONCLUSION

One returns to the question posed at the beginning. Is there a political culture specific to the *beurs*? There is no unequivocal answer. The earlier model of integration and individual social mobility, which was tried and tested on previous strata of immigrants, still works but it no longer constitutes the sole process. On the contrary, there has been a development of a neo-communalistic model related to social exclusion. However, although this model exists in France, it is has not replaced the older model and it is no more prominent than such a model in the United States or other European countries. Indeed, some of the Islamic group behaviour appears not to be related to exclusion but to represent a kind of group individualism negotiating collectively its integration in the face of a weakened nation-state. This raising of Muslim consciousness could be seen as a kind of collective answer to stigmatisation of the better integrated, who counter with such a threat each time their privileges are put in question. From this perspective, does not the political culture of the *beurs* constitute simultaneously a kind of adaptation to the fears of the globalised society and a means of maximising its advantages while managing the prevailing logic of integration? New empirical studies concerning, for example, the wearing of the headscarf *today* by Muslim girls or about young Muslims' reactions to FIS activities in Algeria and France may put such analyses to the test.

REFERENCES

Dazi, F. and R. Leveau (1988) 'L'intégration par le politique – Le vote des "beurs"', *Etudes*, September, pp. 139–88.

Etienne, B. (1989) 'Islamic Associations in Europe', *Contemporary European Affairs*, 2, pp. 29–44.

Gallup/IFOP/*Le Monde*/RTL (1989) 'L'islam en France'.

Gallup/IFOP (1991) 'Les musulmans et la guerre du Golfe'.

Kepel, G. (1987) *'Les Banlieues de l'Islam: Naissance d'une Religion en France* (Paris: Editions du Seuil).

Kepel, G. (1993) *Des mouvements islamistes au neo-communautarisme* (Paris: Institut d'Études Politiques thesis).

Leveau, R. (1991) 'Mouvement associatif et transition ambigue vers le politique dans l'immigration maghrébine', in *Etudes politiques du monde arabe*, document of the CEDEJ, Le Caire, pp. 265–77.

Leveau, R. and D. Schnapper (1987) 'Relition et politique, juifs et musulmans', in R. Leveau and G. Kepel (eds), *Les musulmans dans la société française* (Paris: Presses FNSP) pp. 99–140.

Mission de Réfléxion (1991) *Rapport a Madame le Premier Ministre de la Mission de Réfléxion sur la Commaunite Repatriée d'Origine Nord-Africaine*, xerox, May.

Nielsen, J. (1992) *Muslims in Western Europe* (Edinburgh: Edinburgh University Press).

Noirel, G. (1987) 'Immigrations et traditions politiques', *Pouvoirs*, 42, 83–92.

Peach, C. and G. Glebe (1995) 'Muslim Minorities in Western Europe', *Ethnic and Racial Studies*, 18, pp. 26–45.

9 Islamic Vision and Social Reality: The Political Culture of Sunni Muslims in Germany

Werner Schiffauer

An underlying notion in the sociology of religion of Weber (1973a,b) and Troeltsch (1922) is the idea that religion is a dynamic phenomenon. Religion is not to be understood as a static and coherent system of symbols, but rather as an ongoing process of constructing a world view. The direction of the religious search is conditioned by the transcendent (formulated in myths and articulated in rituals) attempt to connect an ideal relation of individual and society with the actual experience of the other and the self in existing society. This approach implies an analysis of the religious process in terms of problems and solutions. It is in this respect that I want to analyse the political culture of Sunni Turks in Germany with particular reference to 'fundamentalist' groups.

The use of the term 'fundamentalism' is disputed, while the inner diversity of the presumed fundamentalist camp is usually underestimated (cf. Riesebrodt, 1990). When I use this term I do so for two reasons: (1) the term points out that movements with similar structures of thought are emerging all over the globe and therefore are not restricted to one religion or ethnic group; and (2) the term alludes to a characteristic feature of all-these movements, namely the search for a stable 'fundament' on which the edifice of an all-encompassing social theory can be erected.

This study involves ethnographic material collected in the Southern German city of Augsburg. In the first section I reconstruct the history of Muslims there, a history showing a similar pattern to that in other

German Cities (see Blaschke, 1984; Mıhçlyazgan, 1990, Amiraux in this volume). After this historical sketch, I proceed to a sociological analysis reconstructing systematic reasons for conflicts among Sunni groups.

A HISTORY OF ISLAM IN AUGSBURG

The history of Islam in Augsburg is characterised by a continued process of fissions which can be represented in the form of a kind of genealogy (see Figure. 9.1).

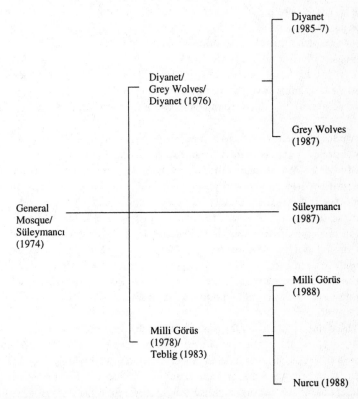

Figure 9.1   A genealogy of Islamic groups in Augsburg

Islam was brought to Augsburg by Turkish migrants arriving at the beginning of the 1960s. This generation of workers – all young men who came with the intention of staying only for a short period in Germany – was not very religiously inclined. There were only very few believers who met for the Friday prayer in rooms set apart in the workers' homes. This changed in the beginning of the 1970s when the workers started to bring their families to Germany. A growing concern for the religious education of the next generation, as well as the possibility of a prolonged stay in Germany, may have led to an increased interest in the institutionalisation of Islam. In 1974, somewhat later than in Germany's other cities, a general mosque was founded in Augsburg. At this time there had been a declared intention among members to avoid the split that already had occurred in other places. As one of the founding members explained, 'When we founded that mosque here we said: "We do not want any politics [*siyaset*] here, we want to restrict ourselves to religious services. We will install Qur'an courses, and offer religious services".'

This proved to be an illusion. In the same year (1974) the general mosque was taken over by the Süleymancı brotherhood by an action which can only be called a coup. According to one informant:

Among the believers there had been one or two friends who had connections to the Islamic Cultural Centre [i.e. the Süleymancı] in Munich.... We of course did not know about that. There had been a certain Ali Hoca [*hoca*: preacher, teacher] in Munich.... With the help of this Ali Hoca they brought a constitution. They said: 'Let us make it official.' 'Alright,' we said, 'let us make it official.' But we did not know that they would thus align us officially to the Islamic Cultural Centres. We just thought that it would be helpful. Well, and with time passing, they only brought Hocas of the Islamic Cultural Centres to Augsburg.... They tried to develop the Süleymancı teachings here.... We could not agree with that.

There are two reasons for the seeming naïvité of the majority of the believers: (1) the statute which turned the mosque officially into a *Verein* (association) was written in German and probably only very few of the believers were able to understand its bureaucratic and juridic language; (2) the idea of organising a religious group in the form of a corporate group was very alien to the Turkish believers (and to the Islamic tradition in general) – they probably just thought 'that it would be helpful' without spending much thought on the implications.[1]

The fact that the general mosque was now in the hands of one particular group triggered off a process of segmentation. In 1978 a mosque of the Diyanet Isleri Türk Baskanligi ('office of religious affairs', or DITIB) representing official Islam in Turkey was founded. This mosque was taken over by the Grey Wolves (a fascist movement fighting for a kind of synthesis of Islam and Turkism) by shifting majorities and was later taken by the Diyanetçiler. This again led to the setting up of a mosque exclusively for the Grey Wolves in 1987.

Also in 1978, a mosque had been founded by the National Sight, i.e. the European branch of the Religious Salvation Party/Welfare Party of Necmettin Erbakan. Under the impact of the Islamic Revolution in Iran, there had been a growing radicalisation among the followers of this group in the beginning of the 1980s, a radicalisation which finally led to a split in 1983. The Teblig Movement (Annunciation Movement),[2] headed by Cemaleddin Kaplan and favouring an Islamic revolution on the lines of the Iranian model, broke away from the National Sight. In the Augsburg community these dissenters were in the majority and took over the mosque. The group which remained loyal to the National Sight set up its own mosque in 1988. In the same year, a group of mostly young people, migrants of the second generation whose fathers had been in the Milli Görüs/Teblig Movement, set up a small lodge of the Nurcu group. This was the only foundation which did not result out of a conflict.

This short sketch shows that the history of Islam in Augsburg is conflict-ridden, a history characterised by coups, by fissions and by takeovers through shifting majorities.

In turning now to the structural reasons for these conflicts, I want to restrict myself to the four 'fundamentalist' groups, i.e. to the groups which fight for the reintroduction of the Şeriat (system of Islamic law) in Turkey:[3] The National Sight, the Süleymancı, the Nurcu, and the Annunciation Movement.

These groups comprise a sort of religious revitalisation movement which has always cropped up when the gap between religious vision and social reality grew too great (at least for a certain part of society) – when the religious model of and for society, to put it in Clifford Geertz's (1983) terms, could no longer be related to actual society. In such moments there is a desire to guard, or to regain, a feeling of one's identity in society. As individual identity and collective legitimacy are closely related to each other, this has direct political implications. The question refers as much to the aims of the individual life as to the aims of modern society as a whole. Religiously inclined persons tend to answer this question, as Troeltsch (1922) has brilliantly shown, by an orientation 'back to' the origins.

This also holds true for the fundamentalists, who seek an answer to the question of identity in modern society by way of a mythical regress (Riesebrodt, 1990), i.e. by the attempt to revitalise the social order of a golden age, which in this case would be the early phase of Islam: 'A holy and universal system of law was revealed to Muhammad which serves for all needs of mankind before doom' (Kaplan[4]). This system of law was put into practice during the age of Muhammad and the four caliphs. In this time, Islam conquered the whole Middle East and reigned in three continents. According to this view, all problems of mankind result from the departure from this divine order. This philosophy of history is reapplied in a generative way to the modern history of Turkey: with the introduction of a laicist order the Republic of Turkey, the early Fall of Man was repeated.

Seeing that all these convictions are held in common, what then are the reasons for the conflicts among the fundamentalists?

THE HYPOTHESIS

With the declared intention to fight for the *şeriat*, a central question arises immediately – one has to decide *how* to fight for the *şeriat*. The hypothesis I want to formulate is as follows.

(1) There are different answers to this core problem. The four groups in the fundamentalist camp differ on the question of how to organise for the fight and how to conduct the fight.

(2) These are only seemingly mere questions of strategy. I want to show in the following discussion that the answers given to these questions are related to deep-seated convictions about the (actual and ideal) relation of the individual to society, that they imply certain concepts about the self and the other. This may explain why questions of strategy are so seldom settled at the conference table, and why they are so bitterly disputed. It may also explain why the

factions do not disappear when the aim is reached (i.e. when the revolutionary groups are successful). By reconstructing the ideas about the relation of the individual to society I hope to get down to' the real questions' which divide the fundamentalist camp.

(3) Every position concerning strategies implies further characteristic problems, which again can be assumed to structure future religious quests and – possibly –future fissions. I want to reconstruct these problems by quoting the comments the groups make about each other. This has the advantage of giving an impression of the views held by those involved (and not only of the sociologist's construction).

In order to arrive at a description of the different ideas about the relationship of the individual to society, I divide this relation into two aspects: (1) the relation of the individual to secondary groups (in our case the religious community); and (2) the relation of the secondary groups to the society in general (which in our case implies the question of the kind of political action they should take). These two dimensions are independent from each other, which allows for the scheme depicted in Figure 2.

One might add that when talking about 'society', the point of reference is 'Turkish society'. That is, the four groups are strictly oriented toward Turkey. Germany for them is seen as a 'country of emigration', sometimes explicitly paralleled to Muhammad's stay in Medina. The

		COMMUNITY:SOCIETY	
		Ethics of conviction (methodists)	Ethics of responsibility (strategists)
INDIVIDUAL:COMMUNITY	Mystics	*Nurcu*	*Süleymancı*
	Ascetics	*Teblig*	*Milli Görüs*

Figure 9.2 Types of relationship between individual and community, and community and society

institutionalisation of Islam in Germany is of only secondary importance to the fundamentalist believers: it is more or less a defensive
measure. It seems to be more important not to lose Islam in that intermediary phase of diaspora than to develop permanent institutions which
negotiate the continued presence of Islam in Germany. This correlates
with a marked disinterest with regard to German society. It is telling
that in the bookstores of the Islamic communities in Augsburg I was
not able to find one single tape-recorded sermon which discusses the
problems of Muslim migrants in Germany (for example, with regard to
Islamic education). It is also striking that – at least in Augsburg (cf.
Gür, 1993) – there are no initiatives directed to building up Islamic
institutions (like Kindergarten, for example), while at the same time
money is collected for the foundation of Islamic schools in Turkey. So
the interest in Germany is mostly strategic: it is the interest of having a
base abroad in order to fight at home, and one does everything in order
not to threaten the existence of this base.

I shall now proceed to describe the two dimensions and show how
the four fundamentalist groups differ in these aspects.

THE RELATION OF THE INDIVIDUAL TO THE RELIGIOUS COMMUNITY

There are two models of the religious community in the Islamic tradition. On the one side, there is the tradition of orthodox, scripturalist,
ascetic Islam of the mosque community. On the other side, there is the
tradition of the mystical, charismatic, esoteric Islam of the Sufi brotherhoods with the central institution of the *tekke* or convent see (Kissling,
1954; Gellner, 1981; Trimingham, 1971). The opposition between the
two traditions should not be overstated: most of the time they exist side
by side. One can show, however, that *şeriat*, the law, and *tarikat*, the
mystical way, were put into different structural relations to each other
in different phases of Islamic history.

This is also true for the groups discussed here. Although the two
groups which are referred to as mystics in the scheme, the Nurcu and
the Süleymancı], are not pure mystics anymore, one might characterise
them as 'reform mystics'. Said Nursi, the founder of the Nurcu movement, and Süleyman Hilmi Tunall, the founder of the Süleymancı
movement, both reacted to the challenge of the establishment of the

laicist Turkish republic by giving up the inimical or indifferent attitude to the world (Max Weber's *Weltfeindichkeit*), which was characteristic for the classical brotherhoods. They stressed the need to work for the *şeriat* within the world.

Süleyman Hilmi Tunalı did that by establishing Qur'an courses, the purpose of which was to answer to the need for training *hocas*, a need which was created with the destruction of the system of religious education in Turkey in the 1920s and 1930s. Whereas the Süleymancı still have the classical structure of a mystical brotherhood (they consider themselves to be part of the Naksibendi, one of the most important mystical brotherhoods in Islam; see Algar, 1976, 1985), it is questionable whether this still holds true for the Nurcu. Said Nursi's intent was to interpret the Qur'an in order to propagate Islam in a changed and modern world and thus to re-establish the Islamic spirituality and influence. He was building up his own organisation for the distribution of his works during his exile in Isparta between 1925 and 1934 (Spuler, 1973). He himself called this organisation a 'school' (rather than a brotherhood) and never considered himself to be a *seyh* (the spiritual leader of a brotherhood). Still, there are so many parallels with the classical brotherhoods that it seems justified to treat the Nurcu as a developed (or transformed) mystical brotherhood.[5] The inner hierarchy of 'student', 'brother', 'friend' and 'beloved' (Spuler, 1981, p. 428) closely resembles the structure of mystical groups, as does the central ritual, the *ayin* (a meditative contemplation of the works of Said Nursi), which was explained to me to be a structural correlate of the Sufi *zikr* (mystical practice of the repetition of the name of God in order to achieve knowledge by way of contemplation). Further, the spirituality of the movement clearly has its roots in the pantheist outlook on nature in mystical Islam (which sees God reflected in all things; cf. Ritter, 1955), but transforms it too by extensively taking note of the results of modern science.[6]

The relevance of this inner-worldly turn of the mystical tradition can hardly be overstated. The mystical exercises are no longer seen as an end in themselves, but rather as a source of strength or an additional source of knowledge (Dinçer, 1983). The two groups thus intend to use the – original or transformed – *tarikat* (mystical way) for the reintroduction of the *şeriat* (Islamic law).

The two scripturalist groups do not reject mysticism altogether. Their position is that mysticism can be a beautiful exercise once the *şeriat* is established. Under the present circumstances, however, mystical exercises would only distract from the principal task which is to fight for the introduction of the Islamic order. These groups do not see mystical exercises as a source of strength but rather as a source of weakness. The following quotation of a leading member of the Teblig Community in Augsburg is characteristic of the attitude in this camp:

> Today we have despotism because nobody, starting from the head of the government down to the head of the family, practices Islam any more. One of the most important *hadiths*, however, states that he who proclaims the law in opposition to a despotic government and in doing so risks prison, torture, death ... has the strongest faith. This man has the strongest faith, the strongest moral, he is a man of the law, a man of God. We do think that this is the task of the day, and that a scholar has to put that into practice ... and that it is a sign of weakness to put this aside and to occupy oneself with the *tarikat*.

The decision for or against the mystic tradition has several implications for the organisation of the community. The first difference refers to the social structure of the groups. While the two reform mystic groups tend to be hierarchical and to allow for different degrees of initiation, the two scripturalist groups tend to be egalitarian. Among the latter, an idea is prominent which may be referred to as the *hocack* (priesthood) of all believers. Or, as they would put it themselves, everybody is a *hoca* according to his/her degree of knowledge.

A second difference is closely related. Whereas leadership in the mystical groups is charismatic (or traditional), leadership in the scripturalist groups tends to be rational. Whereas the former tends hardly to be questioned, the latter is subject to evalutation or criticism. The events which led to a split of the Milli Görüs in the early 1980s are telling in this respect. As mentioned above, there had been a growing radicalisation among the members of Milli Görüs during these years. At the same time, the party establishment in Turkey came under considerable pressure from the military government. The result was increasing unrest. In this situation the party decided to send the *müftü* of Adana, Cemaleddin Kaplan, to Germany. The following quotation shows how this was received by the common followers:

> Well it was not only me personally, there had been several persons who worked within Milli Görüs, among them several *hocalar* and

scholars. They were thrown out by the executive committee.... At that time the movement started. When they realized that they could not suppress the movement, they brought Cemaleddin Kaplan from Turkey in order to appease them.... When they brought him here we watched him exactly: Is he a true scholar; will he be a master of his Islam, will he master them? [They went to Munich in order to listen to him.] Judging from our experience we said to some of our friends: 'He is not like the other scholars, he will not conform.... He puts Islam in the first place, he will not agree with them.'

This quotation reflects a remarkable self-confidence. The believers in the scripturalist camp feel that they are in a position to judge their spiritual leaders. It is *they* who decide whom to follow. There were several believers in the Teblig Community in Augsburg who said that they would definitely leave Kaplan if they ever realised that he did something wrong.

A third organisational difference refers to limits. The two reform mystic groups keep a tight hold on information. With regard to the Nurcu, Spuler (1981, p. 426) remarks that while it is quite easy to establish a first contact, it is very difficult to establish a closer relationship. This holds even more true for the Süleymancı. It is extremely difficult to get reliable information about them; when contacting the group, one is immediately referred to an official spokesman or even trained public relation officers.[7] The two scripturalist groups, on the other hand, are much more accessible: their view is that secrecy is irreconcilable with the Islamic spirit.

A fourth implication of the difference between the reform mystics and the scripturalist camp refers to political practice. The reform mystics tend to take the position that consciousness-raising should come first and political institutions next, whereas the scripturalists tend to the position that one should not separate consciousness-raising from political action (Kaplan) or that one should reach out for political institutions and engage in consciousness-raising on the basis of political power (Milli Görüs). Both mystics and the scripturalists refer to the *sunna*, to the practice of the prophet.

For the Süleymancı, Dinçer argues:

When our Prophet (Peace Be Upon Him) started to propagate the Islam among the Polytheists in Mecca he provoked a strong reaction by them. He decided to withdraw into a certain quarter of the city where he could pray calmly and preach Islam. *The fundamental task of all prophets consists in passing on the divine revelation they received, in teaching their followers and in passing judgements.* Our Prophet chose the apartment of Erkan bin Ebü-l Erkam bin Esed one of the first Muslims.... He lived in this apartment, prayed, taught Islam to the visitors and trained the Muslims up to the time that Hz.Ömer converted to Islam. In this house the Muslims experienced his spiritual guidance.   (1983, p. 17; emphasis added)

The message is clear: in a situation of relative weakness (which is comparable to that faced by true believers in present day Turkey), one should withdraw from society and teach the true Islam in clandestine meetings. The aim of these courses is nicely conveyed in an image:

While there is fierce fighting in front of the castle of the infidels these courses are underground tunnels leading right into the core of the castle. [The tunnels] are an extremely great invention ... comparable only to the invention of Sultan Mehmed with which he had his war ships pass the mountains and glide into the Golden Horn.   (Dinçer, p. 6)

Here, success does not lie in the open battle, but rather in the (very literal) underground operation! It may be mentioned that the image of the mines is very familiar to Turkish schoolchildren who are taught extensively about Ottoman warfare strategies in their history lessons.

The counter position is formulated by Kaplan in a sermon which is distributed on tape under the title 'Sermon in the *hicret*':

The Arab's say: If you don't jump into the sea you will not learn to swim. Without practice you will not become fighters for the faith. There is no necessity to build up a special cadre with special methods. For this is a question of method, of belief, of courage and of capabilities. The preachers who were sent out by our master and prophet – did they have a special training? No: The Islamic belief is in itself a school. It is an educational institution. It is the perfect educational institution. Abu Bakr, Omar, Ali Musa – did they go to a university? That is why all practice appeasement politics who say: Let us first train a cadre, let the cadre get occupation in state service and let us then speak of state, of proclamation and politics. That is nothing but laziness and fear.

Three aspects seem to me to be remarkable in this passage. (1) Esoteric spirituality is here confronted with spirituality of the fight. One does not become a *mücahit*, a fighter for the faith, by a special training (Qur'an courses or esoteric exercises) but by going out into the street and taking up the fight. By doing this one learns to believe, to love, to be courageous and one acquires competence. There is another passage in the same sermon where Kaplan takes up the mystics' Symbolic analogy of the love to a girl and gives it an activist turn (see Ritter, 1955, p. 347ff.). This passage can thus be read as a direct reply to the mystics.

You have to believe in our matter, you have to love our matter. A young man loves a girl; he feels a deep affection to her. Day and night, while waking and dreaming he thinks of her. He, who believes in the movement and identifies with it, must have a feeling toward this faith which is comparable to this love. Even while eating, while sleeping, while working he has to think: 'O what could I do, how could I behave to promote my affairs – even if it is by a minute detail.'

(2) The task is not education. A recurrent theme of Kaplan is that everything is manifest. The task of the day is open preaching and political action. Those who preach that one should first educate and then become politically active, will get nowhere.

(3) A third aspect is hinted at in the double usage of the word 'special'. It is not the question to build up with *special* methods a *special* cadre. In this usage the particularist aspect of mystical brotherhoods is referred to. The argument was more explicitly stated by a leading member of the Augsburg branch:

We can commit all Muslims to the Qur'an; that is easy. But it is not possible to commit all believers to the Risal-i-Nur of Said Nursi – he was an *alim* but he was not a prophet. For that reason mass mobilisation is impossible with Nurcu or Süleymancı. The Süleymancı have that *tarikat* (Brotherhood) thing. If somebody does not join the *tarikat* he is not accepted. We cannot commit all Muslims to one *Tarikat*.

THE RELATION OF THE RELIGIOUS COMMUNITY TO SOCIETY AS A WHOLE

The horizontal axis in our scheme (Figure 9.2) refers to the other dimension of the relation of the individual to society; that is, to the question of how the community should relate to society as a whole. The scheme implies that a basic difference can be made between strategists and methodists. This distinction refers to Max Weber's distinction between *Gesinnungsethik* (ethics of conviction) and *Verantwortungsethik* (ethics of responsibility). In his article 'Der Beruf zur Politik' ('The Vocation for Politics'; 1973a), Weber argues that any political action has to face the difficult (and often conflicting) relation of means and ends. This is particularly true for religiously motivated politics, which in a quite radical way is confronted with the problem of pursuing noble aims in a bad world.

Following Weber, there are two answers to the problem. The methodist *(gesinnungsethische)* answer would be: the believer does what is commanded by God, and success is in God's hand. The methodist thus would not allow for any compromises with the world – he would in a way reject the position that there is a tension between means and ends. The strategist, on the other hand, would regard the methodist's point of view as an illusion. His position would be that it is simply not true that well intended actions necessarily show good results; ethically doubtful actions can prove to be very effective, whereas ethically acceptable actions can lead into a disaster. The strategist thus takes into account the world as it is. It is not implied that strategists have no conviction or that they are pleading for machiavellian politics, but rather that they take responsibility for their actions in the world (a responsiblity the methodist delegates to God).

The distinction between *Gesinnungsethik* and *Verantwortungsethik* is closely related to other key concepts of Weber's sociology of religion. In the above-mentioned article, he points out that these concepts are related to the problem of *Theodizee*, which he regards to be crucial for religious development, and he proceeds in the same article to show how different religions have found different answers to this problem.[8]

It is evident from the scheme in Figure 9.2 that I suggest that the distinction between strategists and methodists cuts cross the distinction between mystics and scripturalists. Let us now discuss the four different positions which result from that.

1. The Süleymancı very clearly have a strategical outlook. Their politics could be summed up as follows. The Süleymancı try to lay the foundation for successful educational work (concentrating on the establishment of Qur'an courses) by pursuing pragmatic politics, including aligning themselves with the powers in office. In Turkey – where they are officially forbidden – it is claimed that they have good relations to the Demirels Party of the Right Way (Dogru Yol Partisi).[9] In Germany they claim to be purely religious, having no political aims whatsoever. They are much more concerned than the other groups to stress the fact that their activities are strictly within the limits set by the German constitution. The already-mentioned very strict information politics is related to this. Mystics who pursue inner-worldly aims with a strategical outlook almost necessarily organise themselves in the way of a cadre party. A tightly knit and hierarchically structured inner group with a clear task is clearly distinguished from an outer group of mere sympathisers. The criticism of the other groups refers to the structure and the politics of an elitist cadre.

A first criticism refers to the arrogance of the politics. Actions, such as the above-mentioned coup, with which they took over the mosque in Augsburg, created a reputation of trickiness: 'They are tricky [*kurnaz*]' remarked one member of the Teblig community, 'they are foxes'. A second criticism refers to the absolute loyalty the Süleymancı show to Kemal Kaçar, their present leader. They would accept all twists and turns without protesting. Particularly, shifting alliances are criticised. In fact, the inner structure of the Süleymancı movement seems to allow for changes which in the scripturalist camp would create considerable unrest – and probably segmentation. A third criticism refers to the separation of the inner and outer group: the exclusiveness of the inner group is regarded with suspicion. It is frequently insinuated that the Süleymancı would just withdraw in order to watch pornographic movies. Although this is extremely unlikely, it reflects the scripturalists' attitudes toward all kinds of exclusiveness.[10]

The separation between the inner and outer group also allows for a relaxation of the demands on the 'normal believers'. The members of the other groups frequently mention that the Süleymancı would 'make it easy on the believers' in order to be attractive. They refer in this context to decrees (*fetva*) supposedly issued by Kaçar allowing for interest on loans and sending women to work while resident in the *dar ul harb* ('the territory of war' as opposed to the *dar ul Islam*, the 'territory of Islam').

(2) The Nurcu have a methodist outlook. Their work does not aim at missionary mass mobilisation but rather at spiritual gathering. Their educational and contemplative work is primarily addressed to intellectuals (see Spuler, 1981). They do not seem to make compromises – and I personally know several migrants from rural backgrounds who feel repelled by that. To them, the Nurcu are too intellectual. 'They only read the Qur'an in Arabic', complains one informant (in Schiffauer, 1991, p. 211), 'and there is nobody who explains it. That is good for people who have studied and know much. They do not have a *hoca*, who explains the meaning in Turkish.'

For methodist mystics who pursue inner-worldly aims, a secret society seems to be a particularly appropriate type of organisation. The secrecy allows for single-mindedness; the strong bilateral tie (*rabıta*) between *mürid* and *mürsit*, mystical student and mystical teacher, allows for the setting up of clandestine networks. In fact, that is what the Nurcu do when they set up lodges (*nur daireleri*) with high-ranking officials or officers. The idea seems to be to infiltrate the state apparatus.

The problem with secret societies is that their political efficiency is hard to measure. While sympathisers of the Nurcu claim that it is very high, their opponents think that it is almost non-existent. A general criticism in the fundamentalist camp is that the Nurcu only pay lip service to the idea of the Islamic revolution: they would betray the example set by Said Nursi.

One does, in fact, get the impression (at least with regard to the Nurcu in Augsburg) that their outlook is much more quietist than political. The young men who felt attracted by the Nurcu showed much more interest in existentialist than in political questions. They loved to discuss questions such as the meaning of life, the inevitability of death and the phenomenon of time, and to reflect on the divine wisdom in nature.

(3) The strategist's position in the scriptural camp is represented by the National Sight. The aim of the Welfare Party with which it is affiliated is to re-establish, by political participation, the Islamic presence in Turkey. This poses several problems. In the eyes of the other groups there are four points which make this position problematic.

The first problem has already been touched upon in the discussion of the split of the National Sight in the early 1980s. Political rationality forces a party to control their representation in the public sphere. Control over members has to be exercised in order to protect the party's reputation. This political rationality can easily be interpreted as a betrayal of Islamic principles as one of the followers of Kaplan mentioned:

> We said, that we wanted to use the party for Islam but not Islam for the party. They [the party representatives] said: 'If this is the case, then we cannot work, then the party will be closed.' But why should we reduce Islam. We want to remain free.

A second problem is related to this: in order to run for elections a political party has to accept the constitutional framework. This again appears to the methodists as a compromise with an idolatrous system – a compromise which is dangerous because it serves to strengthen the system rather than weaken it.

The third problem from a fundamentalist point of view is that the political rationality of an established party does not allow for much spirituality. This at least seems to be the point made by Kaplan when he implicitly compares the Teblig community to the National Sight:

> Our community is a community of love and not a community of reason. He who has love sacrifices himself for the cause or for the faith. He who has only reason is satisfied with taking measures.

The most interesting criticism, however, comes from those who claim that the organisation as a party is incompatible with Islamic principles from a structural point of view. The argument is that the structure of a party stresses dissent and that conflicts are started for strategical reasons. One of the members in the Teblig community expressed that in the following way:

> No party in Turkey has anything to do with Islam. It is politics, games, traps, deceit. But Islam is clean. In Islam there is no deceit, no lie, no deception... . But the work of parties consists in lying, in defamation of character. In order to strengthen their own party they cast aspersions on the characters of their opponents.

The structure of parliamentary action is here opposed to an ideal of an Islamic formation of opinion – that is, the ideal of a discourse of scholars and specialists in which solutions to open questions can be found by means of rationality.

(4) The methodist scripturalist position is represented by the Teblig movement. Their basic assumption is that an Islamic revolution (one which deserves its name) can only be brought about by a mass movement. The task of the day is the open proclamation, the open annunciation with the aim of political mobilisation. With this outlook the Tebligci try to avoid the pitfalls of institutionalisation. These are: (a) the separation of inner and outer circles, with its problems of control and (b) the constant need to reconcile institutional demands and political aims (which, after all, are their *raison d'être*) – either by compromises (like the Süleymancı or the Milli Görüs) or by refuge to secrecy (like the Nurcu). By insisting on the organisation as a *movement*, the Tebligci try to remain diligent *and* outspoken. Or, to express it with the words of one member of the Augsburg community, 'Well, I told myself the parties go only so far as it is legal. Then they say "Stop." That means: You cannot put into practice there what is demanded by Islam.'

It is this methodist orientation which leads to very strong irritation with the Süleymancı who – as the Tebligci tend to say – 'make it easy on the believer'. Whereas there exists some contact with other groups (including even the Diynetci), there is a strict avoidance of the Süleymancı.

An open movement like Teblig is dependent on a certain 'drive'. It has to grow or else it vanishes. If it is in decline, its only chance to survive is to change its particular character. It has to institutionalise and thus turn into a party or a quietistic circle. In short, it has to face the problem for which Max Weber coined the term routinisation (*Veralltäglichung*).

NEW DEVELOPMENTS

In December 1991, the Refah Partisi made considerable gains during the general elections in Turkey. This success led to euphoria among the followers of the Milli Görüs in Europe – it was considered to be a confirmation to be on the right path. The success of the Milli Görüs must have been a particular problem to Kaplan because of the closeness of the position of the two groups – both being in the scripturalist camp. Furthermore, it came at a time of slow but continued decline of the Teblig movement.

In this situation, Kaplan evidently decided to radicalise. On 18 April 1992, he gave the speech entitled 'Hakkl sahibine iade' ('Return the right to the owner'), in which he declared the Islamic State with himself as the acting caliph who would be in office until the real caliph was elected. This radicalisation was severely criticised (and sometimes mocked) by the other organisations. It also led, however, to unrest within the community. Some of the leading members of the Augsburg community left, feeling that instead of remaining an open movement, Teblig had turned itself into a party. In fact, one of the consequences was an increasing articulation of boundaries. This turned into clashes between young members of the Milli Görüs and the Teblig movement after Tebligci activists had attached posters to the mosque of the Milli Görüs which condemned the party system as idolatrous and all who would vote and stand for election as idolaters and, therefore, '*melun*' (damned). However, this new and radicalised position proved to be attractive to many young men of the second generation (most of them coming from religious families), among them many engineers and medical doctors. In Augsburg, young Turkish men aged between 15 and 30 nowadays occupy the leading positions in the community. Overall, the number of followers is now increasing again. It may have been the success of the radicalisation which led Kaplan, in Köln on 8 March 1994, to take a further step and declare himself the actual caliph.

At the same time, the other organisations became closer to each other, probably due to the success of the Islamic cause in Turkey. The differences between the different positions play less of a role now than five years ago. There is more co-operation now. One sign is that the Süleymancı, the Nurcu and the Milli Görüs were able to set up an Islamic list for the *Ausländerbeirat* (a foreigner's advisory committee) in Augsbrug. The Nurcu became somewhat less methodist after they were allowed to act more openly in public in Turkey. Thus they opened Islamic boarding schools and allowed the display of portraits of Atatürk (this symbolic reference to the republic is a prerequisite for obtaining permission to open a school). The Süleymancı are said to be more open and co-operative than five years ago. The Milli Görüs, too, seem to have become more pluralist, thus integrating different currents within the party. All these tendencies are, however, severely criticised by the

Kaplanci who feel that they are the last to hold up the true banner of Islam.

NOTES

1.   It seems to me that this necessity to organise in corporate groups implies a strengthening of the borders *vis-à-vis* the other groups. Thus the different groups appear more clear-cut in the diaspora than they would in Turkey, even if they were not under political pressure there. In Turkey a loose and overlapping network could be expected. This implies also that the processes of fission which we discuss here take place in a more clear-cut way in the German diaspora than at home. Some Turks' astonishment about this is reflected in an article by Ugur Mumcu: 'The mosques and the prayer houses abroad are split up among the sympathizers of the Süleymancı, the Milli Görüşçü, the Diyanetçi, the ülkücü [Grey Wolves] and of Kaplan *hoca*. Different associations, different mosques, different communities' (*Cumhurityet*, 10 March 1987, p.6).

2.   The organisation has been known officially as the Islami Cemaatlar Birligi – The Union of the Islamic Communities. As will be described below, the name was changed from 'Türk Federe Islami Devleti' ('The Federal Islamic State of Turkey') into 'Anadolu Federe Islami Devleti' ('The Federal Islamic State of Anatolia'). Among the other communities they are known as 'Kaplancı' – the followers of Kaplan. For reasons of clarity I shall use the programmatic term Teblig Cemaatl or 'Annunciation Movement', a term which was coined by Kaplan in a programmatic sermon.

3.   The *Şeriat* was abolished during the Turkish revolution in a series of legislative measures, starting in 1924 with the abolishment of the caliphate and ending in 1928 with the declaration of the secular character of the Turkish state.

4.   All quotations from Kaplan in this article refer to his programmatic sermon: Hicret Konuşması (a sermon in the emigration). Like the other sermons of Kaplan, this sermon is distributed on tape and can be purchased in the mosques of the movement.

5.   The discussion about these structural characteristics is obviated because of the political relevance of this point — the *tarikats* are forbidden in Turkey. Thus one finds an exaggeration of the continuities among the opponents of this movement, whereas sympathisers tend to play the parallels down and stress the differences. The best characterisation of these dynamics is still Spuler (1981).

6.   This stance again is characteristic of the group. The classical mystics did not show a marked interest in natural explanations, but rather saw God's working directly reflected in nature and tended to reject causal explanations as *slırk* or polytheist tendencies.

7. This is confirmed by Metin Gür's (1993) experiences. One of the few documents giving inside information is the typescript by Dinÿer (1983), who was one of the leading members of the brotherhood in Germany. The writing of the text was evidently a private initiative with the intention of introducing the Süleymancıs to the German public. However, the text caused disputes and the leadership of the brotherhood decided not to distribute it.

8. Another key concept which seems to me to be closely related to that distinction is the concept of 'routinisation' (*Veralltäglichung*). In fact, institutionalisation and routinisation of a religious movement implies a shift from *Gesinnungsethik* to *Verantwortungsethik*.

9. Before elections, the newpapers are full of reports of alleged meetings of Kemal Kaçar, their leader, with the heads of the different right-wing parties. It is speculated whether Kaçar promises the votes of his followers to one or the party (Hottinger, 1993, p. 149).

10. The accusation of sexual orgies is often voiced against mystics. I heard similar insinuations voiced against the Bektashi. This might be related to a too-literal interpretation of the mystics of love.

BIBLIOGRAPHY

Algar, H. (1976) 'The Naqshbandi Order: A Preliminary Study of its History and Significance', *Studia Isalmica*, XLIV, pp. 123–52.

Algar, H. (1985) 'Der Naksibenid-Orden in der republikanischen Türkei', in J. Blaschke and M. v. Bruinessen (eds), *Islam und Politik in der Türkei* (Berlin: Express Edition).

Blaschke, J. (1985) 'Islam und Politik unter türkischen Arbeitsmigranten', in J. Blaschke and M. v. Bruinessen (eds), *Islam und Politik in der Türkei* (Berlin: Express Edition).

Dinçer, N. (1983) *'Wer ist Süleyman Efendi (K.S.)? Was ist 'Süleymancık' (Süleymanismus)*, Köln (unpublished manuscript).

Geertz, C. (1983) *Dichte Beschreibung* (Frankfurt: Suhrkamp).

Gellner, E. (1981) *Muslim Society* (Cambridge: Cambridge University Press).

Gür, M. (1993) *Türkisch-islamische Vereinigungen in der Bundesrepublik Deutschland* (Frankfurt/Main: Brandes und Apsel).

Hottinger, A. (1993) 'Der Islam in der heutigen Türkei', in J. Schwartz (ed.), *Der politische Islam – Intentionen und Wirkungen* (München: Schöningh) pp. 143–155.

Kaplan, C. (not dated) *Hicret Konuşması*, transcribed sermon.

Kissling H. J. (1954) 'The Sociological and Educational Role of the Dervish Orders in the Ottoman Empire', in G. E. v. Grunebaum (ed.), *Studies in Islamic Cultural History: American Anthropologist*, vol. 56, no. 2, part 2, memoir no. 76, pp. 23–35.

Mıhçlyazgan, U. (1990) *Moscheen türkischer Muslime in Hamburg. Dokumentation zur Herausbildung religiöser Institutionen türkischer Migranten* (Hamburg: Hersg. von der Behörde für Arbeit, Gesundheit und Soziales).

Mumcu, U. (1987a) 'Avrupa'daki Islamcı Örgütler' ('The Islamic Organisations in Europe'), a series of seven articles in: *Cumhurityet*, 22 February 1987, p. 13; 23 February 1987, p. 13; 24 February 1987, p. 7; 25 February 1987, p. 13; 26 February 1987, p. 13; 27 February 1987, p. 13; 28 February 1987, p. 13.

Mumcu, U. (1987b) *Rabıta* (Istanbul: Tekin Yaylnevi).

Nagel, T. (1981) *Staat und Glaubensgemeinschaft im Islam* (Zürich: Artemis).

Riesebrodt, M. (1990) *Fundamentalismus als patriarchalische Protestbewegung* (Tübingen: J. C. B. Mohr-Siebeck).

Ritter, H. (1955) *Das Meer der Seele – Mensch, Welt und Gott in den Geschichten des Fariduddin Attar* (Leiden: E. J. Brill).

Schiffauer, W. (1991) *Die Migranten aus Subay* (Stuttgart: Klett-Cotta).

Spuler, U. (1973) 'Nurculuk' in O. Spies (ed.), *Studien zum Minderheitenproblem im Islam*, vol. 1 (Bonn: Bonner Orientalische Studien, Selbstverlag des Orientalischen Seminars der Universität Bonn).

Spuler, U. (1977) 'Nurculuk. Eine moderne islamische Bewegung', in W. Voigt (ed.), *XIX. Dt. Orientalistentag, Vorträge* (Wiesbaden: Franz Steiner) pp. 1246–54.

Spuler, U. (1981) 'Zur Organisationsstruktur der Nurculuk Bewegung', in H. R. Roemer and A. Noth (eds), *Studien zur Geschichte und Kultur des Vorderen Orients. Festschrift für Bertold Spuler zum siebzigsten Geburtstag* (Leiden: E. J. Brill).

Trimingham, J. S. (1971) *The Sufi Orders in Islam* (Oxford: Clarendon Press).

Troeltsch, E. (1922) *Die Soziallehren der christlichen Gruppen und Kirchen* (Tübingen: J. C. B. Mohr).

Weber, M. (1973a) 'Der Beruf zur Politik', in M. Weber (ed.), *Soziologie – Universalgeschichtliche Analysen–Politik* (Stuttgart: Kröner) pp. 167–85.

Weber, M. (1973b) 'Einleitung in die Wirtschaftsethik der Weltreligionen' in M. Weber (ed.), *Soziologie – Universalgeschichtliche Analysen-Politik* (Stuttgart: Kröner) pp. 398–440.

Weber, M. (1973c) 'Richtungen und Stufen religiöser Weltablehnung', in M. Weber (ed.), *Soziologie – Universalgeschichtliche Analysen-Politik* (Stuttgart: Kröner) pp. 441–83.

Part IV
New Representations

10 To What Extent is the Swedish Muslim Religious?

Åke Sander

The aim of this paper is to raise and to discuss some methodological issues involved in determining the number of Muslims and, particularly, the number of religious Muslims in a country in the absence of official statistics. My aim is not to give definite solutions to problems or definite answers to questions. It is only, more modestly, to try to identify the relevant questions and problems, to elucidate some of the conditions for acceptable solutions and answers, to describe the methods I used, and to stimulate a debate about the methods and the results. Undoubtedly, some loose ends will remain.

My discussion takes its point of departure in descriptions of two different empirical investigations (in the late 1980s and in the early 1990s) relevant to the problem I undertook within the framework of a larger project.[1]

BACKGROUND TO RELIGION AND IMMIGRATION IN SWEDEN

Sweden has, for all practical purposes, been a monoreligious Christian society for about one thousand years, of which roughly the latter half has been effectively dominated by an, on the whole, strongly nationalist, authoritarian, conservative and xenophobic Evangelical-Lutheran state church. With very few exceptions, an individual had to be a member of this officially recognised state church to be a Swedish citizen and to be able to live and work in Sweden. The formula

179

Table 10.1a   Number of Muslims in Sweden from different countries,
31 December 1993 (people with foreign background according
to country of birth and citizenship)

Country of origin (CO)	Total number of immigrants in Sweden	Percentage of Muslims in CO	Estimated number of Muslims in Sweden
African countries			
Algeria	1 340	99	1 327
Arab Republic of Egypt	1 823	92	1 677
Ethiopia	13 596	60	8 158
Gambia	1 683	98	1 649
Ghana	726	33	240
Kenya	768	30	230
Liberia	523	45	235
Libya	324	99	321
Morocco	3 428	99	3 394
Nigeria	405	45	182
Senegal	157	90	141
Somalia	5 636	100	5 636
Sudan	485	90	437
Tanzania	668	55	367
Tunisia	2 410	99	2 386
Uganda	1 891	40	756
Africa total	**35 863**		**27 136**

according to which Sweden was governed was: 'One nation, One
people, One religion.' Dissidents from the 'Right Faith' could, for
example, be both punished and expelled from the country up to the end
of the nineteenth century, and the Swedes were not formally granted a
Freedom of Religion Act until 1951.

It has only been since the 1960s, and particularly during the last
10–15 years, that this situation of religious homogeneity has changed
in any relevant respects.[2] This is mainly owing to the arrival in
Sweden of a relatively large number of immigrants and refugees. As a
result of immigration, the number of people with foreign backgrounds[3] living in Sweden today is estimated at about 1.3 million

Table 10.1a *Continued*

Country of origin (CO)	Total number of immigrants in Sweden	Percentage of Muslims in CO	Estimated number of Muslims in Sweden
Asiatic countries			
Afghanistan	959	100	959
Bangladesh	2 021	85	1 718
United Arab Emirates	259	90	233
India	9 745	12	1 169
Indonesia	1 455	90	1 310
Iraq	16 836	97	16 331
Iran	49 796	99	49 298
Jordan	827	95	786
Kuwait	344	90	310
Lebanon	21 597	75	16 198
Malaysia	877	54	474
Pakistan	2 561	97	2 484
Palestine	913	44	402
Saudi Arabia	317	95	301
Syria	8 546	87	7 435
Turkey	36 001	98	35 281
Asia total	**153 054**		**134 689**
European countries			
Former Yugoslavia	57 212	21.5	12 300
Sum total	**246 129**		**174 125**

(that is, about 15 per cent of the Swedish population). From the mid-1980s onward, most of the net immigration to Sweden[4] has come from countries dominated by a Muslim cultural tradition. The total number of people with backgrounds in these countries can be estimated to be around 200 000 (cf. Table 10.1a,b). The largest groups have come from Iran, Iraq, Lebanon and Ethiopia. Generally speaking, it is probably no exaggeration to claim, as Jørgen Nielsen does (1992, p. 80), that Sweden has undergone a greater transformation in character as a result of immigration than any other European country since the Second World War.

Table 10.1b Number of Muslims in Sweden from different countries, 31 December 1993 (people with foreign background according to country of birth and citizenship)

Country of origin (CO)	Total number of immigrants in Sweden	Percentage of Muslims in CO	Estimated number of Muslims in Sweden
African countries			
Algeria	1 340	97	1 300
Arab Republic of Egypt	1 823	91	1 659
Ethiopia	13 596	40	5 438
Gambia	1 683	85	1 431
Ghana	726	19	138
Kenya	768	10	77
Liberia	523	15	60
Libya	324	98	318
Morocco	3 428	95	3 257
Nigeria	405	85	344
Senegal	157	82	129
Somalia	5 636	99	5 580
Sudan	485	72	349
Tanzania	668	24	160
Tunisia	2 410	92	2 217
Uganda	1 891	10	189
Africa total	**35 863**		**22 646**
Asiatic countries			
Afghanistan	959	99	949
Bangladesh	2 021	85	1 718
United Arab Emirates	259	87	225
India	9 745	11	1 072
Indonesia	1 455	90	1 306
Iraq	16 836	95	15 994
Iran	49 796	95	47 306

ISLAM AND MUSLIMS IN SWEDEN: THE THEORETICAL PROBLEM

Our first problem, then, is to try to determine how many of these roughly 200 000 people with their backgrounds in a country with a

Table 10.1b *Continued*

Country of origin (CO)	Total number of immigrants in Sweden	Percentage of Muslims in CO	Estimated number of Muslims in Sweden
Jordan	827	93	769
Kuwait	344	87	299
Lebanon	21 597	51	11 014
Malaysia	877	44	386
Pakistan	2 561	97	2 484
Palestine	913	44	402
Saudi Arabia	317	95	301
Syria	8 546	85	7 264
Turkey	36 001	96	34 561
Asia total	**153 054**		**126 050**
European countries			
Former Yugoslavia	57212	20	11442
Sum total	**246 129**		**160 138**

Source: SCB Tabell C 16, *Personer med utländsk bakgrund efter födelseland, medborgarskapsland, kön och ålder 1992-12-31 enligt indelningen 1993-01-01.*
Notes: The differences between the two ways of estimating the number of Muslims in CO is 174 308 − 160 138 = 14 170. It is, in other words, a difference of about 10 per cent. The mean is 167 223.

To the number given in the table should first be added individuals from other countries with Muslim populations including Albania, Burkina Faso, Djibouti, The Ivory Coast, Guinea, Guinea-Bissau, Mali, Mauritius, Mozambique, Sierra Leone, Chad, Togo, Zaire, Zambia, Surinam, Bahrain, The Philippines and Yemen. The numbers from these countries are small, however. Given the same principles of estimating used above, the total number of ethnic Muslims from these countries is most likely between 1000 and 1500.

significant number of Muslims can be said to be Muslims in any relevant sense of the term. We are faced with two types of problem: one theoretical and the other empirical. The first of these problems can be roughly formulated as follows: 'Muslim' is a term used with several different meanings, denoting different concepts among different people in different contexts. And until we know *what* we are going to count or measure, it is obviously impossible to get any accurate measure. The second problem can roughly be formulated as follows: given the facts that there are no official statistics about the ethnic, cultural and religious backgrounds of the people living in Sweden, and that my resources when it comes to time, money and staff are very limited, what is the best way to arrive at a reasonable figure for the number of Muslims (defined in a particular way) in Sweden?

To solve this problem in a relatively simple way, I stipulate four different definitions of 'Muslim' which also have difference in scope. I will, for want of a better term, call the first, and widest, an *ethnic* definition, the second, and somewhat narrower, a *cultural* definition, the third, and still narrower, a *religious* definition and the last, and narrowest, a *political* definition. In this paper the first and the third are the focus of attention.

I define *ethnic* Muslim as anyone born in an environment dominated by a Muslim tradition, belonging to a Muslim people, of Muslim origin, with a name that belongs in a Muslim tradition and/or who identifies her/himself with, or considers her/himself to belong to this environment and tradition. This definition is independent of cultural competence, attitudes toward Islam as a cultural, political or religious system and its various representatives, and leaders, religious beliefs, and whether or not the individual actively practices Islam as a religious system.

I designate as a *cultural* Muslim anyone who is socialised into, and has to some extent internalised, the Muslim cultural tradition – the Muslim 'cognitive universe'[5] – and who has Muslim cultural competence. In this sense, someone is a Muslim if the 'Islamic cognitive universe' functions as her/his 'frame of reference' or 'pattern of thought, life and communication' and thereby as that which gives her/his world and its objects, words, situations, behaviours, their meaning and sense (see Sander, 1988). In other words, if the Islamic cognitive universe is the phenomenon 'through' which the individual constitutes and experiences her/himself and her/his life-world. Cultural Muslims can have very different norm- and value-systems, very different political opinions, very different attitudes towards Islam as a religion and very different degrees as well as ways of practising religion from one another. But, and this is what is important, they all have a certain common knowledge, in the wide sense of the term, owing to which they can use the same terms, the same religious, political, etc.

words of prestige and abuse, the same metaphors, allegories, proverbs, symbols, pictures and jokes, with the same meaning in relevant respects. Stated differently, when they hear a word or a phrase, see an object, picture, gesture or human behaviour, they get the same associations in relevant respects. In other words, they understand each other, in both direct and indirect means of communication.

I define someone as a *religious* Muslim if (s)he professes specific beliefs, participation in religious services and other religious practices, personal piety and other elements of personal life style. In other words, if (s)he 'measures positive' on a set of criteria designed to measure religiosity (such as is presented below).

Finally, I define someone as Muslim in the *political* sense if (s)he has specific ideas about the place, role and function of religion (Islam) in society. A person is a political Muslim if (s)he claims that Islam in its essence or primarily is (or ought to be) a political and social phenomenon. In other words, if (s)he in an activist manner underscores and claims the 'dogma,' 'belief' or idea of unity under, or oneness of, God (*Tawhid*) and the exclusive transcendental sovereignty (*hakimiyya*) of God as the most central and important characteristics of Islam; that is, if (s)he – usually in the spirit of al-Maududi or Sayyed Qutb – sees Islam as a *total* way of life for the individual as well as for society at large. In other words, from the point of view of political Islam, on the one hand belief in God, his angels, and acts of worship, and on the other, acts of 'worldly' affairs, such as political, legal and economic aspects of society, form one seamless garment woven by God to enwrap man's entire being (cf. Choueiri, 1990; Esposito, 1992).

The definition that, explicitly or implicitly, is the most commonly used in statistics about the number of Muslims in the world or in Sweden is the first and widest one: the ethnic definition. This is also the one I use in my attempt to arrive at a reasonable estimate of the number of Muslims in Sweden.

ON THE NUMBER OF ETHNIC MUSLIMS IN SWEDEN

When trying to explore the matter of numbers of ethnic Muslims, we face the empirical problem already mentioned: how to find what we want to count when the only available statistics are based on nationality, which, for at least some national groups, is a poor indicator of which religious tradition people from there belong to, even in the ethnic sense. Here the only feasible method – given a reasonable amount of money and work – is to start out from the number of people with foreign backgrounds from countries we know to have sizeable Muslim populations and adjust that with what we know from other sources about these countries, their populations, the structure of immigration from the various countries, and so forth. Yet this procedure carries with it the obvious criticism that its results will be afflicted with a considerable uncertainty and a large margin of error.

The most essential factor to adjust for is what we know about the percentage of ethnic Muslims in the various countries of origin. However, when trying to do this, we again run into the problem of a lack of reliable figures. Various sources give different, sometimes very different, figures for the percentage of Muslims in a country. Generally speaking, it seems that what we can call 'Muslim sources' on the whole give higher figures for the percentage of Muslims in a country than do what we can call 'Western sources'. There are, of course, different ways of dealing with this problem. In this paper I have compared country by country in several sources[6] and compiled two tables, Tables 10.1a and 10.1b. Table 10.1a can be considered to be a sort of a 'maximum table' and 10.1b a sort of a 'minimum table'. Then I have taken the average of the two as the point of departure for my discussion.

The next thing of importance to correct for is our knowledge about the structure of emigration from the different countries. The most important of these is related to the figures for Turkey. Here we know that the Turks[7] in Sweden have a very different composition and structure when it comes to ethnic group membership and religion than the Turks in Turkey. The Turkish population in Sweden consists of between 30 and 40 per cent non-Muslims, especially people referred to as *Suryoye* (Assyrians/Syrians) from the east of Turkey, above all from the province of Mardin. Most of these people belong to different 'Oriental Christian Churches'. The figure for Muslims among the Turkish immigrants in Sweden – including a few thousand Alevis and Muslims Kurds – should therefore be reduced by roughly 10 000–13 000.

Other countries in the table for which the bias might be considerable, both with regard to the actual percentage of Muslims in the country of origin and their numbers in Sweden, are Ethiopia, Kenya, Lebanon, Liberia, Malaysia, Palestine, Sudan, Tanzania and Uganda. However, the numbers of people in Sweden with backgrounds in these countries are, with the exceptions of Ethiopia and Lebanon, so small that the problem, given the large margin of error following from the method used here, probably is negligible (see Sander, 1990, 1993).

The ethnic, linguistic and religious diversity of the approximately one hundred different groups living in Ethiopia is large, even though it has been played down for political reasons both by the Haile Selassie and the Mengistu governments. Due to this fact, and the many years of problems of various sorts, no precise information on the balance of religions in Ethiopia today is available. However, it seems clear that the percentage of Muslims is unevenly distributed over the various groups and provinces in the country. The Muslims claim that they have been discriminated against by, as well as being strongly under-represented in, the armed forces and political administration, also seems correct. There also seem to be reasons to believe that they have been over-represented in the various liberation movements at large. These facts, as well as the little that is known about the Ethiopian population in Sweden (for example, that a large part of them are from the now independent state Eritrea), seem to indicate that the percentage of Muslims in the Ethiopian population in Sweden can be expected to be at least as high as in the country of origin. The estimation that around 50 per cent of the Ethiopian group in Sweden are ethnic Muslims therefore does not seem unreasonable.

The situation in Lebanon resembles, in many ways, the situation in Ethiopia. For example, the country is very heterogeneous in several respects and the balance of religions has long been a politically very sensitive question. In the last census, in 1932, Maronite Christians comprised the majority, with 55 per cent of the population. Since then it seems clear that their relative size has been decreasing at an accelerating pace, and many sources claim that their relative size has now fallen to no more that between one-third and one-quarter. Although it is a matter of discussion as to which figure is correct, there seems to be no reason to doubt the general opinion that the various Muslim groups together now comprise the majority religious tradition in Lebanon. Given what we can know from the little precise information available about the structure of emigration from Lebanon, as well as the structure of the group in Sweden, it seems reasonable to believe that ethnic Muslims make up at least 60 per cent of the Lebanese group in Sweden today.

To the sum total in the table should also be added the individuals from the second generation not already included – that is, individuals born in Sweden as Swedish citizens with at least one parent born abroad as an ethnic Muslim. This number can be estimated to be between 8000 and 10 000 (Sander, 1993).

Another category of ethnic Muslims not included in the figures given in Tables 10.1a and 10.1b are immigrants from the third and following generations. It is difficult to make any qualified estimation about the size of this population. Given the history of Muslim immigration to Sweden, this number is most likely not larger than would fall within the large margin of error associated with the general method of calculation used here.

To reach a complete figure of the number of Muslims in Sweden in early 1993, we should perhaps also – even if they do not fit the definition of 'ethnic Muslim' given above – include the Swedes who have converted to Islam. This group is also hard to estimate with accuracy, but 4000–5000 seems a reasonable figure from the information available.

On the basis of these considerations, it does not seem unreasonable to me, even given the rather large margin of error that our methods force us to deal with, to conclude that the number of ethnic Muslims in Sweden in early 1993 was at least 160 000.[8]

ON THE DEFINITION OF 'RELIGIOUS MUSLIM'

How many of these approximately 160 000 ethnic Muslims in Sweden can also be said to be Muslims according to a religious definition? Not surprisingly, the answer depends on how one defines 'religious Muslim' in greater detail. How 'religion' and 'religious' should be defined is a controversial and much debated question. There have been, as anyone familiar with the literature will know, major controversies among priests and theologians as well as among philosophers, psychologists, anthropologists and scholars in religious studies about the correct definition of 'religion', 'religious' and other cognate terms, as well as about what (which and how large) the area of competence and application of religion in society ought to be. That a person's opinion on the second issue not only has political relevance, but also implications for his or her opinions about what is (or ought to be) 'religious,' should be obvious. In this connection I will, in a perhaps oversimplistic way, allow myself to summarise this complex issue by saying that religiosity is a matter of kind as well as of degree, and which conditions should be suggested as necessary and/or sufficient conditions for somebody to satisfy being considered a religious (a genuinely religious, an authentically religious)[9] person is, to a large extent, a matter of choice and, of course, of what is most suitable given a specific interest or research task (see Sander, 1985, 1988, 1993).

In this context I suggest that, in line with much Islamic self-understanding, we use a rather inclusive definition of religiosity. This is to say, one that stipulates relatively low demands on the individual when it comes to having knowledge about, and agreeing with, the various doctrines of the religious tradition in question, when it comes to frequency of participation and degree of activity in religious services and the like, when it comes to having had (or reporting having had) religious experiences, of having been 'reborn' and the like, as well as when it comes to the degree of actually following the different rules and regulations the religious tradition in question claims, a good ad-herent should follow within her/his religious as well as every-day life.

Against this background I suggest we count anyone a Muslim in the religious sense who: (1) accepts (or claims to accept) the words of the declaration of faith that there is no god but Allah and that Mohammed is his last messenger; (2) believes and has faith in Allah as the highest authority, his angels, his books, his prophets, the day of judgement and the final resurrection; (3) by virtue of this has (or claims to have) as her/his, at least long-term, goal in life to try, to the best of her/his ability, to realise the commands and intentions of the Qur'an and the example of Mohammed (the *sunna*) in her/his life; and (4) that because (s)he, inde-pendently of how (s)he is living right now *de facto*, seriously believes (or claims to believe) that a life in accordance with the Qur'an, etc. con-stitutes the right, good, correct or valuable life. Included in this goal in life should be, among other things, that (s)he, to the best of her/his ability, shall perform the daily prayers (*salawat*), visit the mosque with reasonable regularity, fast (*Swam*) during Ramadan, perform the pilgrim-age (*Hajj*) and follow the basic rules of Islam in matters of food, dress, ethics, family relations, etiquette and so on as (s)he understands them.[10]

ON THE NUMBER OF RELIGIOUS MUSLIMS IN SWEDEN

As mentioned in the introductory paragraph, in my attempt to find an answer to the question of the number of religious Muslims in Sweden, I use results from two empirical investigations I have carried out among Muslims in Sweden. From the first one, I use some results from a questionnaire investigation among the Muslims of Göteborg carried out during 1987 and 1988. Later in this paper I use results from the second one, an investigation into the number of people visiting the various Muslim congregations during Ramadan in 1991 and 1992.

At the time of the questionnaire investigation, the number of ethnic Muslims in Göteborg aged 15 years and older was 5000–6000. The number of codeable questionnaires ultimately collected was 385. In other words, the questionnaires were answered by roughly 7 per cent of the total population. Of the different national groups participating in the investigation – individuals with backgrounds in Turkey, Iran, Iraq, Morocco, Tunisia, Pakistan and 'other countries' – Morocco was slightly over-represented and Turkey somewhat under-represented in the sample. The questionnaire consisted of 109 questions, most of them of 'thermometer' type, with pre-formulated alternative answers. Of all the questions, thirty-nine dealt with issues directly relevant to the task of measuring religiosity. Altogether, the questionnaire contained roughly 350 variables.[11]

As a first step towards arriving at a reasonable answer to the question of how many of the ethnic Muslims in Sweden are also Muslims according to a religious definition, I constructed two indices for measuring different dimensions of religiosity: one focusing more on attitudinal aspects and the other more on behavioural ones. Thereafter I weighted the two indices together.

To get an intuitively reasonable, and at the same time relatively simple, index I decided to use the results from the following nine questions as 'religious-making characteristics' in the first index. The answers to more and/or other questions could of course have been used. The suggested ones give, I think, a relatively good relation between simplicity and what might be called 'cost and result relevance'.

Religiosity Index 1

The questions[12] I chose for the first index were:

(1) Do you believe in God?
(2) How interested are you *personally* in religion and questions and problems connected with religion?

(3) How important do you consider it to be for a person to belong to a religious tradition and to have religious faith (to be religious)?

(4) How important is Islam (your religion) to you personally?

(5) How important is it for *you* personally to try to live a correct Muslim life – to live in accordance with Islamic tradition, its rules, norms, manners and costumes – to the best of your ability here in Sweden?

(6) To what extent do you consider yourself to be living a correct Muslim life in Sweden?

(7) How important is it for you that your children receive a proper Muslim upbringing, that they acquire, preserve, maintain and live according to the norms, manners and customs of your country and become/remain good Muslims?

(8) How often do you visit a Mosque (or *musalla*) here in Sweden?

(9) How often do you practice *salat* [prayer] in Sweden now?

Religiosity is, as mentioned, a matter of both kind and degree. To get a relatively simple way of handling this problem I categorise individuals as *exclusively* religious, as *inclusively* religious or as *non-religious* depending on how they answered on questions 2–9 above. For the first question there are, of course, only two alternatives: religious and non-religious. In relation to the second question, an individual is classified as exclusively religious if (s)he has answered that (s)he is 'very interested', as inclusively religious if (s)he answered 'quite interested' or 'fairly interested'. For other answers (s)he has been classified as non-religious. For the questions (3), (4) and (5) the answer 'very ... ' classified an individual as exclusively religious, the answer 'quite ... ' classified her/him as inclusively religious and other answers as non-religious. For the sixth question, the answers 'very high' and 'quite high' were classified as exclusively religious, 'fairly high' as inclusively religious and other answers as non-religious. For question (7), an individual is classified as exclusively religious if (s)he answered 'very important', as inclusively religious if (s)he answered 'quite important' and as non-religious if (s)he gave any of the other answers. An individual who answered 'every day' or 'at least once a week' to question (8) was classified as exclusively religious, and as inclusively religious if (s)he answered 'at least once a month'. All other answers are classified as non-religious. For the last question, people were classified as exclusively religious if they answered 'every day', as inclusively religious if they answered 'at least once a week' or 'at least once a month'. All other answers were classified as non-religious.[13]

It is, as we shall see, clear from the answers to the questions in Index 1 that we will find the largest amount of religious people in the total population if we use questions focusing on attitudes as our main 'religious-making characteristics' – questions concerned with the interest in and the importance of things – and the least number of religious people if we use questions focusing the behavioural aspects of religiosity – for example, frequency of practising *salat* and visiting mosques. That this is associated with the general phenomenon that it is easier to say something than to do something should be clear. Whatever the reasons, as far as I can see this is a factor we have to take into consideration somehow when we construct a compiled index of religiosity. One of the easier ways of doing this is to give the different variables included in the index different values or weights when we compile them together as a compound index. Even this can be done in different ways.

The way I have chosen is 'normatively adapted', i.e. I have decided to apply the normative principle that the more personal commitment I expect a person to manifest in answering one of the questions on the basis of which (s)he is going to be classified as (exclusively or inclusively) religious, the more weight I give to that answer when compiling the compound index of religiosity. From this principle it follows that I count behavioural questions as having greater weight than attitudinal ones. To reach my compiled index I have intuitively rated the various questions in terms of weight as follows. An individual statement that (s)he considers it important to be religious (question (3)) is given relatively little weight as a religious-making characteristic. It is given a quarter of the weight of 'the average question'. An individual statement that (s)he is personally interested in religion (question (2)) is given relatively more weight than the previous statement. These answers have been given half the weight of 'the average variable'. To claim that Islam is important to oneself personally (question (4)) is given even more relative weight. This question is chosen as 'the average question', and given a value of one. The questions 'importance of trying to live a correct Muslim life', 'how important it is that one's children receive a proper Muslim upbringing' and 'frequencies of practising *salat*' (questions (5), (7) and (9)) have been considered to be of relatively greater importance than 'the average question' and have been given one-and-one-half times as great a weight as the 'average question'. Questions

(6) and (8) – extent of living a correct Muslim life in Sweden and mosque visiting frequency – have been deemed to be the most important and have been given the greatest relative weight: two and two and one quarter times that of 'the average question'. With this way of compiling our first index of religiosity, we find that 43.8 per cent of the total population qualify as exclusively religious, 21 per cent as inclusively religious and 35.2 per cent as non-religious. The ratio between religious and non-religious people is, in other words, 64.8 per cent to 35.2 per cent (Figure 10.1).

The level of religiosity varied among the different sub-groups that make up the total population. As it turned out, the total population divided rather naturally into four sub-populations: the Iranians, the Iraqis, the Turks and 'the rest'. Breaking down Index 1 into these four sub-populations, the data appear as Table 10.2 and Figure 10.2.

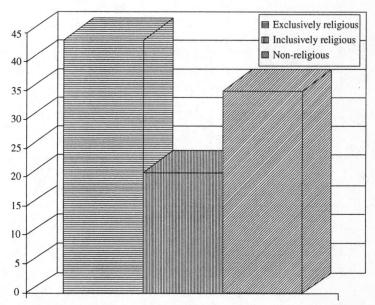

Figure 10.1   Religiosity Index 1. Number of exclusively, inclusively and non-religious Muslims in the total population according to a 'weighted' compiled religiosity index.

Table 10.2 Percentage of exclusively, inclusively and
non-religious Muslims in the four main sub-populations
according to a 'weighted' compiled religiosity index

Population	Exclusively	Inclusively	Non-religious
Iran ($n = 107$)	7.6	11.4	81.0
Iraq ($n = 38$)	23.1	7.7	69.2
Turkey ($n = 145$)	72.4	22.1	5.5
the rest ($n = 93$)	48.9	35.9	15.2
Turkey + the rest	63.0	27.3	9.7
Iran + Iraq	11.7	14.5	73.8

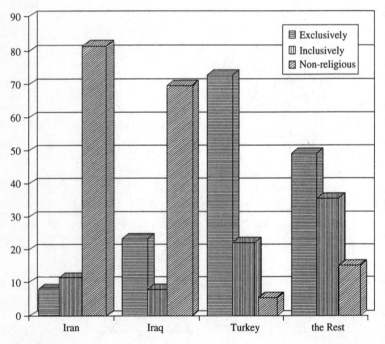

Figure 10.2 Number of exclusively, inclusively and non-religious Muslims in
the four main sub-populations according to a 'weighted' compiled religiosity
index.

Here we see that 19.0 per cent of the Iranians and 30.8 per cent of the Iraqis are religious in some sense, while the corresponding figures for the Turks and 'the others' are 94.5 per cent and 84.8 per cent respectively.

Religiosity Index 2

This second index has been constructed from the reactions to seven of the statements in the part of my questionnaire intended to measure the informants' attitudes to determine their degree of religiosity. The reactions to more and/or other statements could have been used here, as with the construction of Index 1. Those suggested below give, I believe, a good relation between simplicity and 'cost and result relevance'. The seven statements suggested are:

(1) That children of Muslims ought to be able to receive education *about* and *in* their own religion and cultural tradition from Muslim teachers within the framework of the normal school, as they do with home language instruction.
(2) That the Swedish parliament should decide that Muslims may apply the Islamic legal system, *Shari'a*, to matters of civil law, family law, inheritance and the like.
(3) That the most important Islamic holidays (*Eid*) should be proclaimed official holidays for Muslims so that they obtain the legal right to be absent from work and school.
(4) That Muslim children, especially girls, should be able to attend school in special uni-sex classes.
(5) That day-care centres, pre-schools and schools with Muslim children should offer *halal* food.
(6) That Muslim teachers should have the right and opportunity to teach Muslim children about Islam as a culture and religion within the framework of the state school system.
(7) That Muslims should be granted the legal right to about two hours of leave from school and work every Friday in connection with *salat al-djuma*.

The basic principle behind the division of individuals into the different degrees of religiosity was that an individual should be classified as exclusively religious in relation to a particular statement if (s)he claims to 'agree completely' with the given statement, as inclusively religious if (s)he claims to 'agree on the whole' and as non-religious if (s)he have answered that (s)he agrees 'only partly' or 'not at all'. When a specific individual's answers to all the seven questions are weighed together (s)he had to have (the equivalent of) at least three 'agree completely' and four 'agree on the whole' to be classified as religious in the exclusive sense. To classify as inclusively religious (s)he had to have (the equivalent of) at least three 'agree on the whole' and four 'agree only partly'. If an individual did not fulfil these conditions (s)he was classified as non-religious.

Using this method, we arrived at the following results: 39.7 per cent of the total population is exclusively religious, 24.9 per cent inclusively religious and 35.4 per cent non-religious. We get roughly the same, but a little less 'extreme', 'hammock distribution' as in Index 1 (see Figure 10.3).

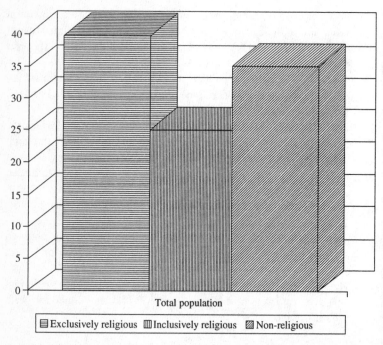

Figure 10.3 Religiosity Index 2. Number of exclusively, inclusively and non-religious Muslims in the total population accorded to a 'weighted' religiosity index.

The range of variation in religiosity among the four sub-populations can be seen in Table 10.3 and Figure 10.4.

The Indices Combined

In light of the figures just given,[14] and in combination with considerations based on the total material from my Göteborg investigation, it is reasonable to conclude that roughly 40 per cent of the total population can be said to be religious in a rather clear sense – i.e. exclusively religious – and an additional 20 per cent can be said to be religious in a somewhat less clear sense – i.e. inclusively religious. It seems to me reasonable to consider the remaining 40 per cent non-religious.

If we break these figures down into sub-populations, we get the following numbers: among the Iranians we find roughly 10 per cent to be exclusively religious, 10 per cent to be inclusively religious and the remaining 80 per cent to be non-religious. Among the Iraqis the corresponding figures are: 20 per cent, 10 per cent and 70 per cent respectively, among the Turks 65 per cent, 25 per cent and 10 per cent, and among 'the rest' 55 per cent, 25 per cent and 20 per cent. These results are summarised in Table 10.4 and Figures 10.5 and 10.6.

Before I move on to describe the results from the second investigation, I will make a few comments on the figures. Of the questions and statements I used to determine the degree of religiosity among Muslims in Sweden, four, given the total population, showed a particularly high degree of non-religiosity, two in the first and two in the second index.

Table 10.3 Percentage of exclusively, inclusively and non-religious Muslims in the four main sub-populations according to a 'weighted' compiled religiosity index

Population	Exclusively	Inclusively	Non-religious
Iran (*n* = 107)	11.1	7.8	81.1
Iraq (*n* = 38)	32.3	16.1	51.6
Turkey (*n* = 145)	53.9	34.0	12.1
the rest (*n* = 93)	72.3	8.4	19.3
Turkey + the rest	60.8	24.5	14.7
Iran + Iraq	16.6	9.9	73.5

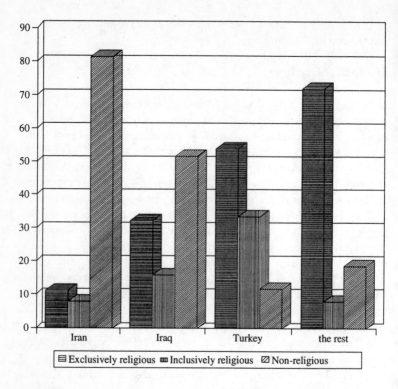

Figure 10.4 Number of exclusively, inclusively and non-religious Muslims in the four main sub-populations according to a 'weighted' compiled religiosity index.

The ones included in the first index are frequency of visiting mosque and practising *salat*, and, in the second, agreeing with the statement that Muslims should have the right to apply *Shari'a* and that Muslim children should be allowed to attend school in uni-sex classes. The segments of the total population that were non-religious on the basis of these four questions were, given the way of calculating used here, 66.2 per cent, 51.1 per cent, 55.0 per cent and 65.9 per cent respectively. Of the results from these four variables, I particularly want to comment on the first – frequency of mosque visiting. There are two main reasons for this: on the one hand, many people consider this variable to be of special importance and, on the other hand, I think that there are special factors we have to reflect on when interpreting the results.

Table 10.4   Summary percentage of extent of religiosity:
four sub-populations

Population	Exclusively	Inclusively	Non-religious
Total population	40	20	40
Iran	<10	10	>80
Iraq	>20	>10	<70
Turkey	>65	25	<10
the rest	55	25	20

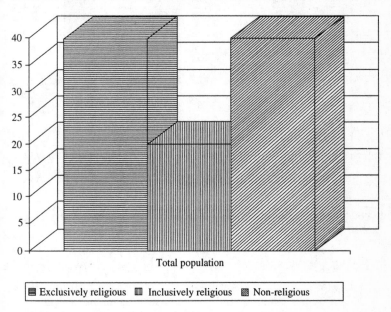

☒ Exclusively religious   ▥ Inclusively religious   ▨ Non-religious

Figure 10.5   Summary of Religiosity Index 1 and Religiosity Index 2: total population.

In this connection, I limit my comments to a request to the reader, here as well as in connection with the discussions about mosque visiting frequency in the next part of this paper, to consider the following:

(1) The statistics used above are based on the total population, a population of which 37 per cent consists of women, for whom visiting

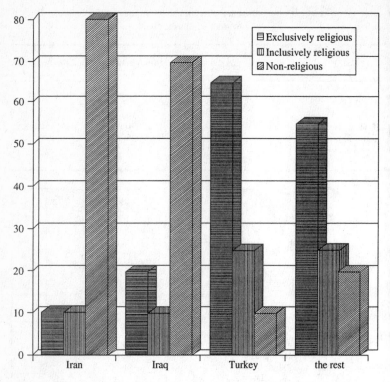

Figure 10.6 Summary of Religiosity Index 1 and Religiosity Index 2: sub-populations.

the mosque is not an obligatory part of being a good Muslim. If we use only the results from the male population on this question, we find the proportion of non-religious people to be 60.5 per cent rather than the 66.2 per cent, as was the figure for the total population. The number of males claiming to visit the mosque at least once a week, and thereby considered to be exclusively religious, was 32.3 per cent.[15]

(2) The day it is obligatory for a Muslim man to pray in the mosque – Friday – is a normal working day in Sweden.

(3) The number of mosques and prayer halls in Sweden is, relatively speaking, very limited (see below).

(4) The Muslims in Sweden constitute a very heterogeneous group: they have different cultural, national, ethnic, linguistic, political and educational backgrounds, and they represent several different Islamic religious schools or traditions. These are factors which, taken together, often make for limited possibilities of finding 'a suitable' mosque within reasonable distance.

(5) The existing prayer halls are, with very few exceptions, located in basements which are sometimes ill-suited for their present function and are generally in poor condition.

(6) A large part of the congregation also suffers from a lack of knowledge and competence. They have a shortage of religious and other leaders and officials who have a high degree of competence in and about Islam, on the one hand, and about how to run such a complex organisation as a religious congregation in such a bureaucratically complex society as prevails in Sweden. They lack, in other words, leaders who have the necessary double knowledge and competence in Islam and the Swedish language and the way Swedish society and culture function.

All these are factors that, at least superficially, should tend to have a negative effect on mosque attendance rates. Imagine what would happen to church attendance at the different Christian churches in Sweden or any other Western European country, given the conditions described in (2)–(6) above.

The figures used in Index 1 above – according to which 25.5 per cent of the respondents claimed to visit a mosque at least weekly, 6.7 per cent at least monthly, 15.1 per cent only on special occasions and holidays (*Eid*) and 49.9 per cent never or almost never – are based on the Muslim population of Göteborg in the late 1980s. For various reasons, they cannot simply be extrapolated to the country as a whole. Trying to compensate for as many of the known relevant factors we can – for example, the difference in size of the total group as well as of the relative size of the various sub-groups, the difference in relative size of the sex and age groups, the different density of Muslims in various regions of the country and the difference of mosque density/availability – I estimate that the corresponding figures for the country as a whole in the early 1990s are: approximately 17 per cent of the Muslims visit a mosque at least on a weekly basis; 7 per cent at least on a monthly basis; 22 per cent at least on holidays and special occasions; and 54 per cent never or almost never.

THE RAMADAN STUDY

The background to the second empirical investigation, briefly presented here, is that in Sweden all religious movements or communities are classified into two groups: the Lutheran church of Sweden, the tax-financed state church; and 'the rest', which are termed 'non-state' or 'free churches'. The latter category also includes, besides various Lutheran churches and denominations, the Roman Catholic church, the Orthodox churches and the Jewish and Islamic religious organisations.

During the 1950s and 1960s, the role and position of the state *vis à vis* the various free churches were discussed, sometimes heatedly. During these two decades the view developed that the state should welcome and support differences in religious view, life style and organisation. The general idea behind this was that the state should be impartial towards the various religious communities.

As a result of this debate, and as an attempt to establish this 'impartiality' even on the economic level, The Council of Swedish Free Churches was created in 1972. On the Council, members of the various free churches were represented. Its main tasks were to provide economic support to the various non-state churches and their congregations that qualified for such support. In 1991, altogether thirty-three national religious organisations or federations qualified for such support. Three of them were Islamic.

Financial assistance is distributed through the various free churches' national federations, and is thought to parallel the church–state co-operation; for example, the church tax. The principles according to which this support is distributed between the different free churches and their congregations do not need to be discussed here. It is sufficient to say that one of the criteria determining the relative size of the total support a particular church or denomination receives is related to the net number of individual people it serves during a year, known as 'units served'.[16] In other words, there is at least a partial correlation between a religious organisation's number of 'units served' and the amount of state support it receives. That this situation has a high potential for generating problems of various kinds among the different 'free churches' should not be hard to imagine, particularly because of the above-mentioned absence of official statistics concerning religious affiliation and attendance. It is up to the religious organisations to collect and keep such information if they choose, and the Islamic congregations have, for various reasons, so far not proved to be very 'statistically minded'. Whatever the reasons, the Islamic congregations have, over the years, been rather heavily criticised for reporting too high numbers of 'units served' to the Council, in order to receive disproportionately large shares of the total amount of support available.

As an attempt to clarify this, the Council asked me to investigate the matter. Given the magnitude of the problem and the limited finances the Council could allocate for the project, it was obvious from the start that all that could reasonably be aimed for was a pilot study. The main result would be a somewhat clearer picture of the number of people served by the various Islamic congregations. Another, possibly more important result would be a better idea about more exactly *what* needed to be done to acquire the desired information and *how* one practically could go about acquiring it.

In meetings with the leaders of the three Islamic national federations, we decided together on a 'traditional' investigation in the sense that I would have field workers visiting all the official mosques and prayer halls[17] on a certain number of Fridays to 'count heads'. As it was spring, we decided to do the counts at Friday prayer on 22 and 29 March and 12 April 1991, all during Ramadan. In addition, the congregations were to be visited on a specific week on a day of their choice when they had activities especially for women and children.

When the national leaders tried to confirm this procedure at the local level, problems arose. To make a long story short, local congregational leaders objected to having their congregations counted in this way during prayer. The main official reason given was with reference to (an interpretation) of the Qur'an 9:17–18.[18] Other reasons were fears that many Muslims would regard this kind of counting as an attempt by the Swedes to gain control over the Muslims in Sweden or the like, a particularly sensitive issue in the wake of the Rushdie affair and the recently concluded Gulf War. Other reasons were also given.

After new rounds of negotiations with Muslim leaders, we arrived at the conclusion that the only practical way of doing it was to let 'trusted staff' at the various prayer halls do the counting and report it on a special form and have the local prayer halls' imam verify the correctness of the results with his signature.[19] We also decided to add the prayer at *'id al-Fitr* to the list of times to be counted.

The forms were then distributed to all official mosques and prayer halls – at the time, a total of 61.[20] It turned out, for various reasons, that not all of them were actively operative during the time of the investigation.[21]

In the autumn of 1991, when the results had been compiled and partially analysed, they were presented to a group of representatives of the different Islamic organisations, as well as members of the Council, the 'project group'. The intense discussions that followed at subsequent meetings in the project group during the fall and winter culminated in a common decision in the group that I should carry out 'sample-tests' during the next Ramadan at a number of the congregations that had been criticised for reporting suspiciously high figures. My co-workers and I visited seven congregations on two different Fridays during Ramadan 1992. The visits were unannounced. These sample-tests showed between 10 and 15 per cent fewer participants than were reported the year before. Given such facts as Ramadan in 1991 but not in 1992, partly coinciding with the Easter holidays, tougher conditions in the labour market in 1992 than in 1991, and that what a Muslim leader called 'the mobilising effects of the Rushdie affair and the Gulf-war', were less in 1992 than in 1991, it does not seem unreasonable that the figures were lower in 1992 than in 1991, although it is difficult to say how much lower. After more meetings and more discussions in the project group, we decided that it probably was reasonable to count on a certain level of overestimation of the numbers of participants in the 'self-reporting' system used during 1991. The extent to which this was due to 'conscious fraud' or to more 'unconscious factors' is impossible to say. Personally, I believe that the amount of 'conscious fraud', if any, was extremely limited. However, to take care of this problem we decided to count using two sets of figures, one as if the reported figures were unquestioned and one where we had reduced all the figures from 1991 by between 5 and 10 per cent.

Given these considerations, the official mosques and prayer halls in Sweden were visited every Friday during the time of the investigation by roughly 6000 individuals. Of these, 78 per cent were men, 9 per cent women and 13 per cent children under 15 years old. What can this tell us about the total *net* number of individual visitors ('units served') per year? Some speculations follow.

Based on my work among the Muslims of Sweden in the last 7–8 years, I feel fairly confident in making the following assumptions:

(1) An average population at the Friday midday prayer at a prayer hall in Sweden consists of about 80 per cent of regular visitors and about 20 per cent of irregular visitors.[22]

(2) The relation between possible visitors/actual visitors at a Friday prayer varies over the year, depending on 'what kind' of Friday it is. For example, a large proportion of the possible visitors actually visit the prayer halls during Ramadan and other Fridays that coincide with other 'special occasions' in the Muslim religious calendar, than on an 'average' or 'normal' Friday. It also seems clear that a smaller proportion of the possible visitors, due to vacations, etc., actually visit the prayer halls during the summer months than during the rest of the year. On the basis of these observations I give 'Special Fridays' a value of 100 per cent, 'Normal Fridays' a value of 75 per cent and 'Summer Fridays' a value of 50 per cent. I have further assumed the total number of 'Special Fridays' to be ten, 'Normal Fridays' to be 32 and 'Summer Fridays' to be ten in a year.

On the basis of these assumptions, the *total* or *gross* number of prayer hall visits on Fridays in Sweden during one year is around 215 000 (235 000). According to principles of calculation which are beyond the limits of this paper to discuss (see Sander, 1993), we arrive at the following conclusions about the *net* number of individuals who make this total number of visits: (1) the net population of 'Special Friday' visitors is around 22 000 (24 000); (2) the net population of 'Normal Friday' visitors is around 40 000 (45 000); (3) the net population of 'Summer Friday' visitors is around 9000 (10 000).

As the individuals constituting the net number of 'Summer Friday' visitors are probably a proper sub-set of the net number of 'Normal Friday' visitors, they should not be included in the final sum. In other words, the number of individuals who visit the prayer halls only during the summer months is most likely negligible.

Thus we find the total number of net Friday prayer hall visitors in Sweden during 1991 to be estimated to be around 62 000 (69 000). Granted that the total number of Muslims – given the same way of calculating as used above – was around 130 000 at the time of the investigation, we find that around 30 per cent (35 per cent) of the total population, measured in terms of frequency of prayer hall visiting, could be considered to be religious in a fairly exclusive sense of the term and that about an additional 17 per cent (18.5 per cent), giving a total of 47 per cent (53.5 per cent), could be said to be religious using a more inclusive definition. The remaining 53 per cent (46.5 per cent) is, then, non-religious.

CONCLUSIONS

If we compare the figures for mosque-visiting frequency from the Ramadan study with those based on the Göteborg study[23] we get, on the whole, quite a homogeneous picture. Just above half the population turns out to be non-religious in the sense that they never or rarely visit a mosque or prayer hall, while just under half visit prayer halls, at least on special occasions. When it comes to the visiting frequency among those who claim to visit prayer halls there is, however, a difference in the proportion of exclusively and inclusively religious people between the two studies. This difference can have many explanations. I will just point to one: the proportions of men and women differ in the two studies[24] and when it comes to mosque visiting frequency, women rank lower than the men.

Since religiosity measured according to the variable 'mosque visiting', as we have seen, gives a lower proportion of religious people than measurements according to the other suggested variables, it seems reasonable to conclude that the results from the two indices for measuring religiosity used above – according to which around 60 per cent of the population is called religious if we use the term inclusively – corresponds with reality.

As a final comment, I would again like to underscore the fact that the results presented in this paper are both based on relatively weak empirical grounds and on a relatively large number of stipulations and assumptions. A larger and sounder empirical base in combination with different definitions, stipulations and assumptions might have given somewhat different results. The reader is therefore advised to take the results *cum grano salis*.

As the primary aim of this paper was not to give a definite answer to the question in its title, but to propose and discuss some methods or ways of reaching such an answer, the uncertainty of the results is of limited relevance in judging the value of the project. What is important is if the study, with all its shortcomings, and the discussion it might generate can be helpful in our continued attempts to answer the question in the title.

NOTES

1. The project was entitled 'Muslims Immigrants' Encounter with Swedish Society' and was sponsored by The Bank of Sweden Tercentenary Foundation.
2. One official investigation of all religious groups in 1963, denominations and churches in Sweden commissioned by the Swedish state – there is, for example, no mention of Islam or any Muslim group. One Islamic 'congregation' had, however, been established in Stockholm in 1949. It was started by a group of Tatars originating from Russia.
3. In the category 'people with foreign backgrounds' the following are included: (1) 'first generation immigrants' (people with present or previously foreign citizenship born outside of Sweden); and (2) 'second generation immigrants' (individuals born in Sweden with at least one parent born abroad). Of the total number of people with foreign backgrounds in Sweden, roughly 800 000 belong to category (1) and the rest to (2).
4. In the late 1980s this was over 30 000 people per year. In 1992 it was close to 40 000. This made Sweden the largest per capita recipient country in Europe.
5. The Muslim cognitive universe includes, among other things, the cultural, political and religious history and tradition as it is seen and defined from a Muslim point of view, as well as their literature, mythology, art, architecture and popular beliefs and customs.
6. My primarily sources have been Weeks (1978), Kettani (1986) and Shaikh (1992). I have also consulted several other 'minor' sources, like various area- or country-specific books. However, almost all sources give figures between Weeks (on the low end) and Kettani (on the high end).
7. The term is used here to denote people with origins in the state of Turkey, i.e. the term is *not* used in its normal *ethnic* sense, referring to one specific ethnic group among the others that make up the population of the state of Turkey.
8. At present there are, according to the immigration authorities, around 100 000 people in refugee camps in Sweden waiting for their asylum applications to be processed. Even though nobody knows for sure, probably about half of them fit the definition of 'ethnic Muslim'. These people are not included in the figures given in Table 10.1a and 10.1b above.

9. Many typologies of the different ways, different degrees of intensity, etc. an individual can be religious have been suggested in the literature. See, for example, Batson and Ventis (1982).

10. More exactly, what 'empirical' forms this understanding takes in real life for a specific individual can vary with a number of factors. What is important, however, is not the exact empirical forms of manifestation, but what correspondence there is between what the individual seriously considers it to be for a Muslim to live a good or correct life according to Islam, on the one hand, and the life (s)he *de facto* is (thinks (s)he is) leading, on the other.

11. The questionnaire existed in the following languages: Swedish, Turkish, Arabic, Persian and Urdu.

12. Question (1) has, for obvious reasons, only two different possible answers. Questions (2)–(9) were 'thermometer questions' with five alternative answers.

13. Exactly which, and how 'strict', criteria should be formulated for an individual to be considered religious in different senses of the word, and thereby where the borders between the different types should be drawn, is, as with all formulations of definitions, to some extent arbitrary and a matter of decision and stipulation. The ones suggested here are no exceptions. Discussions with my informants make me believe that the ones suggested here are defensible. Of the different 'borders', I deem the one between exclusive and inclusive religiosity the most questionable, in the sense that I might have put up too 'soft' demands for an individual to be exclusively religious.

14. Where the figures in Indexes 1 and 2 differ in any relevant respect I have given the figure in Index 1 slightly more weight than the figure in Index 2, due to the fact that the first index includes the, to my mind, more important behavioural variables.

15. To put this figure in some perspective, it can be mentioned that only 3–4 per cent of Swedes claim to visit their church at least once a week.

16. The definition of 'unit served' is discussed in Sander (1993). Here it is enough to say that individuals taking 'regular part' in a congregation's religious services play a important role in the definition.

17. A prayer hall being 'official' in this case means that it is a member of one of the three Islamic national federations and fulfills the requirement of being eligible to receive financial support by the Council.

18. In 'Abdullah Yusef' Ali's translation (which is recommended by Swedish Islamic leaders), it says: 'It is not for such as join gods with Allah, to visit or maintain the mosques of Allah while they witness against their own souls to infidelity. The works of such bear no fruit: in Fire shall they dwell. The mosques of Allah shall be visited and maintained by such as believe in Allah and the Last Day, establish regular prayers, and practice regular charity, and fear none (at all) except Allah. It is they who are expected to be on true guidance.'

19. Given the facts that (1) there is a certain rivalry between the various national federations, as well as between various local congregations;

(2) that there are power, prestige and money connected with the relative size of a particular congregations/national federations in relation to the other congregations/national federations; and (3) that I had made them aware of the fact that I would have the figures given by one congregation checked by their 'rivals', the uncertainty of the procedure used might not be as large as first might be feared.

20. It is impossible at the moment to have any clear idea about how many 'unofficial' prayer halls or places where Muslims meet to pray at relatively regular frequency (and that for various reasons are not registered at any of the Islamic national federations) there are. As far as I can estimate at the moment, there seem to be at least 20–30. It should also be added that many of the Swedish refugee camps are equipped with what can reasonably be called a prayer room, and that the number of people frequenting them on a regular basis, according to camp staff, is relatively high. At present there are, as we have seen, about 100 000 people in Swedish refugee camps. Of them, about 40 000 are from Bosnia-Herzegovina. Most of them are guessed to be Muslims. Of the remaining 60 000, many estimate that approximately half of them come from countries dominated by Islamic cultural traditions. In late June 1993 the Swedish government decided, owing to the extraordinary situation in Bosnia-Herzegovina, to depart from the normal procedure of judging each applicant individually, and grant the refugees from there refugee status collectively. This decision increased the population of ethnic Muslims in Sweden by several tens of thousands. According to Swedish law, an acceptance of a person's refugee status also extends to her/his husband/wife and children. This makes the immigration authorities estimate that the decision of the government will increase the number of Bosnians in Sweden by 70 000–80 000 rather than by 40 000.

21. Such reasons were, for example, that they were under repair, at the time they did not have an imam and that they had decided to 'join up' with a neighboring prayer hall during Ramadan because it had a visit from a well-known 'guest imam'.

22. To be regarded as a regular visitor, an individual shall visit the mosque at least once a week if (s)he does not have any legitimate reasons not to be able to go. Given this, a regular visitor is defined as a person making at least forty-two visits a year. To qualify as an occasional visitor, an individual has to make at least ten visits per year. People making less frequent visits are considered to be in the margin of error that follows with our speculations.

23. Which can be very roughly summarised in the table on p. 210.

24. In the Göteborg study, the division between the sexes was 63 per cent men and 37 per cent women, and in the Ramadan study this relation was 78 per cent men, 9 per cent women and 13 per cent children. In the Göteborg study there was only one individual under the age of 15 years.

Mosque visiting frequency/study	Inclusively	Exclusively	Non-religious
Göteborg total population	26	23	51
Göteborg population men only	33	17	50
Göteborg extrapolated to Sweden total population	17	29	54
Göteborg extraprolated, population men only	22	24	54
Ramadan total population	30	17	53
(Ramadan total population)	(35)	(18)	(46)

BIBLIOGRAPHY

Batson, C. D. and Ventis, W. L. (1982) *The Religious Experience: A Social–Psychological Perspective* (New York and Oxford: Oxford University Press).

Choueiri, Y. M. (1990) *Islamic Fundamentalism* (London: Pinter).

Esposito, J. L. (1992) *The Islamic Threat. Myth or Reality?* (New York: Oxford University Press).

Kettani, M. (1986) *Muslim Minorities in the World Today* (London: Mansell).

Nielsen, J. (1992) *Muslims in Western Europe* (Edinburgh: Edinburgh University Press).

Sander, Å. (1985) 'Religion och Religiositet', Institutionen för filosofi, Göteborgs universitet, Göteborg (unpublished manuscript).

Sander, Å. (1988) *En Tro – En Livsvärld: En fenomenologisk undersökning av religiös erfarenhet, religiöst medvetande och deras roller i livsvärldskonstitutionen*, vols I and II, (Göteborg: Göteborgs Universitet).

Sander, Å. (1990) 'Islam and Muslims in Sweden', *Migration: A European Journal of International Migration and Ethnical Relations*, 8, pp. 83–134.

Sander, Å. (1991) 'The Road from *Musalla* to *Mosque*. The Process of Integration and Institutionalization of Islam in Sweden', in W. A. R. Shadid and P. S. van Koningsveld (eds), *The Integration of Islam and Hinduism in Western Europe* (Kampen, The Netherlands: Kok Pharos).

Sander, Å. (1993) *I vilken utsträckning är den svenske muslimen religiös? Några överväganden kring problematiken med att ta reda på hur måga muslimer som deltar i verksamhenten vid de muslimska 'församlingarna' i Sverige*, KIM-rapport no. 14 (Göteborg: Göteborgs Universitet).

Shaikh, F. (ed.) (1992) *Islam and Islamic Groups. A Worldwide Reference Guide* (London: Longman).

Weeks, R. (1978) *Muslim People: A World Ethnographic Survey* (Westport, Conn.: Greenwood).

11   Muslim Minorities in Italy and their Image in Italian Media

Stefano Allievi

Islam in Italy is characterised by a *statu nascendi* (state of coming into being). It is more a movement than an institution. Nevertheless, one may draw, at this moment, a first draft of its image: a picture that, like photographs taken in motion, will not be completely clear, because the situation is not stationary – it is moving, and quite fast.

THE RETURN OF ISLAM

From the historical point of view, the contemporary presence of Islam in Italy is actually a return (Allievi and Dassetto, 1993). In Italy there had been an Arab presence in Sicily since the seventh century – the very beginning of the history of Islam – and an absolute Islamic domination of the island from the ninth through eleventh centuries. But the Islamic heritage is visible elsewhere, indeed up to Aosta Valley, passing through Puglia, Toscana, Liguria and Sardinia. In the eighteenth century in several towns such as Genova, Livorno and Napoli there were mosques for Muslim captive slaves from a variety of Islamic countries, from the Maghreb to Bosnia.

Italy doesn't even have a significant past as a great colonial power. Commercial contacts with the Islamic world, obviously, have always gone on: the Mediterranean Sea, for commerce and trade, has often been more an advantage than a obstacle, more a bridge than a wall. The only political contact of any real importance took place during the fascist period, when Mussolini tried to play the role of a 'protector' of

Islam. He liked to be with the 'sword of Islam', given to him in Tripoli by a group of native chiefs in 1937. Ten years before, he defined Italy not only as a 'friend of the Islamic world', but even as a 'great Muslim power'. Among other historical examples of political links are the Arabic programmes of Radio Bari, founded in 1934, and the frequent visits to Rome of the Great Mufti of Jerusalem. However, these twentieth-century political gestures have had little consequence for Italian culture and society, for which Islam is an unknown reality. If anything, Islam has long been regarded overall as the old enemy, probably more because of the frequent incursions on the Italian coast of the Saracen pirates than because of the Crusades.

From a sociological point of view, however, the Islamic presence is a new phenomenon. Italy was a country renowned for 'exporting' migrants no more than twenty years ago. The symbolic turning point – the year in which the number of Italians returning to the country became higher than the number of those who where leaving it – was 1973. And the real 'boom' of *immigration* to Italy has been quite recent, that is throughout the 1980s and 1990s. This latter movement started with the arrival of different groups of immigrants, largely from the Philippines and other mainly Roman Catholic countries such as El Salvador. This has been particularly an immigration of domestic workers, although it has continued through successive waves with the most recent groups of migrants – both legal and illegal – coming from the countries of Maghreb, some countries of the sub-Saharan Africa, Albania and Peru (Allievi, 1991).

Thus the migratory influx has started in a more recent period in Italy compared with the countries of Central and Northern Europe. But, in some ways, it seems to be faster. This is suggested not by way of quantitative data, but with regard to social dynamics activated by the migrants living in Italy.

What we could call a Muslim process has arguably been faster in Italy as well. In terms of a large community of resident believers, Islam has just arrived in Italy: it is a newcomer. This can be dated to some twenty years ago, when the first mosques were established in several university towns by the Union of Muslim Students in Italy (USMI). In Italy, before the action of the USMI, there was only a single mosque in Rome: but this was not particularly active, being wholly influenced by the embassies of Muslim countries, and much more a service for their members – and eventually their interests – than an institution for a locally based community. What is peculiar in the Italian situation is that the first mosques were created not by and for the communities of foreign workers, but by and for an élite of students, mainly coming from the Middle East (Syrians, Jordanians and many Palestinians). Soon the number of workers heavily exceeded that of the students, and mosques in Italy have changed their role and frequently their legal status (but not very often their leadership).

It is visibly evident that Islam in Italy is establishing itself very quickly, complete with mosques, associations, Sufi orders (*turuq*), political movements, intellectual production, liaison with transnational powers, intervention of states of origin, and converts. All these Islamic phenomena are now to be found in Italy, but due to its new and rapidly founded nature, all this is still obviously at a rather fragile state of organisation. Certainly, questions of leaderships – especially at the national level – are far from defined: the match is still going on.

HIC SUNT LEONES: LOOKING FOR THE 'OTHER'

Given the fact that an internal Islamic presence in Italy is a new phenomenon, it comes as no surprise that it is more or less unknown to the Italian population at large. Only in very recent times have some social agencies started to address the religious aspects of the presence of foreign immigrants. And, not by chance, most of these agencies have been voluntary associations, themselves based on religious principles or managed by religious leaders, predominantly Catholic.

Academic researchers have, on the whole, not followed the lead of the social agencies in addressing questions of religion. This is likely for two main reasons. The first one seems to be a matter of prejudice: the emergence of the religious factor as characterising a social phenomenon is something intellectually alien and ideologically troublesome for a large part of the Italian intellectual camp, particularly that in the sociological field. The second reason is that most research on migration has been based on statistics and official documents, and very little on personal experience or 'the human factor'. And if it is frequently true that the migrants of flesh are not necessarily well represented by the migrants as they are described on paper, this is especially true with Islam: the Islam of the text, as it is described in every introductory handbook, is very different from the Islam of flesh as we can meet it

through the life and the perception of the Muslim communities –
particularly those who are living in a non-Muslim society such as Europe.

Islam, perhaps more than other world religions, seems to bring with
itself a sort of curse: non-Muslims may discuss it much, but by way of
a certain meaning apart from its reality. One need only have a
superficial look at the overall European Press (and the Italian Press is
starting right now in the same direction) to see that Islam *is* news, but
almost automatically of a kind largely seen as a problem. The Italian
Press, in particular, is itself rapidly reproducing this discourse. Hence
Islam is, in a way, known and debated. But actual Islamic communities
are far from being known and discussed with the same level of interest.

As on the ancient geographical maps, we might write on contemporary Islamic 'territory' the phrase '*hic sunt leones*' ('here be lions'). It
is because of the fear of lions – or more probably because of a common
intellectual and practical laziness – that individuals very rarely go to
see and to verify what is said of such territory. These days, however,
that is exactly what is needed: Islam – the 'inside Islam' of Europe –
needs explorers.

The information gap is even less acceptable in a country that is a
bridge in the Mediterranean between Europe and the Arab-Islamic
world. That's why a core of Italian researchers have started with a very
simple but absolutely necessary kind of fieldwork: a cartography, a
map-making, a description of the morphology of Islam in Italy in its
different forms. Starting with such a basic approach has been required
in Italy as, until recently, practically nothing existed on the subject: no
sociological studies by way of research, theoretical approaches, nor
even a sufficient number of empirical descriptions of the Islamic presence. That is why our study has taken the character of an exploration:
in one and a half years we have travelled all over Italy, region after
region, town after town, in a sort of investigative process: to search, to
look for, to inquire into, in order to discover something.

Nearly four months of true *tournée*, more than 8000 miles covered
by car and as many by other means of transport, hundreds of witnesses
and social actors interviewed, an even greater number of contacts made
regarding various related matters, and an indefinite number of hours of
conversation. The results have taken the form of a map of the mosques,
places of meeting, organisations of the Muslim world living in Italy, an
evaluation of their significance, and an initial interpretation of the
social and religious role they are playing.

TOWARDS A MORPHOLOGY OF ISLAM IN ITALY

The Muslim presence in Italy is especially difficult to evaluate for the simple reason that even the number of migrants is far from being known. Italy is one of the countries in Europe with the smallest presence of migrants, but it has one of the highest percentage of non-EU foreigners, and surely one of the highest with regard to illegal immigrants.

Something more than 900 000 (at the end of 1992) foreigners are legally resident in Italy. Among them are some 760 000 non-EU members, with around 280 000 (31 per cent) coming from Muslim countries, or (calculated in percentage) from countries with a Muslim presence in their population. If we add a moderate estimated percentage of illegals, the converts and those who have obtained Italian citizenship, we can suggest a number of 500 000 persons of Muslim origin that are not mere 'birds of passage', continually moving from a place to another. This can be considered the number of those who are well enough established to activate also a religious demand. Yet this number obviously doesn't say anything about their effective and practical 'Islamicity', if the neologism is permitted (cf. Sander, in this volume).

Unlike the predominance of Turks in Germany, Algerians in France or Indians and Pakistanis in Great Britain, approximately one-third of the Muslims in Italy come from Morocco, while the rest are divided between several countries of origin, from Tunisia to ex-Yugoslavia, from Senegal to Albania, from Egypt to Iran, from Somalia to Pakistan, and further. With regard to the illegals, most of them come from the Maghreb (mainly Morocco and Tunisia), but presently there are increasing numbers of Bosnians and Albanians as well. Overall, we can observe here one of the peculiarities of the Islamic presence in Italy: that is, it is a multi-pole presence, with very few Turks, a modest presence of Muslim Asians, and no more than a symbolical presence of migrants coming from former Italian colonies.

From the point of view of religious organisation, Italian Islam is moving along the same course as that of the Islam transplanted in other countries of Europe, but at a remarkably higher speed. Until 1970, as we have already seen, there was only one mosque in Italy. In the 1970s six new mosques were created. Between 1981 and 1990 we witnessed a rapid diffusion of twenty-three mosques in different regions of the country – seven of which in 1990 alone. But the real 'boom' is even more recent, and now we can speak of more than sixty mosques and 100–120 halls of prayer.

The ethnic community at the origin of the mosque, when it is possible to single it out, is frequently Moroccan, but there are also Tunisian, Algerian, Iranian, Egyptian, Pakistani, Libyan, Turkish and ... Italian mosques. More frequently the origin of the mosque is not ethnic but associative and, at least in the past, particularly from the USMI network.

The organisation of the *turuq*, the Sufi orders, is not one of the easiest subjects to study. Even if they are not secret societies, they are always, at least, discrete societies, and those who belong to one or another of them don't declare their membership at the first moment – indeed, they sometimes deny it (that is the case also for members of some religious and political-Islamic movements). The most evident of them is the Senegalese *tariqa* of the Mourides, to which the majority of the Senegalese living in Italy refer, even if they are not explicitly members of it, or if they were not used to be before leaving their country. That is because the *tariqa* plays a role that is not only religious, but also social and even economic.

In Italy one can find the traces of other Sufi orders. Two branches of the Tijaniyya are active: one is Senegalese (and in Senegal is still, probably, the most important *tariqa* in terms of sheer number of adherents), and the other one is mainly composed of converts. The Burhaniyya, an Egyptian *tariqa* that is very active also in Europe and that has its European centre in Germany, is also present among certain groups of converts. Mainly (and sometimes exclusively) composed of converts are the groups which are referred to as the Naqshbandiyya, the Darqawiyya, the Alawiyya, and others, all with some dozens of members at most.

Also of growing importance are political and religious movements that are starting to be present and influential in the Italian Muslim world. Some of them are more established than others: this includes the Tablighi Jamaat (see King, in this volume) and the Muslim Brotherhood, which perhaps is much more important as an ideological reference than as an organised structure, and whose ideas are popular among the leadership of the USMI (Union of Muslim Students) and of some Islamic centres of a certain importance.

Unlike what happens in other European countries, in Italy national organisations (which the French terminology calls *amicales*) play only a modest role, but one which is surely developing. Various subjects are trying to play the role of representation of Islam in Italy, and the match is far from being concluded. What is possible to say is that at the moment no one can pretend to monopolise the leadership of Italian Islam.

The most important actors are, at this moment, the following.

(1) The Islamic Cultural Center of Italy (Centro Islamico culturale d'Italia): This is the group which is primarily associated with the large mosque of Rome. It is possible to define it as a diplomatic-state Islam: the board of the centre is officially comprised of the ambassadors of different Islamic countries, even if the leading role is played by Saudi Arabia through the Rabita, the World Muslim League.

(2) The Union of Communities and Islamic Organisations in Italy (UCOII): founded in 1990 in order to be the representative of the 'real' Islam – in opposition to the 'official' Islam of the centre in Rome – this body has as its promoting committee the Islamic Centre of Milan, historically one of the most powerful and best organised in Italy, and the Union of Muslim Students (USMI), whose role we have already underlined. The UCOII is quite active both in internal organisation and in external public relations with the media and Italian society more broadly. It is the publisher of a new Muslim bi-lingual (Italian and Arabic) monthly, *Il musul-mano,* and its main purpose is to obtain an *Intesa* (agreement) with the Italian state in order to recognise the Islamic religion (along-side others that have obtained a similar recognition, i.e. Protestant churches and Jews) as one of the religions of the country.

In Italy, other Islamic social actors are playing important roles too. In some areas of the country regional networks, with the most ancient or the better organised mosques at their centre, are quite active and relatively independent from the federation and the other bodies quoted above. Transnational powers, like the Rabita and the Libyan Da'wah, are exercising their influence in Italy as well. Some states too – particularly Morocco, Tunisia, Egypt and Iran – are trying to establish certain controls over their citizens. Also, Italian Muslim converts (and, among them, the Shi'ites) recently started to build their own networks at both national and European levels. Finally, we should remember that among the social actors there is a large proportion of what we might call the freelancers, a typology not rare in Europe, even if non-existent in the countries of origin of Islam. These are 'sociological' Muslims, quite often intellectuals, who play a role of interlinking the Muslim world and non-Muslim societies, and are often more recognised as Muslim representatives by the non-Muslim majority than by the Muslims themselves.

Finally, we must emphasise in this phase of the establishment of Islam the role played by the converts. It is they who know better the Italian language; it is they who have the necessary kinds of know-how for organising groups in this context; and it is they who seem to be more able to find necessary financial resources. But all this means that the Italian converts, with their peculiar way of thinking and of living Islam, become the key link with the media and, more generally, with society as a whole. It is probably a temporary phase, but they seem to be capable of influencing in a significant way the image of Islam presented to the wider society: often this image is both more mystical and more radical and militant than is the reality lived by Muslim migrants.

THE IMAGE OF ISLAM IN THE ITALIAN MEDIA

Islam has started to become present and visible in public space. This is especially through the estimated presence, as we have already seen, of some 500 000 persons coming from Muslim countries, much more than through mosques and organisations (indeed, these latter are not only little known by the society that surrounds them, but are ignored by important local government agencies and relevant non-government organisations as well). Islam is perceived more through the individuals seen here and there, on the road or at work, than through Islamic symbols and collective structures. And, obviously, it starts to become visible throug the mass-media system. This process, too, is in an early phase which can be characterised by certain key events and developments.

The Case of the Gulf War

The coverage of Islam in Italy was initially very limited, particularly centering on certain countries of origin (Libya and Iran foremost), and on the 'Islamic danger' in the world generally. The turning point has been, for Italy, the Gulf War, with the fear of a fifth column of Islamic terrorists working inside the territory of the state (see Allievi, 1992a).

On this occasion, for the first time, the Muslim minorities in Italy were perceived by some media not only as objects of interest, but also as a sources of information. For the first time, Muslims were involved in some feedback. Further, some newspapers, local radio and TV programmes discovered that there was a part of the public opinion that reacted quite differently to their messages. For the first time too, the media gave information specifically on Islam by way of special supplements, special pages and instalments. However, there was a very clear dependence on the foreign debate, particularly that of the French and the British. The Italian media discovered that there were no national experts (or at least that they didn't know them): therefore there were frequent references to the French and British ones – the same ones interviewed by French and British newspapers. As often happens, newspapers copy one another. This is what we could call the 'carbon-paper' type of journalism, which represents a world-wide phenomenon and a problem in itself: the number of items of information increases, but the sources of information are very few, and always the same. More media and the same messages.

The image of the internal Arab minorities during the war is exemplified in the *Corriere della sera*, the best-selling newspaper in the period. In its pages a major social problem was postulated from the very first day of the war. On 17 January 1991, an entire page of *Corriere della sera* was dedicated to the notion: 'Fear of the opening of a second front among the immigrants in the name of the Islamic Jihad.' The article was 'imported' from the French situation, to which reference is made. In any case, the concept of a 'second front' entered Italian public space from the very first day, and it went on to make a great career. Even if no evidence of the existence of that front had been found during the whole period of the war, such an idea continued with headlines such as: 'Danger of terrorism, red alarm', or 'A secret plan for the internal front' (in this instance, the plan was one prepared not by the supposed terrorists, but by the government), and 'The terrorist alarm increases'. News that a bomb was found in the disco in a small town in Tuscany stimulated the hypothesis that 'the pro-Iraq terrorists have started to hit'. The story was repeated some days later with respect to the case of a fire in the port of Carrara, for which a Syrian was initially suspected.

Coverage of the war and surrounding issues of interest were often represented by non-news, 'factoids' created by the media themselves (sometimes by secondary press agencies). The idea of the 'Arab-Muslim terrorist' was regularly reproduced because it was the kind of news item that one would like to have – a sort of desire and an expectation within public opinion, at least unconsciously, which also bolstered a general prejudice directed at the Arab immigrants. We could say that within mainstream newspapers like *Corriere della sera*, however, the main character of the period was the double fear/desire of finding the fundamentalists among the resident Arab community. Local radio and TV, however, provided a partial corrective. Here it was possible to find examples of the participation of Arab representatives of the migrant community, and also an increase in the number of Arab listeners during the Gulf War period.

Other Recent Cases

Leaving aside issues related to the Gulf War, general coverage of Islam is, by evidence, subject to the general laws of journalism. One of them is the emphasis given to conflicts among the great powers. This attitude can promote a sort of instrumental use of Islam for objectives that have nothing to do with it.

A good example is the frequent habit of attacking the Catholic church using, in some way, the Islamic argument. This is possibly due to historical reasons in Italy – the most important of which is, probably, the power and the influence of the church in the society and the fact that the process of Italian unification, supported by liberal opinion whose roots were in the French Revolution, has been built in opposition to the church. In intellectual circles, non-Catholic opinion is still more anti-clerical than secular. This background, together with some common, unwritten laws of journalism, can explain the use of Islam in anti-Catholic polemics from the laity. Some examples are given below (cf. Allievi and Dassetto, 1993).

In March 1992, the conference of the Bishops of Triveneto (an area which includes the whole north-eastern part of Italy) approved a document on Christian–Muslim relations. The text goes in the direction of knowledge and broad-mindedness rather than otherwise. But on the day following the appearance of the document, the daily newspaper *La Repubblica* covered its release on the front page under the title 'Don't marry a Muslim: Crusade of the Triveneto's bishops', making of the document an example of the medieval attitude of the Catholic church (the use of the term 'crusade' is explicit enough).

Such an episode would be of little importance if the article didn't register the opinion of the leaders of the local Islamic centre in Padova. 'Absurd, we can't believe it, all this is in contradiction with the speech given by the Pope at the Angelus of New Year's day', he said. 'It's a pity…. To think that just few days ago John Paul II sent us his greetings for the Ramadan'. In a meeting I had with the leaders of the Islamic centre some time later, it emerged that they never read the entire document, but were given only the final phrases by the journalist, with some very calm pastoral considerations on the question of giving church halls for Muslim prayer, common moments of prayer, and the problems that may arise in mixed marriages. A similar event occurred in February 1993 when some rather commonsensical declarations of the Bishop of Rome regarding mixed marriages obtained the honour of being front-page news in *La Stampa* and *Corriere della sera*. This particular piece of misinformation was even repeated by the BBC.

A more serious problem is that surrounding the 'emergence of Islamic radicalism', or the so-called 'Islamic threat'. These notions have often been linked by the media with the presence of Muslim minorities, such that there is a blurring of 'internal' and 'external' 'fronts' in the presumed struggle between the West and Islam. Among many quarters of the Italian media, when a bloody incident happens somewhere (it doesn't matter if it's internal or external) it is automatically linked with the Muslim Brotherhood or some similar, known Islamicist body. This causes two kinds of misunderstandings. With regard to the 'external front', the image is conveyed that the Muslim Brotherhood is *one* organisation (which is not the case), and that it is much more powerful than it is in the reality. With regard to the internal front, it produces a dangerous tendency to identify Muslim organisations in Italy with one or another external source.

An example of this mechanism can be seen in the case of the expulsion of the president of the USMI in August 1992 (which took place, as in similar cases, during a holiday period on a Saturday and at 5.00 a.m. in order to avoid an immediate reaction). The USMI had been frequently identified – too easily – with the Muslim Brotherhood. Omar

Tariq, USMI's president, is a Palestinian. Two days after his expulsion to Jordan, in the relative silence of the Press, there was a *coup de théâtre*: one newspaper, *Il Giorno*, boasted on its front page the sensational title: 'A killer for two Ministers'. In the article Omar Tariq was identified as an anti-Arafat Palestinian extremist who had been contracted by the Italian *mafia* to kill the Minister of Defence, the Minister of Justice and a general of the *Carabinieri* – nothing less! Muslim organisations protested heavily with a press conference, and even the Ministry of Interior denied this interpretation, which in the meantime wholly occupied the media scene.

In reality, Tariq had been expelled by mistake: in fact the motivation for the expulsion was related to troubles among anti-Iranian groups in the town where Tariq lives. But since Tariq is not Iranian: what was going on? There had been, most likely, a confusion with another organisation with similar initials – USMIE (Union of the Iranian Muslim Students in Europe), which is pro-Khomeini. This has never been admitted by the authorities, but some months later Tariq was given the permission to return to Italy, in order to discuss his final thesis at the university. Following a press conference of Muslim organisations, this news was relayed by the majority of Italian newspapers – naturally, with the exception of *Il Giorno*.

This case may not be that important in itself, but it is symptomatic of wider matters. The image of the Muslim terrorist is like an illness, a virus, a toxin of distrust, which once injected into public opinion, starts to live its own life. If the environment is favourable, it can multiply without control. Even if a story such as this one is repudiated, the view of Arab Muslims as potential terrorists remains. And, more than this, it pushes the Muslim communities into an attitude of victimisation and, as a possible consequence, into radicalisation – resulting in a self-fulfilling prophecy.

Among non-Muslim journalists, Islam presents uncertainties of many kinds. Is it to be 'covered' by internal or foreign affairs? social policies or religious problems? immigration or minorities? This conundrum is evident through the professional figures that are asked to work on it: staff journalists, special correspondents on the Middle East, specialists on social problems such as migration, or religion, occasional writers, intellectuals, human- or women's-rights professionals, and more. On the whole, there is no specialisation yet developed, and no knowledge of Arabic in evidence. The result is a maze of distorting mirrors, of reciprocal prejudices and stigmas.

BIBLIOGRAPHY

Allievi, S. (1991) *La sfida dell'immigrazione* (Bologna: EMI).
Allievi, S. (1992a) 'Médias, minorités, information européenne. Le cas italien', in S. Allievi, A. Bastenier, A. Battegay, and A. Boubeker (eds), *Médias et minorités ethniques. Le cas de la guerre du Golfe* (Louvain-la-Neuve: Academia-Sybidi).
Allievi, S. (1992b) 'Le due guerre del Golfo', *Dimensioni dello sviluppo*, 1.
Allievi, S. (1993) 'L'évolution des pratiques sociales et des références religieuses des musulmans en Italie', in S. Allievi *et al.* (eds), *Politiques d'integration et Islams européens. L'expérience italienne* (Paris: Institut du Monde Arabe).
Allievi, S. and F. Dassetto (1993) *Il ritorno dell'Islam. I musulmani in Italia* (Roma: Edizioni Lavoro).
Allievi, S., A. Bastenier, A. Battegay and A. Boubeker (eds) (1992) *Médias et minorités ethniques. Le cas de la guerre du Golfe* (Louvain-la-Neuve: Academia-Sybidi).
Dassetto, F. (1991) 'Islam in Europa, Islam d'Europa: identità a confronto', *Prospettiva sindacale*, pp. 79–80.
Dassetto, F. (1993) 'L'Islam europeo. Evoluzione e sviluppi futuri', *Orientamenti*, pp. 4–5.
Dassetto, F. and A. Bastenier (1991) *Europa: nuova frontiera dell'Islam* (Roma: Edizioni Lavoro).
Gabrieli, F. (1989) 'Storia, cultura e civiltà degli Arabi in Italia', in F. Gabrieli and U. Scerrato (eds), *Gli Arabi in Italia* (Milano: Garzanti-Scheiwiller).
Lucrezio-Monticelli, G. (1991) 'L'appartenenza religiosa degli imigrati esteri in Italia', in L. Di Liegro and F. Pittau (eds), *Per conoscere l'Islam. Cristiani e musulmani nel mondo di oggi* (Casale Monferrato: Caritas-Piemme).
Riccardi, A. (1989) *Il mondo musulmano in Italia, in Comunità di Sant'Egidio, Cristianesimo e Islam. L'amicizia possibile* (Brescia: Morcelliana).
Volli, U. (1989) 'Per un'ecologia della comunicazione molecolare', in M. Manzoni (ed.), *Etica e metropoli* (Milano: Guerini e Associati).

12   The Islamic Broadcasting Foundation in the Netherlands: Platform or Arena?

Nico Landman

In September 1993 the Dutch Islamic Broadcasting Foundation (IBF) concluded its seventh season of broadcasting on Dutch radio and television. They did not have much reason to celebrate, however, since afterwards the responsible authorities did not allow them to continue their activities, but transferred their broadcasting authorisation to a rival organisation, the Dutch Muslim Broadcasting Council (DMC). The history of the IBF illustrates the complex nature of the representation of Muslims in a Western-European country. The complexity is due to the ongoing process of institutionalisation of the various Muslim communities, and the fluctuation and the changes of leadership within their organisations and of the relations between them.

THE ALLOCATION OF BROADCASTING TIME IN THE NETHERLANDS

The Netherlands have a decentralised media system in which most of the available broadcasting time and funding is distributed among nine parties: the National Broadcasting Foundation and eight broadcasting associations representing various religious and cultural tendencies in society. This system was based on the notion of a segmented society where the various denominations had separate institutions in most social fields (a system known as 'pillarisation'). Although the system

224

hardly exists any more officially, the system of distribution of resources is still in force, while competition with new commercial channels compels the old associations to co-operate and to give up their idiosyncrasies. Access of new religious or cultural groups to the system is possible but not easy, as an association with a minimum of 150 000 paying members is required. For Muslims this option is not a very realistic one because of the diversity of the communities with Muslim background and the weak organisational position of most of them.

Since 1980, however, Muslim organisations have explored other legal possibilities for making their voice heard in the Dutch media. Article 17 of the Broadcasting Act of 1967 gives the Minister of Culture the opportunity to allocate broadcasting facilities to 'associations with a spiritual root' for broadcasting in the area of religion or philosophy. The phrase 'associations with a spiritual root', which is used in several Dutch laws, refers to Christian churches in the first place, but includes other religious or non-religious communities whose functions are accepted to be similar to those of the Christian churches.

Although a clear and generally accepted definition of the concept is absent in Dutch jurisprudence (in cases of conflict about its applicability to a specific group, an *ad hoc* decision has to be made in court), there is no serious doubt that it can be applied to the Muslim community.[1] Neither is there serious opposition to the idea that it should be applied to them, in order to prevent legal inequality between Muslims and the Christian churches. Nevertheless, it took Muslims six years to get these legal possibilities implemented. One of the reasons was the absence of a legal body that could be recognised as representative of the Muslim community. The heterogeneous character of the Muslim community as such was never the main obstacle, rather the unclear nature of the representation of this community by specific organisations.

Although various programmes with a Christian inspiration and content are made by some of the general broadcasting associations mentioned above, each of the main Christian denominations in the Netherlands has been given the opportunity to broadcast religious programmes for their believers. In this way, both the religious ceremonies of the different denominations and Christian comments on current events are presented in the media. The authorities of the different churches have transferred their responsibilities in this area to an ecumenical broadcasting foundation in which they co-operate. This transfer is not a condition for the churches to obtain their broadcasting authorisations, but is their own choice made for reasons of efficiency.

The situation for the Muslims was different in at least two ways: their numbers were smaller and there was no established and accepted way to legitimise the leadership. To address the problem of representation it is necessary to discuss the situation of the Muslim organisations in the Netherlands at the end of the 1970s and the beginning of the 1980s.

MUSLIM ORGANISATIONS OPERATING AT THE NATIONAL LEVEL

By 1980, the process of institutionalisation of Islam in the Netherlands had reached a stage at which mosques were established or being established in about hundred Dutch towns (see Landman, 1992; van Bommel, 1992). On the national level, however, there were two processes progressing simultaneously: the involved efforts to create a platform for all Muslim organisations in the Netherlands, and the establishment of rival federations of mosques, based on discrete ethnic communities.

Prior to this time, a limited number of Muslim organisations with various backgrounds (Dutch, Indonesian, Surinamese, Pakistani, Turkish and Moroccan) co-operated in the Federation of Muslim Organisations in the Netherlands (FOMON). Although FOMON could in no way formally represent the Muslims, it was the only Muslim organisation operating on the national level which tried to bring the religious and social problems of the overall Muslim minority to the notice of the Dutch public and politicians. By the end of the 1970s, however, its position was challenged by the establishment of the Turkish-Islamic Cultural Federation and the Union of Moroccan Mosques in the Netherlands. As 46 per cent of the Muslims in the Netherlands are of Turkish origin and 38 per cent are Moroccans, successful organisations within these two communities have the potential to become major forces in organised Islam in the Netherlands. The Turkish federation, which co-operated with the Directorate of Religious Affairs in Ankara (Diyanet; see Schiffauer and Amiraux in this volume), was especially to become a major force since most of the Turkish religious organisations joined it instead of the multi-ethnic FOMON.

These developments made it clear that FOMON in its old form could no longer represent – not even informally – the Muslim communities in the Netherlands. In 1980 an attempt was made to put FOMON on a new and more representative basis. During a congress attended by ambassadors of Muslim countries and 120 Dutch Muslim organisations, it was decided to abolish FOMON in its old form and let a small committee look for a structure that was acceptable for all parties. The result of the negotiations, in which the Turks played a dominant role, was a structure based on ethnic background: the seats in the board were to be distributed among the ethnic communities according to an estimation of their numbers. Moreover, the Turkish and Moroccan Muslims were to be represented by the Turkish-Islamic Cultural Federation and the Union of Moroccan Muslim Organisations in the Netherlands respectively, excluding other Turkish or Moroccan organisations. However, this newly designed structure was never put into effect and the new federation existed on paper only.

At the beginning of the 1980s, when Muslims tried to obtain access to the Dutch media, the situation can therefore be summarised as follows: (1) there was an absence of a single legal body representing the different Muslim organisations; (2) internal debates continued in Muslim organisations concerning co-operation and representation; (3) much discussion was dominated by the Turkish-Islamic Cultural Federation; and (4) this federation tried to solve the problem of representation by distribution of power along ethnic lines, they themselves representing the Turks.

BROADCASTING AUTHORISATION FOR THE TURKISH FEDERATION

In the early 1980s, Muslims applied to the Minister of Culture for a broadcasting authorisation. The main actor in this effort was the chairman of the Turkish-Islamic Cultural Federation, Mr I. Görmez, who also led the Turks in the negotiations with other Muslim organisations about co-operation. In 1980, together with a representative of the Moroccan mosque federation, he founded the Islamic Broadcasting Foundation. Its application for broadcasting time was turned down in 1981 because the IBF could not be regarded as an 'association with a spiritual root' as meant in the Broadcasting Act. Formally, this was correct beyond any doubt: judging from its articles of association, the IBF was simply a foundation with a board of three members and nothing else, even if these three happened to be leaders of Muslim organisations. But not only formal and bureaucratic arguments led the Ministry to turn down the application. An evaluation of the representativeness of the IBF was also taken into consideration and, as explained above, the period was characterised by uncertainty about the representation of Muslims on the national level.

Also in the second attempt representativeness played a decisive role. In this attempt, it was the Turkish federation which applied for a broadcasting authorisation for Islamic programmes. The Broadcasting Council – the advisory agency of the Ministry – advised in this case granting permission on the condition that the authorisation would be transferred to a supra-ethnic organisation in order to prevent Islamic broadcasting becoming purely a Turkish matter. To meet these conditions, the IBF was redefined as a broadcasting company to which Muslim organisations which obtained a broadcasting authorisation could transfer this authorisation. Thus, the way in which the churches had structured their broadcasting authorisation functioned as a model for the IBF.

Nevertheless, the Minister turned down the application because he regarded as insufficient the guarantees against a Turkish monopolisation of Muslim broadcasting time. A close look into the articles of association of the IBF do indeed raise suspicions about the intentions of the Turkish initiators of the IBF with respect to allowing it to become a broad and open platform for Muslim organisations: for instance, they could dominate the organisation simply by controlling the admission of new member-organisations.

It was only after a year of intensive lobbying and several changes in the articles that the authorities finally agreed to give the Turkish federation a broadcast authorisation on the condition that the authorisation would be transferred to the IBF. In his decree, the Minister showed his awareness of the Turkish-Islamic orientation of the federation, but he showed he was confident that the IBF would function as a platform for the various Muslim organisations. Thus, he judged, there were enough guarantees for the introduction and presentation of 'Islam' instead of just a Muslim group in the Dutch media system. This decision led to an annual allocation of 13 hours of television time and 52 hours of radio time to the federation. It also enabled the IBF financially to become an institute with paid personnel, including a director, clerical staff, translators, ten broadcasters and a chief editor.

The acceptance of the IBF by the Dutch authorities was a major success for the Turkish-Islamic Cultural Federation, half of whose biannual report for the period 1986–7 was devoted to the issue. Also, it was the personal triumph for its energetic chairman Mr Görmez, who saw his efforts rewarded with a well-paid job as director of a broadcasting institute. In some Turkish press reports the simple fact of a fully state-funded Muslim broadcasting organisation was celebrated as a major step in the institutionalisation of Islam in Europe.

In the process, the Turkish initiators had done all the work and drawn all the attention. They had negotiated with the authorities and designed an organisational structure acceptable to the Minister. The other Muslim organisations had seemingly disappeared from the scene. It was only after the success of their Turkish brothers in obtaining a broadcasting authorisation that something was heard from them. They turned out to be highly critical of the behaviour of the Turkish initiator, whose actions, they claimed, had excluded them from the IBF. Indeed they were excluded, because the IBF was turned into a platform for Muslim organisations *with a broadcasting authorisation*. But the spokesman of the largest Moroccan Muslim organisation made the interesting statement that his organisation had *refrained from applying* for a separate broadcasting authorisation because they had chosen to support the Turkish application. This suggests that he and his organisation had been unaware of the model chosen more than a year before, i.e. the model of different Muslim organisations applying for broadcasting authorisations and transferring them to the IBF.

As a result either of a seemingly deliberate monopolising attempt by the Turkish federation or of insufficient communication between them and other Muslim groups in the early 1980s, the IBF started its broadcasting as an organisation that was exclusively controlled by Turks. Moreover, within the Turkish community only the organisations co-operating with Diyanet were represented.

IBF BECOMES A MULTINATIONAL

The first two years after the broadcasting authorisation of the Turkish federation were characterised by two developments: sharp conflicts about the management of the newly established institute and attempts among other Muslim organisations to be admitted to the platform.

The internal conflicts among staff members arose from frustrations about the autocratic style of management of the director, who, according to his critics, ran the institute as a family business, dismissing employees arbitrarily and interfering in the production of programmes. In the autumn of 1988 the conflicts surfaced when the personnel, supported by the Christian National Trade Union, went on strike and occupied the IBF building. Only after the director had been forced to resign did the IBF experienced a short period of calm.

As for the non-Turkish Muslim organisations, in order to be admitted to the IBF they – like the Turkish federation before them – had to apply for broadcasting authorisations. Not all of the Muslim organisations who had criticised the monopoly of the Turks applied for a separate authorisation. But two Moroccan organisations and three organisations with a predominantly Surinamese background did.

In considering these applications, three elements played a major role the authorities' decision: the status of the applicants as 'associations with a spiritual root', an estimation of the number of Muslims involved, and a fierce public debate about the political affiliations of one the Moroccan applicants. The first criterion was used twice to turn down an application. The second criterion, too, served as a basis to reject two applications. In evaluating the representative character of Muslim organisations the authorities did not demand a formal list of members or adherents. They accepted messages of support from local mosques as proof of broad support for the Union of Moroccan Muslim Organisations in the Netherlands (UMMON). But it was here that the third element of consideration came into play.

Although UMMON is generally recognised as a federation in which the majority of the Moroccan mosques in the Netherlands co-operate, its position has always been disputed because of its loyal attitude to Moroccan government authorities and claims of its being an instrument of the Moroccan regime's attempt to control subjects abroad. They were accused of being an undercover organisation of the Amicales, the organisation established by the son of King Hassan for his subjects in Western Europe.

Two left-wing Moroccan organisations fiercely opposed the application of UMMON for a broadcasting authorisation. Their opposition came not only by way of an ideological commitment but also by way of a strategic one: they competed with UMMON for admission to a formal Dutch government advisory council for minority affairs.

Although the case against UMMON has never been strong enough for the Dutch national and local authorities to refrain from co-operating with them, it does affect the relations with, and a range of decisions about, UMMON. In this case, however, a new Media Act gave the authorities the opportunity to escape from having to decide about the nature of UMMON. The new Media Act, which came into effect on 1 January 1988, created the possibility of granting a broadcasting authorisation not just to associations with a spiritual root themselves, but also to organisations with which such associations co-operated. Therefore, the indirect construction used by the Turkish federation and the IBF became superfluous: the broadcasting authorisation could be granted to the IBF directly. The IBF responded to this new legal possibility by reopening negotiations with UMMON and a Surinamese Muslim organisation (the World Islamic Mission, WIM) about a new federative structure for the IBF and by announcing a forthcoming application for a broadcasting authorisation, this time directly to the IBF. The Commission for the Media, the organ which under the new law had to decide upon the matter, seized this opportunity to turn down all individual applications of Muslim organisations, including UMMON, 'in order to give the new initiative of the IBF a real chance'.

In the summer of 1989, the IBF was formally restructured into a platform of Muslim organisations which were regarded as representative of ethnic communities: the Turkish federation for the Turks, UMMON for the Moroccans and WIM for the Surinamese. The Turks continued, however, to have a dominant position by occupying five of the ten seats in the board. To this reorganised IBF a broadcasting authorisation was granted in 1990, with the allocated time being doubled.

THE BOARD OF THE IBF: A PROBLEMATIC COALITION

The coalition which was created had more or less been imposed upon the partners by the Dutch authorities. For the Turks, it was a condition for the continuation of their broadcasting authorisation. For the others, it was the only way to get one. But spokesmen of UMMON and WIM had in the past strongly criticised the Turkish federation and, especially, its chairman, the later director of the IBF. The departure of the disputed director provided for a new start between the three coalition partners.

The new coalition did not lead, however, to a more efficient and satisfactory management. The vacancy created by the dismissal of the director was never filled and the position of the chief editor was constantly disputed. From time to time, the personnel complained again to the trade union about their weak position, as most of the broadcasters were freelancers who worked on short-term contracts. Moreover, the lack of adequate leadership resulted in the absence of a comprehensive broadcasting policy.

In the summer of 1991 a new crisis broke out within the IBF. This crisis was related to an internal power struggle within the Turkish federation. There, an opposition group had managed to get the board dismissed by the congress and had taken over control. But the old leaders refused to give up their positions and disputed the procedures which their opponents had followed. It is hard to be sure about the real issues at stake. The opposition group claimed that the board had been infiltrated by fundamentalists and 'Grey Wolves' (adherents of the extreme nationalist Turkish party of Alparslan Türkes), but no details are known to substantiate these accusations. For half a year the federation had two groups of leaders, each claiming to be the legitimate board. The controversy was brought before the courts, where finally the new board was legitimated.

The effect of this internal controversy was immediately felt in the IBF because the dismissed leaders had appointed themselves as the Turkish representatives in the broadcasting company. There, too, they refused to give up their positions, supported in this by the Moroccan and Surinamese delegates. As a consequence, the IBF refused to accept the new Turkish representatives who were appointed by the new federation leaders. As the new leaders of the Turkish federation were to put it in a press declaration of 1 November 1992, 'for months they [the ousted individuals] conspired with fundamentalists who had infiltrated the former board of our federation' and refused to admit the 'democratically chosen leaders' and their representatives. The winning federation leaders demanded not only that their delegates to the IBF be admitted by the other IBF members, but also that all the decisions taken by the (in their eyes) illegitimate board – that is, all decisions in the second half of 1991 – be cancelled, including some changes in personnel.

This case was brought before the public courts as well, where a compromise was found to the effect that the new Turkish delegates were accepted, yet their number would be reduced to four, against the already present three Moroccans and two Surinamese. This was done so that the Turks could no longer dominate the IBF.

In conclusion, the board of the Islamic Broadcasting Foundation was an arena in which a struggle for power and jobs was going on. The balance of power shifted in the beginning of 1992 by a reduction of influence of the Turkish contingent. But in the same period it had become clear that the basis of co-operation was very weak. The new board was unable to govern the institute adequately, and in June 1992 the personnel once again protested by occupying the building. The contribution of an independent mediator helped to settle matters, but not for long.

The end of co-operation – and of the IBF – was initiated by a new controversy surounding the Moroccan federation, UMMON, beginning in the Autumn of 1992. Old accusations that UMMON was an undercover agency of the Moroccan regime, using intimidation against its opponents, were put forward by the Moroccan director of the state-funded National Centre for Foreigners. This action against UMMON attracted much public attention through a published report of the National Centre for Foreigners which detailed among Moroccans living in the Netherlands cases of intimidation for which the leaders of UMMON were held responsible (Rabbae, 1993). Although the allegations were not proven, and although some commentators suggested that they were not motivated by moral considerations but by political ones, the report had incriminated the Moroccan mosque federation. Their Turkish coalition partner in the IBF responded by publicly announcing a severance of connections with UMMON in all fields, including the IBF. This implied a stalemate on the IBF board, which had by then stopped guiding the institute. Taking the problematic history of the coalition into account, one must conclude that the UMMON affair was not the reason but only the occasion for the Turkish federation to end co-operation. The reason was both a lack of mutual trust and a loss of Turkish control over the institute.

The Commission for the Media reacted to events by forcing the IBF board to suspend its activities for half a year to put the daily management of the institute into the hands of a non-Muslim substitute director. In the meantime, research would be carried out on the possible ways in which the Muslim voice in the Dutch media could be continued. In June 1993 this research led to the conclusion that new efforts toward reconciliation of the coalition partners were not realistic. The IBF was informed that its broadcasting authorisation would not be continued in the next season.

The fact that the IBF was an arena for conflict did not stop its being a platform for presenting Islam in Dutch public space. This latter role is underscored in the following section, which describes some of the goals, contents and development of IBF programmes.

IBF PROGRAMMES

After obtaining broadcasting authorisation, the IBF started with personnel hardly qualified for the job. Only some of the broadcasters had a journalistic background or were graduates of a journalist academy. Many had to learn the basic professional skills. Due to lack of experience, the quality of the programmes was variable and some of them made an rather amateurish impression.[2] I do not intend to give a general judgement about the journalistic quality of the IBF productions, however, but will examine the goals which the IBF strived after in their programmes and the types of programmes with which they tried to attain those goals.

The goals were expressed in a report about past and present activities and future intentions of the IBF, published towards the end of their first year. In the report, the general tasks of the organisation are formulated as follows: 'With Islam as its guide-line, the IBF will have to bridge the gap between the different groups among the Muslim community in the Netherlands and at the same time between this community and the non-Muslim majority of the Dutch population. This demands a positive approach of the differences'. For the programming this implies, according to the authors, that both Islam as a religion and the social reality of Muslims in the Netherlands have to be paid attention to. Islamic faith is regarded as something shared by all Muslim groups, and has to be presented 'in its essential form'. But a sympathetic presentation of the different cultural and social traditions of the various Muslim groups is also required so as to improve mutual knowledge and understanding. The aim of improving acceptance of Muslims by the non-Muslim public leads to the rejection of missionary goals, although a reference is made to disappointment among some Dutch Muslims about this policy. Also, the relations between Islam, Christianity and Judaism – as the three Abrahamic religions – must be presented in a sympathetic way.

We have to keep in mind that these recommendations were written in the period that Turks controlled the institute. They clearly were not only meant as internal guidelines, but also as a form of public relations, in which the openness of the IBF to all Muslim groups and to the non-Muslim surroundings had to be underlined. During the internal troubles which occurred later, an IBF journalist expressed to me rather sceptical views about this document, which he regarded purely as an outward facade. Still, it is worthwhile to see to what extend the stated purposes and choices made in the report are realised in the actual programmes.

In its first four seasons the IBF broadcasted 45 minutes on radio, divided into three programmes, in Dutch, Arabic and Turkish. On television they broadcasted 15 minutes a week, in which the three languages were used. Since the fifth season, after the Moroccans and Surinamese had joined the board, the broadcasting time has been doubled. For practical reasons, I restrict myself to the television programmes and examine the choice of topics and the way they were discussed.

Short recitations from the Qur'an were a component of many IBF programmes. In addition, short prayers (*du'a*) were said in programmes during Ramadan. Apart from these, the 15-minute programmes of the first four years were usually devoted to one item, whereas in the 30-minute programmes more often a magazine with two or three items was broadcast, including a brief story for children. Apart from the recitations, *du'as* and stories for the children, in total about 420 items were presented. The topics, covered in nearly 400 programmes spanning a variety of subject categories (Table 12.1), can be described by way of three broad rubrics: (1) Islamic religion and ethics in general; (2) the situation of Muslims in the Netherlands and surrounding countries; (3) history, culture and the contemporary political situations in Muslim countries.

Programmes about Islamic Religion and Ethics

The IBF never produced a coherent series of programmes in which all the aspects of Islamic religion and ethics were presented systematically,

Table 12.1 Categories of items in the IBF programmes by season[*]

Category	Season							
	1	*2*	*3*	*4*	*5*	*6*	*7*[†]	*1–7*
Islamic doctrine	12	9	9	4	14	12	6	66
Women in Islam	5	3	–	1	4	4	3	20
Other ethical issues	1	2	2	2	6	9	1	23
Muslims in the Netherlands	22	7	7	7	20	40	22	126
Social problems of migrants	2	3	3	1	7	15	5	36
Islam in Europe	1	11	1	1	1	–	–	15
Islamic history/culture	4	7	10	15	5	8	10	59
Politics: Muslim world	1	2	3	5	7	12	10	40
Other topics	–	–	2	2	3	3	2	12
Total	48	44	37	39	67	103	59	398

[*] The categories overlap. If a programme belonged in two categories I put it in the one I regarded as being more central to the programme.
[†] For the last season, which ended September 1993, my data were incomplete.

but there was a constant flow of information, mostly connected to one or other of the Islamic feasts. This resulted in very regular attention being paid to the obligation of fasting in the month of Ramadan, the pilgrimage to Mecca, and the life of the prophet, which was dealt with annually at the occasion of *mawlud*. Also the *mi'raj*, the prophet's nightly journey to heaven, was discussed every year.

Other aspects, like the obligation of *zakat* (charity), the role of the Qur'an and hadith in Islam, or the nature and content of Islamic *sharia* (law) received far less attention. It would seem therefore, that the IBF presentation of religious information was not guided by an elaborated view about the aspects of Islam which needed explanation to the Dutch public, nor by long-term planning about the distribution of this information over the years.

In most cases, the programmes about Islam had an introductory and informative character. The information was often given by a Muslim theologian (in some cases by a non-Muslim scholar) who usually

addressed a broad audience, including non-Muslims. Other programmes – specially purchased Turkish or Arabic films – were aimed at
a Muslim public and were of an edifying nature.[3] Apart from a few of
these films, Islamic propaganda and programmes with a missionary
character were virtually absent in the IBF programmes.

If we look into the background of those who presented aspects of
Islam, it is clear that the Dutch and Turkish Muslims dominate, while
the Moroccan and Surinamese are hardly seen. Only since 1992 have a
Moroccan and a Surinamese imam contributed on a more or less
regular basis to the programmes of the IBF. So here the Turkish domination of the administration of the institute is reflected in the programming. This does not necessarily imply that theologians from other
ethnic communities were excluded, because there are other factors
involved such as availability and accessibility. But it did contribute to
the image of the IBF as being a predominantly Turkish broadcasting
organisation.

While the general principles of Islam received ample attention, the
IBF was slow in raising ethical issues. Only in its third season, were
two programmes devoted to organ transplantation, a field where tension
exists between traditional Islamic values and modern technical possibilities. The way the issue was dealt with was typical for the first years of
the IBF: a professor from the Faculty of Divinity in Ankara showed
himself a supporter of organ transplantation and explained that it was,
under certain conditions, acceptable in Islam. The programme was entitled: 'Giving from the Heart'. Two years later, after the IBF had
become a multi-ethnic organisation, the issue was discussed in a rather
different way: this was among a panel comprised of a Moroccan imam
who raised theological objections, a doctor who explained the technical
possibilities and an ex-patient who survived because of organ transplantation. The very fact that conflicting ideas were presented within
the same programme is an indication of a more professional journalistic
approach to ethical issues, even though no serious attempt was made to
confront the views in order to get the differences sharp. In general, a
tendency from general and basic information towards discussion of
issues – including some controversial ones – can be observed in the
short history of the IBF programmes. The method of confronting different views directly was, however, utilised only exceptionally. Instead, at
the end of 1991 a so called 'religious rubric' was introduced, in which
imams (in most cases a Moroccan theologian, in some cases a

Surinamese religious leader) answered questions sent in by spectators, both about religious and moral issues. The principle of *fatwa* (pronouncement) was preferred instead of the principle of discussion. The Moroccan religious specialist of the IBF clearly had a Muslim audience in mind and based his answers on the classical works of Islamic theology and law, not caring too much about how non-Muslim spectators would appreciate his words.

One specific issue raised repeatedly was that of the position of women in Islam. In the religious rubric the (male) imams gave a somewhat apologetic, but also traditional, account of the relation between men and women in Islam, including a defence of polygamy and a discussion of the issue of shaking hands with women. This last practice was permitted, according to the Moroccan imam, 'provided that no sexual desires were implied'. However, the more dominant way of dealing with the issue was giving the floor to Muslim women who tried to offer a counterweight to the general idea of inferiority of women in Islam. The visibility of headscarved and very self-confident and emancipated Muslim women in the Dutch media has been greatly increased in recent years. This development was stimulated by the presence of an Islamic broadcasting organisation.

Programmes about the Situation of Muslims in the Netherlands and Surrounding Countries

Islam as a social fact in the Netherlands and the life of Muslim individuals and groups in the country were the most discussed subjects in the first year of the IBF; however, afterwards this was overshadowed by reports about Muslims in other European countries and programmes about the Muslim world. From its fifth season of broadcasting, the Muslim in the Netherlands returned high on the agenda of the IBF.

These programmes included documentaries about the immigration of Muslims to the Netherlands, the establishment of mosques, religious education, the establishment of Islamic primary schools, ritual slaughter, the role of imams and the celebration of Islamic feasts by Muslim families in the Netherlands. In other programmes an impression was given of the experiences of Muslims living in the Netherlands: their religious and social life, and their relations with their non-Muslim surroundings. In addition, there were short reports about events within the Muslim communities, like the opening of new mosques, Qur'an recitation festivals, conferences, visits of prominent religious leaders, the publication of books about Islam, and so forth. By showing all these activities of Muslim groups and individuals to the public, the IBF ended the seeming invisibility of the Muslim religious communities in the eyes of the outside Dutch world.

Although the religious aspects of the Muslim presence received the bulk of attention, there were also programmes about social problems with or without a link with religion, such as migration policies of European countries or runaway children of migrants. The IBF had a slight tendency to 'Islamise' these social issues by labelling them as problems of Muslims or by trying to find religious aspects in them. For instance, Bosnian refugee girls were pressed by the interviewer in order to describe the importance of Ramadan in their lives, although the only thing they could talk about it was the nice food and biscuits they ate in this period.

In the coverage of the life of Muslims in the Netherlands we can observe a rather equal distribution of attention between the various ethnic groups among the Muslims, although the Moroccan community was not given proportional attention. Based on anecdotal evidence, I would ascribe this to the low accessibility of the Moroccan community for journalists, especially television broadcasters. The fear of expressing one's views before a camera is strong among the Moroccans in the Netherlands and hampers journalistic activities among them, even if the journalist is a Muslim.

More than the area of religious ideas, Islam as a social reality in the Netherlands provided an opportunity for enhancing discussion, including topics surrounding the institutionalisation of Islam and the relation between the Muslim organisations. The IBF did enhance discussions, but predominantly about issues which are controversial among the non-Muslim majority, and almost never about sensitive issues within the Muslim communities. Thus, the establishment of Islamic schools was a subject which appeared repeatedly in the IBF programmes, both in the form of impressions of the existing Islamic schools and in the form of interviews with supporters and – in some cases – opponents of those schools.

During the 'Rushdie affair', the IBF gave the floor to moderate Muslim leaders who expressed their disagreement with the *fatwa* of Khomeini and who detached themselves from anti-Rushdie demonstrations in The Hague and Rotterdam. The Gulf War was also discussed widely in IBF programmes, drawing attention to the negative impact of the war on the image of Islam in the West and to the hostile reactions with which Muslims in the Netherlands were confronted.

As for the conflicts within and between Muslim organisations, they were, until recently, hardly covered by the IBF. Unlike their Christian counterparts, the Ecumenical Broadcasting Company in the Netherlands, the IBF broadcasters did not aim to follow the Muslim leadership critically, nor did they try to analyse conflicting interests. They were not in the position to do so, because it would have required a more independent position than they actually had. A more critical treatment of Muslim organisations and their leaders would also have required a completely different style of journalistic work, as most IBF broadcasters tended not to interrupt interviewees nor to raise serious objections to their statements.

Only in its last year did the IBF broadcasters make more audacious attempts to deal with sensitive issues concerning the institutionalisation of Islam. Thus, when one of the participants of the IBF board, UMMON, was attacked for being a puppet of the Moroccan regime, the IBF produced a programme about the controversy in which the conflicting opinions were presented in a realistic way. Another example of a realistic coverage of Islam in the Netherlands was a programme about Javanese Muslims. In this community, traditional pre-Islamic customs – including a ritual meal in which the spirits of the ancestors are addressed – are cherished by some and criticised by others. Where one might have expected a condemnation of pre-Islamic elements on theological grounds, both the traditional and the puritanical tendency were shown in an objective manner.

Programmes about History, Culture and the Contemporary Political Situation in Muslim Countries

The last category in IBF programming comprises items about the Muslim world in the past and the present, social, political and cultural. Presentations of calligraphy, architecture and other forms of Islamic art were either purchased as video tapes, mostly from Turkey, or produced by the IBF on the occasion of exhibitions in European museums. Turkish films about 'Mevlana' Jalal ad-Din Rumi and about the religious life of Muslims in China ('East-Turkestan') were repeated several times.

During the summer of 1989, IBF journalists travelled with their camera teams to various Muslim countries, which resulted in a series of programmes about Pakistan, Turkey, Egypt, Tunisia and Surinam. Although these programmes were put together in one series (under the title 'Where we come from') they lacked internal cohesion, because some of the broadcasters had focused their attention entirely on history and its legacy in the form of monuments, while others gave an account of the present-day economic situation of the country visited. The conclusion must be that there had been the idea of making programmes in those countries, but little more: no agreements about the type of information to be gathered, nor a central idea upon which the series would be based.

A few other times the IBF sent camera teams abroad to collect material for documentaries about religious and cultural events, but also about political conflicts in the Muslim world. While covering dramatic events, such as the Gulf War and the drought in Somalia, the IBF followed the example of other broadcasting organisations and invited (mostly non-Muslim) experts into the studio to analyse the situation.

More often, however, coverage of conflicts had a kind of accidental character: the opportunity for the programme was often provided by a visit to the Netherlands of a politician, scientist, journalist or activist from the region in question. They were put before a camera and they talked. But these programmes were seldom guided by or based on an analysis of the problem by the responsible broadcaster or the chief editor. In short, the contribution of the IBF to this field was somewhat disappointing to Muslims and non-Muslims alike.

CONCLUSION

The granting of a broadcasting authorisation to a Muslim organisation in 1986 constituted an important event in the institutionalisation of Islam in the Netherlands. A platform was created on which Muslims could present their ideas to a large public and show the lives of their communities independently. The hope was expressed that this platform would contribute to the mutual acceptance between Muslims and non-Muslims in this country and would improve the relations between the various Muslim groups.

This last hope did not come true, as the IBF itself became a major battlefield for rival groups. Poor management and continuous internal strife prevented the IBF from becoming a stable and well-organised institute. As a result, there was no climate for developing a coherent broadcasting policy. The production of programmes could not but suffer from the tensions in the institute.

Even given more favourable conditions, however, some difficult questions would have needed an answer in order to ensure success. These are related to the way in which the Islamic identity of a broadcasting organisation can be translated into concrete choices of topics and manners of covering them. Of the three categories discussed in this paper, two were a logical consequence of being a Muslim broadcasting organisation in the Netherlands: Islamic faith and ethics, and Islam as a social fact in this country.

The presentation of Islamic faith and ethics by the IBF raises questions about who is the key informant and who is the audience. As long as one sticks to very basic information, the problem is not urgent. But for discussing complex ethical problems, more clarity is required about the role of the traditionally trained imams who function in the Dutch mosques. Does one want his *fatwa* to see what 'Islam says about a question', or does one want to show the variety of opinions among Muslims about a complex problem? Choices made in this respect are connected with the public one has in mind.

For the second category, the experiences of the IBF lead to questions of how a Muslim broadcaster can find a balance between loyalty towards the community he represents and a critical coverage of the activities of their leaders. A more independent position of broadcasters is desirable, but even then dilemmas remain about revealing or covering up sensitive issues within these communities.

Within the third category, the topics of Islamic art and culture provide a welcome opportunity for presenting a counterweight against the negative accounts of Islam in the broader, non-Muslim media. The IBF coverage of political controversies in the Muslim world, however, raises serious questions about the specific contribution which a Muslim broadcasting company in the Netherlands should make. Also here, choices have to be made between critical, probing journalism and protecting Muslim countries and their leaders against Western misunderstanding.

Notwithstanding the critical remarks that can and must be made about IBF programmes, they did enrich the Dutch media in the sense that Muslim communities were made far more visible than they had ever been before. Many of the cultural and religious events within these communities which used to pass totally unnoticed were now covered on television and radio. This holds true for various ethnic groups within the Muslim population in the Netherlands. Furthermore, the fact that public information about, and portrayal of, Islam was no longer the privilege of non-Muslim specialists is an important development. In these respects the demise of the IBF is regrettable.

The failure of the IBF did not mean the end of the Muslim voice in the Dutch media, however. In 1993 another Muslim body presented itself as an alternative. This was the Dutch Muslim Council (DMC), a council in which ten Muslim organisations from different ethnic backgrounds co-operate. As the larger Turkish–Moroccan–Surinamese coalition which had dominated the scene in the late 1980s and early 1990s had lost its credibility, DMC constituted the only alternative Muslim organisation on the national level. Although DMC includes members of the different ethnic groups which comprise the Muslim population of the Netherlands, this council is led by Muslims of Dutch origin. They argue that Islam in the Netherlands should no longer be organised along ethnic lines and that the organisational structures which were based on the ethnic divisions and numbers of the different ethnic groups no long have legitimacy.

The broadcasting authorisation which DMC received has substantially strengthened their prestige. It is not impossible that the council will also be recognised in other fields as the representative of the Muslim communities in the Netherlands, which would mean a major shift in the relative influence of the different Muslim organisations. But since only a small minority of the present Muslim organisations participate in this council, the problem of representation of Islam in the Netherlands remains far from solved.

NOTES

1. I will not enter into the discussion about whether or not the concept 'Muslim community' is a correct one in the Dutch context, where a variety of Muslim groups share a religious affiliation but are divided along ethnic and linguistic lines. The decision-makers simply took the concept to mean 'the total of the adherents of Islam', and so will I.
2. For example, a programme about Islamic education, broadcast on 5 and 12 February 1987. This resulted in a complete confusion between

Islamic primary schools and Islamic instruction in the framework of the lessons entitled 'Own Language and Culture' for migrant children in ordinary Dutch schools.

3.   The IBF has often been criticised for depending heavily on outside, purchased productions instead of making their own programmes for which their journalists were paid. A simple count can contradict this criticism: of the 398 items examined for this paper, 335 were IBF productions. It is true, however, that the purchased films were the longer ones, used to fill the long Ramadan programmes.

REFERENCES

Landman, N. (1992) *Van mat tot minaret. De institutionalisering van de islam in Nederland* (Amsterdam: vu-Vitgeverij).

Rabbae, M. (1993) *Naast de Amicales nu de UMMON. De mantelorganisaties van de Marokkaanse autoriteiten in Nederland* (Utrecht: Nederlands Centrum Buitenlanders).

van Bommel, A. (1992) 'The History of Muslim Umbrella Organizations', in W. A. R. Shadid & P. S. van Koningsveld (eds), *Islam in Dutch Society: Current Developments and Future Prospects* (Kampen, The Netherlands: Kok Pharos).

13 Turkish Islamic Associations in Germany and the Issue of European Citizenship

Valérie Amiraux

Most research on questions of immigration and Europe regard immigrants as victims of 'obscure forces they cannot understand' (Leveau, 1989). These studies usually focus upon common European policies concerning the flow of immigrants, the uniformity of natural-isation requirements, or the definition of the right to asylum. In the fol-lowing study, I choose an alternative point of view, not only dealing with the political management of the presence of foreign populations in Europe, but also studying the reactions of immigrant people themselves to the construction of the idea of 'Europe' and especially to the setting up of one of the most controversial aspects of the 1991 Maastricht Treaty on Economic and Monetary Union (EMU), the definition of European citizenship. Such an approach is premised on the idea that every study concerning migration necessarily involves structural issues such as citizenship, nationality, the capacity of nation-states as host-countries to assimilate a certain number of persons into the national area, and the recognition or acceptance of collective mediation.

Here, 'citizenship' as a concept helps identify the discrepancy between the idea of citizenship as activity and, the predominant modern understanding, citizenship as status. This involves, further, a more tra-ditional question concerning the separation between citizenship, the right to vote and the process of naturalisation (that is, change of cultural and national references to become a citizen). In this study, notions of citizenship have been chosen within the context of migration research, both as a means of exploring attitudes of four Islamic associations, and as a rhetorical tool.

Although arrived at with no little difficulty, there are now no more obstacles to the actual application of the Maastricht Treaty. The acceptance of the Maastricht Treaty by the member states of the European Union has been accomplished with the help of referenda (in Denmark, France, Ireland, Greece) or by parliamentary process (in Great Britain and Germany). Germany was the last country to give its position on the Treaty, finally announcing in October 1993 that the Treaty is in accordance with its constitution. The idea of European integration, which had quite abstract political premises until now, seems to have become a reality.

Through the European unification process, Maastricht aims to create a transnational collective power which, through the creation of a European citizenship, will give rise to two categories of Europeans who vote and the others who do not yet vote. These categories will result, for the first time, in the partial recognition of a right derived from residence. As explained in the Maastricht Treaty (7 February 1992), article 8:

Every European citizen has the right to move ... freely.   (8a, p. 6)

Every citizen who is resident of a member state in which he is not a national has the right to vote and the right to be elected.   (8b, p. 6)

While formally recognising the linkage of rights for citizens, this dimension of the official process of European integration carries with it the basic fact that non-Europeans are excluded from social and political recognition.

Local understandings, forms of refusal and acceptance of Maastricht-constructed 'European' citizenship have varied considerably. Here, I assess ways in which different Turkish-Islamic associations based in Germany have engaged supranational concepts such as 'European citizenship' by way of their own mobilisation strategies (for recognition, participation and representation, legal equality, special rights) in a European, even global, system, while their specific claims are still focused on local levels of the federal state (especially regarding religious education in state schools and formal legal recognition as *Körperschaft des öffentlichen Rechts*, or public corporate bodies; see the Introduction to this volume).

The groups described are perhaps the most representative Turkish-Islamic associations in Germany. These are the three largest Germany-wide Muslim organisations – Avrupa Milli Görüs Teskilatları (AMGT), Süleymancı and Diyanet Isleri Türk Islam Birligi (DITIB) – plus one large local organisation, the Islamic Federation of Berlin (IFB). These four were chosen for study because they represent key tendencies of organised Turkish Islam in Germany (see also Schiffauer, in this volume).

AMGT presents itself as, in the words of its General Secretary Hassan Özdogan, 'the biggest non-state Islamic association' in Germany (interview 9 April 1992). Its origins importantly lay in Turkish party politics. For reasons of non-conformity with the national requirements of secularism, the National Order Party (Milli Nizam Partisi) was prohibited in Turkey in 1971; although re-established as the National Salvation Party (Milli Salamet Partisi) it was once again prohibited in 1980. Since 1976 the AMGT has been established in Cologne, where, in a variety of ways, it was easier to develop political activities none the less directed toward Turkey. Today AMGT is a subsidiary of the Welfare Party (Refah Partisi) in Turkey, which had considerable electoral success in March 1994 by winning twenty-six towns and cities including Ankara and Istanbul. In Turkey the Refah Partisi is known for campaigning for the adoption of the *Shari'a* as Turkish constitutional law. In Germany, where the AMGT comprises thirty branches and 200 sister associations, the politics of its leaders is aimed at securing the status of *Körperschaft des öffentlichen Rechts* for Islam so that Muslims can 'be officially exempted from the legal order and allowed to follow the Shari'a instead' (Abdullah, 1989, pp. 438–9).

The 'official' Islamic organisation in Germany is Diyanet Isleri Türk Islam Birligi (the Turkish-Islamic Union for Religion), or DITIB. In Turkey DITIB manages religious affairs in the name of the state. Therefore DITIB officials are state employees; in Germany, where DITIB first appeared (in Berlin) in 1982, its representatives are controlled by the Turkish consulate. While at present DITIB in Germany is responsible for sixteen cultural associations and officially almost 10 000 members could be registered, one of its primary roles is to control, on behalf of the Turkish secular state, what it considers 'Islamic deviance'.

Representing a mystical rather than political tendency, the branches of the Süleymancı are in Germany usually referred to as

Islamische Kultur Zentren (IKZ). The Süleymancıs, whose founder
was Süleyman Hilmi Tunahan (1888–1959), have since 1925 organised their main activities in Turkey around education and religious
training of young people. This Süleymancı speciality still has the
support of the IKZ's considerable network of Qur'an schools,
throughout Germany. For example, in 1979 – seven years after their
arrival in Germany – IKZ offered some 1500 courses for 50 000
Muslim pupils (Özcan, 1989).

Finally, the Islamic Federation of Berlin was founded in 1980. It
differs from the other Islamic associations in its composite structure
(although it must be pointed out that the IFB's ideological tendency is
parallel to that of AMGT). Specific to Berlin, the IFB aims at organising the visibility of a collective cultural identity – in this case, Islam –
by using its special capacity for liaison with local government
authorities in Berlin.

The Turkish community in Germany has inherited a variety of social,
political and religious trends reflecting those affecting Islam in Turkey
itself (Amiraux, 1994). Given the nature of the secular state in Turkey,
Islam has for long been excluded as a legitimate political idiom. The
advocates of Islam in Turkey, therefore, have had to foster and to
bolster expressions of Islam within a predominantly secular milieu.
Tension has also been reproduced among the Turkish diaspora, where
many Muslim activists direct attention and energy toward the situation
in Turkey itself (see Schiffauer in this volume). At the same time,
however, the latter do not forget that Turkish Muslims live as residents
in Europe and have some specific advantages coming from this situation. 'As persons, as families, we want our rights. For example,
freedom of confession and also the possibility to make the prayer and
to practice the religion we want. We've got it here for 90 per cent ... in
our own countries, we haven't got it 100 per cent' (DITIB, Cologne,
13 April 1992).

The reconstruction of Islam by Turkish associations in Germany
takes the form of a synthesis of Islamic and Turkish elements. This is
combined with a strategy of collective mobilisation of Turks in
Germany based on identification with Islam as a common denominator.
Motivations toward Turkish-Islamic synthesis and strategies are shared
particularly by AMGT and IFB (Süleymancıs are 'pietistic' rather than
political) – while they are considered by the DITIB as manifestations of
'Islamic deviance'. For the advocates of Turkish Islam, the same kinds

of functions performed by political parties in Turkey are undertaken by associations in the diaspora.

In Germany the concept of 'association' authorises the legal recognition of an informal collection of interests, and constitutes the visible, organic and functional expression of a common strategy of identification. An association also helps to gather people in cities into organised structures in order to maintain certain religious, ethnic and cultural aspects of their identity. For ethnic minorities generally, associations embody a level of identity option. Of central importance to many of these are spaces of socialisation where identity is reproduced and concentrated. In the case of Turkish-Islamic associations in Germany, the choice is oriented toward creating and maintaining special spaces such as schools, prayer rooms, mosques, libraries, sport clubs, leisure clubs, radio, and printed media. In comparison with Islamic associations among Muslims in many other places around Europe, these Turkish-Islamic associations, spaces and activities in Germany are not particularly spiritually oriented but, rather, are concerned with a broad range of urban experiences. The reason why I selected these four associations is that they are not only representative of the diversity of Turkish-Islam in Germany, but also because they have dynamic roles in relation to the urban ecology of the host country and to the immigration experience through their part in neighbourhoods and as agencies of solidarity.

My research was carried out in 1991 and 1992, thus before the escalation of anti-foreigner violence in Germany such as witnessed in Solingen (May–June 1993). I tried to find out what the reaction of these associations was to the very concrete construction of Europe as far as citizenship is concerned. At the outset of the study there were no official statements from any of the four associations regarding 'European' policies. My observations on the Turkish-Islamic associations' responses to the creation of a European citizenship (on top of national citizenship) are by way of specific rather than generalised phenomena; that is, I examine particular aspects of a localised German political reality. Ultimately, however, I am concerned with the question of how, at a European level, a religious concern expresses itself amongst people who are fighting for the recognition of their cultural identity. How far are the four associations concerned with the construction of Europe?

In this article, two co-existing visions of Europe among Turkish-Islamic associations are described, one positive and one negative.

Given that the common feelings among the Turkish-Islamic associations reflect apprehensions arising from the local conditions of the
Turkish Muslims' everyday lives set against the ongoing construction
of 'Europeanness', we may analytically abstract two tendencies: the
first is a negative one of 'local situation-European projection,' the
second is a positive one of 'European situation-local projection.'

THE DISCRETE DENIAL OF EUROPEAN STAKES

The discourse relating to the 'negative tendency' involves a number of
constructions by way of which the associations project their own political and social experience of the local situation in Germany towards the
European transnational context. In their view, this means rejecting the
new European order as a perceived enlargement of obstacles for recognition–participation which prevail at a local level in Germany. In this
respect, the fall of the Berlin Wall seems to prefigure the associations'
apprehensions, in turn causing their rejection of the European
construction.

Particularly since 1989, Germany has struggled increasingly with
questions surrounding immigration. Prior to constitutional changes, the
country accepted more refugees than any other European country:
256 112 in 1991 (compared, for example, to 47 000 in France) – 61.5
per cent of whom were from Eastern Europe. With this sudden influx of
people from the former Eastern bloc, a hierarchy has emerged among
the different types of immigrants. Instead of coming to terms with this
historical consequence of a recent past, 'the Germans have begun to
create more problems for foreigners in general', according to the
General Secretary of the AMGT (interview, 9 April 1992). Here and
now, the problem concerns the coexistence of three groups of alien
populations: the *Ausländer* ('foreigners'), *Aussiedler* (ethnic German
Nationals originating from Eastern Europe) and *Übersiedler* (Germans
from ex-DDR). Czarina Wilpert (1991, p. 53) explains:

> While the debate continued about how to assimilate or integrate for-
> eigners into German society, the presence of Aussiedler and
> Übersiedler emigrating from the East became more visible every day.
> Since 1987 the numbers of ethnic Germans emigrating from the East
> had been increasing dramatically. Altogether in 1990 some 397,073

entered the country, 20,000 more than in 1988 and four times as many in 1987. The Volga Deutsch from the Soviet Union were a mere 14,488 in 1987 but 147,950 in 1990. At the same time, while in 1987 some 48,000 ethnic Germans came from Poland, the number had multiplied sixfold by 1989 reaching over 250,000 that year.

This new wave of immigration from the East (including a large number of Balkan refugees) has not improved the status of the long-standing foreigners, who in Germany 'face a system of institutionalised discrimination that bars them from a wide range of occupations in the public sectors' (Baimbridge *et al.*,1994, p. 426). The latter remain stigmatised as inherently external elements, firstly as Turks, and secondly as Muslims. 'We arrived in Germany as *Gastarbeiter* [guestworkers], we today live there as *Ausländer* [foreigners]' explains a Turkish doctor. It is interesting to notice that these two Germans words (*Ausländer* and *Gastarbeiter*) designating immigrants are themselves used by immigrants. 'Germany's language of migratory phenomena is unique', Wilpert (1991, p. 49) observes. 'No other country includes such a plethora of serial categories, specific terms which reveal the extreme diversity of legal rights and access to membership: *Gastarbeiter, Ausländer, ausländische Arbeitnehmer, Migranten aus der ehemalige Anwerbeländer, ausländische Mitbürger, Aussiedler, Übersiedler, Fluchtling, Asylanten, wirtschafts Asylanten.*'

My own Turkish informants make the same distinctions and place themselves somewhere in the hierarchy, considering newcomers in terms of whether they are expatriates of German origin or non-Germans. Many informants drew parallels between the making of Europe and the fall of the Berlin Wall, involving opening of borders and the arrival of a new category of people, neither totally German, nor totally foreign. Questions of vocabulary and rebirth of oriental migration waves suggests the notion of 'migratory concurrence'.

At the same time, this hierarchy of inter-migration (in legal designation) shows very clearly how Turkish populations are excluded from the historical construction of the German nation. German history has its victims (*Aussiedler* and *Übersiedler*) for whom the country should provide compensation. Since the 'Fall of the Wall', history has reasserted itself. But what Turks are reproaching is less this 'historical reparation' than the idea that *Aussiedler* and *Übersiedler* arrive today with the same profile Turks had thirty years ago (that is to say other political culture, other language, other *Weltanschauung*) – but with automatic rights to which Turks still don't have. Neverthless, one Turkish professor of theology claims, 'Turks who live here don't have migrant-problems anymore. There are very few new Turks coming here and those who are here are no longer associated with the problems of first migration waves' (at DITIB, Cologne, 13 April 1992).

The four associations in question all identify a connection between the German reunification and the process of European integration. But the significance of 'Fall of the Wall' can be seen in the parallel drawn between the inflow of people of a new category neither completely German nor completely foreign, and the process of European integration, thus realising a kind of 'mini-Europe'. The already established immigrants consider these inflows as being direct competitors for their political and social rights. The associations mention, for example, the problems of citizenship rights being reserved to those ethnic groups recognised as more authentic and legitimate. 'We thought: Germans should be happy because of the realisation of the unification. They will live together in the end. But in fact, what did happen? The Germans have started to make more problems for foreigners [*Ausländer*] in general' (AMGT's General Secretary, 9 April 1992). And it's particularly relevant for the *Aussiedler* issue (especially because the *Aussiedler* still have German nationality according to the article 116-§1 of the German Constitution). According to one of the leaders of the IFB, the *Aussiedler* 'have a German passport. They consider themselves German – although they don't speak German – and they shout: Foreigners out!'

All four associations complain internally about the competitive aspect resulting from this new political situation without contesting the political pattern which is judged legitimate on the whole. In a Europe where the current configuration already presents serious difficulties for minorities, they discuss the process of Europe's opening-up to the East, without being able to construct a satisfactory overview of the subject. That is to say, there is no single emergent discourse on Europe and immigration among or within the Muslim associations, except to say that they perceive ever more obstacles to recognition-participation. Similarly, they fail to suggest any real ideological solution to the problem, even when they are making some general hypothesis about the way political national authorities could respond. The associations commonly express, for example, the view that if there are nationals with a right to citizenship (Germans from the East), why shouldn't there be a citizenship for others independent of German nationality? If the situation in Germany is as it is, why should it be different at a European level? It remains that the representatives of the different associations take the German model and its profound tradition of cultural differentiation as a reference, and base their claims and range of manoeuvre within Europe on this model.

The four associations point out that obtaining German citizenship is easier for people considered as more authentic and legitimate than traditional immigrants. 'They're asking less for nationality than citizenship', Leca (1990, p. 20) points out, 'and this less because of a civic wish to exercise political rights in a national community to which they identify, than because of the national wish to exercise a power which will guarantee their social security.' However, in Germany, where cultural presumptions underlie access to rights, an 'acculturation postulate' constitutes the main barrier to naturalisation (Fijalkowski, p. 1989). The leaders of the Islamic associations raise the challenge of differentiating citizenship and nationality, a challenge posed by political scientists as well:

> Nationality and citizenship complete themselves. Without a common national identity, there is nothing to make people meet, and no reason to give citizenship only to nationals and not to the others.... . Nationality gives them common identity which allows them to imagine the common construction of their world. Citizenship give them the possibilities to do it. (Miller, in Leca, 1990, p. 52)

Nationality alone no longer makes sense in the construction of Europe, while religion is emerging as a new axis of mobilisation. For many Muslims, the rejection of the European system as a whole correlates to a more general form of rejection which relates to a fear of excessive cultural totalisation, by way either of a complete integration–assimilation of migrants or their complete exclusion. In this sense, Islamic identity is a critical instrument for an active resistance to the process of inclusion–fusion. In effect, by mobilising Islamic identity particularly in the face of the influx of Eastern European migrants, the associations are working to ensure their control of their own 'system of acting', in the Parsonian sense of pattern maintenance (stability of the cultural model, maintenance and reproduction of values, of symbolic systems) and strategies toward the realisation of collective objectives (Parsons, 1953). For these associations, Islamic specificity is the expression of the will to stay at the head of their own system of action, more than a real mobilisation for an Islamic government in Germany. It is the wish of not being deprived of what is their very distinctiveness. Religion seems to be the last place for strong demands in a European context where nationality and citizenship, and in general a host of classic political concepts and categories, are increasingly problematic.

A related question therefore arises: to what extent can the particularities of the Turkish community and the practice of the Islamic religion be tolerated in Germany and then in Europe? The narrow-mindedness of the Germans with regard to the presence and visibility of alien populations still prevails: this includes a fear of 'dangerous classes' or marginal groups and their different behaviours, and a kind of helplessness or disarray when confronted with certain life styles. These are constant reminders of 'the other' in a destabilising and radical way, which are assumed to be latent symptoms of social breakdown in the host country.

The rejection by Turkish-Islamic associations of assimilationist demands is one of the bases for this negative attitude towards the construction of 'Europe'. In their view, Europe means assimilation and negation of national and cultural particularities. These views towards the construction of Europe, which are negative in the sense that they foresee a worsening situation for Muslim populations, are projections based on the experience of local specific situations. Yet among the members of the four Islamic associations interviewed, there were also expressed some positive views of the future of Muslim Turkish people *vis-à-vis* European initiatives.

MOBILISATION AND ACTION WITHIN A 'YES STRATEGY'

A second, paradoxical trend displayed by the Turkish-Islamic associations is a 'favourable attitude' towards the construction of a single European political field. This was not really proposed by way of any concrete argument, but rather as a wish to exploit certain aspects of the initiatives surrounding European unity in favour of the people they represent.

In the views of the spokesmen for the associations, some of these initiatives are considered to be beneficial to the local and national situation of Turkish Muslim people living in Germany. They have positive perceptions of the future place of Islam in a united Europe, drawing upon potential aspects of multiculturalist policies, the emergence of new action fields within – or gates of entry into – public space, and the exercise of new modes of collective mobilisation.

Although European integration seems to imply coexistence as a big international community, immigration and 'minorities questions' are still very often subject to cultural and religious hierarchy: that is, a person's rights and status are affected by their cultural and religious distance from an assumed European Christian model. For the four associations, Europe presents itself clearly as a Christian majority. According to one informant, 'we are obviously here in Europe a minority, and we think that if somebody is Jewish or Christian, he has less problems than we Muslims ... and Turkey will never be tolerated in Europe because Europe is a Christian community' (in FIB, 23 April 1992).

This perception is bolstered by the fact that the German state and the religious bodies are not entirely separate, as in France. In Germany, the only legal attempt to separate church and state was made during the Revolution of 1848 when it was discussed in connection with reformulating the Constitution, but this was never enacted. So that today state and church are really seen as partners in several domains (see Hartweg, 1995). In this context, then, it is logical that the first aim of three of the four associations we spoke with (IKZ, AMGT, FIB) is the right for Islam to have the similar status of a *religiöse Körperschaft des öffentlichen Rechts*. As explained by the legal attaché of the FIB, there is a list of eighteen religious groups which have received this status. Inequality between Islam and other religions could be improved through the European process: 'The hope is to finally see Islam put on the same level as other monotheistic religions' said a member of the AMGT.

The *de facto* multiculturalism of Europe and modern Germany, given that they are societies comprised of people from a variety of cultural backgrounds, is considered by the Turkish-Muslim associations as a positive influence. A major issue of the ongoing debate on immigration in Germany, however, is the denial of such a multicultural reality. 'Muslims hardly receive the protection of the government on the cultural, social and religious level', says a member of AMGT (10 April 1992). 'This situation reflects the German political situation.'

The notion of Europe as a multicultural context is nowadays more popular and politically attractive than the notion of minority integration. Multiculturalism means cultural autonomy and integrity – although this is difficult to operationalise in a Europe which is suspicious of, and which hardly knows or understands, Islam. The people we spoke to rebel against the lack of knowledge and ignorance which make the minority of Islamic believers victims. 'They say that the Qur'an is opposed to the *Grundgesetz* [Basic Law, or Constitution], but in my opinion' said a representative of AMGT, 'there is no more contradiction there than in the Bible or the Torah.'

Islam is not legally recognised like other confessions in spite of the fact that it's not really a new religion for Germany (see Abdullah, 1989). What we may call 'a new Christendom' has the monopoly on authority (in other words, on 'legitimate violence'). This is another field whereby informants thought that certain negative conditions for Muslims could improve through European integration. On the one hand, this would involve the possibility of levelling the statuses of religions and, on the other, the possibility of defending against state trends which seek to limit Islam completely to a private sphere. Even when there is no will to bring Islam into the political structure of the host countries, the associations (except DITIB) made it clear that limiting Islam to a strict private level is not positive at all. A re-visualised public European space should be created to accept Islam like other religions in Germany. The previously quoted theology professor and member of the DITIB explains that 'the most important thing is not that we recognise Christians, but that the Christians recognise us'.

In this respect, the historical legacy of Islam is taken as a model for the coexistence of a multiplicity of confessions. 'Islam has developed an art of living with Christians, Jews and Muslims', the imam for the IFB points out (24 April 1992), 'which is written down in the Qur'an. The Christians have no experience of living with the Muslims in their own territories, whereas Muslims do.'

The debate surrounding the question of the legal recognition of Islam is convincingly and energetically developed among all four associations. As part of the strategy for effecting change, the school – perceived as the main agent of socialisation – has emerged as one of the key sites of struggle, especially for the Süleymancı. This is important at two levels: first of all, school is aimed at the very young. Assimilation appears to be a central function of German education in order to maintain the German national culture. The reaction of the Turkish-Islamic associations has been to adopt a supervising strategy of religious reproduction; that is to say, to develop independent Islamic education. In this way, schools are the ideal way to transmit Islamic cultural capital, to adults and children alike, not in opposition with the German system, but in parallel with it.

An associated demand, then, is to run religious courses within German schools. This would have to be developed in line with the change in legal status for Islam in Germany. 'In Berlin', explains FIB's imam (24 April 1992), 'working on Islam is important: at school, nothing had been done, we try to create religious courses, just as Catholics, Protestants or Jews do. 28,000 Turkish children go to school in Berlin and we still don't have any [Islamic] religious courses. We want them to receive a religious education just as believers of other confessions do.'

Other aspirations concerning all four associations involve basic rights given by the European citizenship such as freedom to circulate, dual-nationality, and eligibility to vote. Following European integration, these rights should be negotiable at a local level. It is clear that the pragmatic motivations of the associations show great presence of mind in this unforeseen situation of inheriting benefits coming from a growing European citizenship. They have hopes of turning the situation to their advantage on the concrete level of active participation in state life.

CONCLUSION

The idea of a multicultural Germany and even of a multicultural Europe is no longer seen as temporary, but as permanent. In this context, religion (specifically Islam) must be seen as a social and cosmopolitan vehicle and can no longer be considered as a strictly private affair. The challenge is not for Europe to deal with strong national and religious identities which are being pushed by this European movement, but for those associations to whom we have spoken to manage this new European ideal as imposed from outside.

Religion performs certain political, as well as social, symbolic and esoteric functions. 'The aim of Islam is the wealth of everyone', stated one informant. 'How can we reach our aim without politics?'

Consequently, mobilisation emerges through negotiations based on collective interests of representative organisations; their conversion into special pressure groups takes place as leaders lobby governmental machinery to address collective concerns.

Despite their presence in many European countries, the activities of IKZ, the AMGT and the DITIB are mostly oriented to national or local arenas. Moreover, for many, Turkey actually remains the primary focus for Islamic-political demands. Even if the AMGT in Germany refuses every kind of official identification with the Refah, for example, it is clear that the actual force of this party is based on the capacity of reconstruction of the network in exile. Refah's presence in Germany could be seen as a kind of 'context effect', not determining the political aims of Islamic associations – which are still directed towards Turkey – but rather conditioning broad cultural aspects of Turkish Muslim migrants' lives.

In this study I have described ways in which Turkish-Islamic associations in Germany view themselves as interlocutors and actors within an emerging European system while their specific claims remain locally based. In spite of the strong political differences between the four associations (especially concerning DITIB, whose activities are largely controlled by the Turkish state), I discovered a real convergence of interests between the four associations as they display a certain unity in their various conceptions of emergent 'Europe', Immigrants are generally more interested in gaining citizenship than nationality, and European citizenship may make the Islamic aspect of community notions more important than ethnic identity. All four associations really wish for Muslims to gain a place in public space regardless of their national status. A recognised place in 'Europe' – particularly through citizenship – could provide for this.

BIBLIOGRAPHY

Abdullah, M. S. (1989) 'Islam and Muslim Minorities in the Federal Republic of Germany', *Journal of the Institute of Muslim Minority Affairs*, 10, pp. 438–49.

Abdullah, M. S. (1993) *Was will der Islam in Deutschland?* (Gütersloh: Gütersloher Verlagshaus Gerd Mohn).

Amiraux, V. (1994) 'Les transformations de l'identité islamique turque en Allemagne', in G. Kepel (ed.), *Exils et Royaumes, les appartenances au monde arabo-musulman aujourd'hui* (Paris: FNSP) pp. 385–98.

Baimbridge M., B. Burkitt and M. Macey (1994) 'The Maastricht Treaty: Exacerbating Racism in Europe?', *Ethnic and Racial Studies*, 17, pp. 420–41.

Fijalkowski, J. (1989) 'Les obstacles à la citoyenneté: immigration et naturalisation en RFA', *Revue Europenne des Migrations Internationales*, 5, pp. 33–45.

Hartweg, F. (1995) 'Eglise, Etat et Société', in M. Le Gloannec (ed.), *L'Etat de l'Allemagne* (Paris: La Découverte) pp. 264–7.

Leca, J. (1990) 'Nationalité, citoyenneté dans l'Europe des immigrations', paper presented at the Colloque pour la Fondation Agnelli, Torino.

Leveau, R. (1989) 'Immigrés, Etats et Sociétés', *Revue Europenne des Migrations Internationales*, 5, pp. 113–25.

Özcan, E. (1989) *Türkische Immigrantenorganisationen in der Bundesrepublik Deutschland*. (Berlin: Hitit).

Parsons, T. (1953) *Working Papers in the Theory of Action* (New York: The Free Press).

Wilpert, C. (1991) 'Migration and Ethnicity in a Non-immigration Country: Foreigners in a United Germany', *New Community*, 18, pp. 49–62.

Part V
Afterword

14 Muslims in Europe into the Next Millennium

Jørgen S. Nielsen

There is a widespread feeling that we are at the present time experiencing a period of rapid change of historical proportions. The collapse of communism and the sudden flurry of attempts to settle long-standing tensions, such as those in South Africa and Palestine, combine with the outbreak of new categories of crisis, such as those in Bosnia and Central Asia, to give a sense of an historical turning point. Ideas of the 'end of history' and a new 'clash of civilisations' appear in prestigious publications across the Atlantic.

Historically there has always been a tendency for millennarian and apocalyptic movements to appear towards the end of a century. But the temptation is not alien to usually more balanced individuals. Towards the end of the nineteenth century, Western churches were talking of the 'Christianisation' of the world by the year 1900. Today some Muslims are talking of the Islamisation of the world by the year 2000 – ignoring the fact that their own new century already started thirteen years ago.

Clearly there is something of this artificial '*fin de siècle*' emotion coming through in such atmospherics, and both religious and political leaders seek to mobilise this to their own ends – and it does make for a snappy title for an article! But there is also substance behind the noise, and the fact that this substance places itself in the 1990s (another artificial chronological period) is coincidental.

Other chapters in this volume present aspects of the situation of Muslims in Europe and developments in that field in more detail than I even begin to suggest here. The task I shall attempt is to seek to identify some of the overarching characteristics of the theme of this volume and to identify some of the factors which are at play in setting constraints and helping to determine future directions. This entails drawing out aspects both of the historical baggage and of forces currently at play.

THE INHERITANCE

The immediate background of the presence of Muslims in Western Europe is familiar. Early small-scale settlement starting in the eighteenth and nineteenth centuries was superseded by large-scale labour immigration as European industry expanded in the economic revival after 1945. As the search for sources of labour spread ever further out, it did so along the routes of imperial connections – and I include here the German–Turkish connection. As it did so, the result was that the majority of immigrants into Western European industrial cities coming from outside Europe originated in Muslim cultures, the only major exceptions being people from the Caribbean in Britain and Hindus and Sikhs of South Asian origin in the Netherlands and Britain. Their children, born in Europe, are now growing up – or have grown up and established their own families – and have, on the whole, refused to follow the path of assimilation often predicted for them by observers three decades ago.

Outside Eastern Europe, the background of the Muslim presence there is less well known. The most significant aspect is, of course, that the presence of Muslim communities in this region is centuries old. Consequent upon the Mongol conquests and the establishment of Mongol successor states in the thirteenth and fourteenth centuries, Muslim communities were established across European Russia: principally the Tatars of the Volga river basin and the areas around the Black Sea. In fact, there was Muslim settlement in the Volga Bulgar kingdoms even before that, over a thousand years ago. The establishment of the Ottoman empire from the fourteenth century in South-eastern Europe led to the creation of Turkish, Albanian and Slavic-speaking Muslim communities across the Balkans. In the case of Russia, as it expanded eastward and re-established its power under the Soviet banner after 1917, it also absorbed colonial Muslim populations, although here the relationship was somewhat disguised, compared to the West European experience, because the territories occupied were contiguous rather than overseas or *outre-mer*.

In the encounter between the European states and the Muslim minorities, however they may have come about, two particular historical paradigms or modes of thinking (*Weltanschauungen*?) have had a long-term bearing on realities in particular areas and at particular times. Both have arisen out of peculiar historical circumstances. On the one hand is the European nation state and on the other, and more ancient, is a complex of Muslim models of state and religion.

Compared to the majority of the regions of the world historically, Europe has developed a unique relationship between community, state and government. The origins can be traced centuries back, but the real foundations of the modern European nation state were laid roughly in the period 1750–1900. Political power had moved from a precarious balance based on the medieval church–monarch duality resting on control of the landed economy to a situation where the initiative was in the hands of urban-based merchants and new industrialists. Regional divergencies were absorbed into a new centrally led state, and the new urban industrial working classes together with traditional provincial communities were co-opted into a new national project. Recalcitrant provincials had their energies diverted into the imperial projects which the merchants and industrialists needed to market their goods and whence they increasingly often obtained their raw materials. Universal obligatory education enabled the formation of a national culture, part of whose content were the historical tribal myths of the romantic movement. Political and military events through the eighteenth and nineteenth centuries became imbued with, and in turn imbued, this development of a 'national consciousness'. Suddenly it was discovered that there were such entities as the German or French or Italian people, entities whose roots could then be discerned in the past with the benefit of hindsight – and a good dose of poetic licence.

The context in which this nation state project arose was one which had already for centuries, under the banner of Christianity, shown itself markedly intolerant of difference of religion. Byzantine Orthodoxy had hereticised and persecuted Eastern Christian churches up until the Arab Muslim conquests of its provinces in the Middle East. The Christianisation of Russia had often been a barbaric process of forced conversions. Western Catholic Europe had found its identity and self-certainty in the aggressive adventures of Crusade, *reconquista* and massacres of Jews, and the independence of Northern European absolute monarchies of the sixteenth and seventeenth centuries was based in the religious wars of the Reformation and the 1648 Peace of Westphalia principle of *cuius regio eius religion* ('the people's religion is that of the ruler').

The new nations abandoned the obsession with religion but they replaced it with the 'people' or '*das Volk*' or some other kind of descent-based collectivity, usually defined by common language (helped along by universal education), law and tribal myth. There were not too many steps from this to the racial mythology of the likes of Alfred Rosenberg and Houston Stewart Chamberlain.

The idea of the nation as a determinant of collective political identity and action spread eastward into the Ottoman Empire. The carrier of the idea was the spread of urban-based education independent of the religious institutions: literacy and intellectual activity asserted their independence from the church. In the process new secular written languages and professions appeared, and so did independent Balkan nations – first the Greeks but soon followed by Serbs, Bulgarians and Romanians, and then most tragically by the Armenians.

Nationalism also spread into other parts of Eastern Europe, although here it ran up against Russian nationalism. Here, at one level, close connections with German intellectual developments had already laid secular foundations for a Russian consciousness with a marked expansionist component and feeling of superiority. At the same time, mystical traditions of Russian Orthodox spirituality were contributing to the process of national myth formation.

Into this complex of Central and East European history, Marxist concepts of hierarchies of nations – concepts further developed by Lenin for sometimes dubious motives before they were blatantly abused by Stalin – provided ideological legitimisation in the Soviet-dominated post-1945 Europe for policies which suppressed forms of collective political identity and action unacceptable to the Soviet Communist party leadership.

One extreme interpretation of this whole history might be that the exclusive intolerance of medieval Christendom was directly inherited by the secular ideologies of the nation state and of Nazi and Soviet ideological dictatorships: an uncomfortable thought for most of us.

But there is another side to the inheritance, namely the Muslim. At first sight, and given a serious historical perspective, this seems so much more positive than that of European Christendom suggested above. Virtually from its inception as an historical reality, Islam was a religion identified with political power. One common image is that of the foundation of the Islamic state with the move (*hijra*) of the Prophet Muhammad to Medina in CE 622. Certainly the Arab expansion out of the Arabian peninsular in the period CE 630–56 was imbued with Islamic enthusiasm, and Islam set the criteria by which the Arab Caliphate, stretching from North Africa to Central Asia, sought to organise itself and by which its government was criticised. But the vast majority of the newly subject populations were not Muslim, neither did they become Muslim except through a very slow process extending over many centuries.

Thus, from the beginning, Islam and its theoreticians and practitioners had to come to terms with the challenges of wielding political power over communities which did not share the presuppositions of their rulers. An assumption that there might be room within the polity for communities different from the dominant one was thus built into the fundamental paradigms of Islam, referring to the Qur'anic passages of tolerance as being of more general validity than those of intolerance. With the passage of time, as Muslims became the majority, such tolerance was increasingly challenged from within the Muslim structures. But further Muslim expansions into the Indian subcontinent and into Anatolia and South-eastern Europe during the twelfth to fifteenth centuries required regular reference back to the fundamental paradigm of tolerance.

The expansion of European power in the eighteenth to twentieth centuries has understandably tested this tradition of tolerance to the extreme, often to breaking point. On the one hand, the majority experience of the Muslim community, the one which has historically set the dominant tone, has not included any significant element of being under non-Muslim rule – thence, for example, the sudden flurry of Islamic revivalist movements in India after 1858 when the Moghul empire *de jure* gave way to the Queen-Empress. On the other hand, the history of tolerance had always been in relation to communities, not to individuals: it was as members of recognised and tolerated communities that Christians and Jews had found their place within the Islamic state. The individual existed only as a member of a community – this was equally true of Muslims. This system reached its peak in the *millet* system of the Ottoman empire. It was therefore a particularly sharp defeat and painful retreat for the Ottoman empire when, in the middle of the nineteenth century, it had on several occasions to accept constitutional reforms implementing European modes of individual civil rights as the price of Anglo-French support against Austrian and Russian expansion.

It should come as no surprise, therefore, that Muslims in the late twentieth century seem paradoxically to be trumpeting the traditional much-vaunted tolerance of the Islamic state and of Muslim history, while simultaneously complaining of the intolerance of Western governments and European society and apparently ignoring the abuse of political power in many of their own states. The paradox depends on where you stand.

PROSPECTS

I have suggested already at the beginning of this paper that we are in a period of significant transition, in which the issues arising from the Muslim presence in Europe play an important role. How that Muslim presence will develop, as it plays its role, depends on a number of factors. By definition, such factors can be discerned only in part with reference to research. Research data are historical in nature, they indicate where we are in relation to whence we have come. In relation to the future they may suggest where we may *wish* to go, but this gives little indication as to where we are likely to go: history is littered with projects which have had very different outcomes from those which were initially intended.

With a token acknowledgement that some totally unexpected development may take place in the future, I would still venture to suggest a number of factors which are affecting and will continue to affect the space within which Muslims, at least in Western Europe, will have to manoeuvre, as well as ways in which the wider European social and political structures will have to adapt. The very idea of a 'space' reflects one of my main contentions, namely that both the European 'host' societies and the new communities within them are presented with an area covering a wide variety of optional routes. In Britain the experience of the Jewish communities, which immigrated from Eastern Europe a century or so ago, shows that no single route of integration was acceptable to everybody; so there has been a variety of solutions, which have been worked out through processes of negotiation between particular perceptions of need on the part of the immigrants and of possibilities on the part of the several sections of the 'host' community. The needs and the possibilities today are naturally different from those of a century ago, but the processes cannot be dissimilar. (It is unfortunate that, in the British context, very little comparative work has been done in this field.)

For purposes of convenience it makes sense to classify these factors into three levels: national, European, and international. At the *national* level, it is obvious that circumstances are most varied. One element of this is the publicly expressed attitude of the state government, and here there continues to be a tension between immigration and ethnic minority defined by origin and nationality, on the one hand, and religious identity on the other. Most recently we have witnessed in Britain the contrast between apparent government policy relating to Muslim schools, whose applications for public funding have been turned down, a policy which in the eyes of many Muslims has been deliberately biased against them and appears to reinforce a growing racist element, and a quite remarkable and widely publicised speech by the Prince of Wales stressing both the positive contribution of Muslims to national development and the necessity of wider international co-operation between Muslims and Christians.

At the same time, we experience not only racist attacks in Germany and France but also a process of targeting of Muslims as part of that process at street level. There is no doubt that at the level of national governments efforts have been made to counter such tendencies. After the headscarves affair of September 1990, the French government's Commission for Reflection on Islamic Affairs has sought to bring together different Muslim interests for the greater common good. So there are now a few Muslim chaplains in the military and health services. But both French and Algerian politics continue to destabilise progress. In Britain, the Department of the Environment has established an Inner Cities Religions Council, and several local authorities have developed a very close working relationship with certain religious communities. As for Germany, the official government attitude of neutrality in religion affects only those communities indigenous to the country. While 'ethnic' Germans can continue to enter the country from Eastern Europe and beyond, and become citizens under a 'law of return', people who have lived in the country for two generations are still regarded as 'guest workers': Germany is not a country of immigration, as the official formula repeatedly states.

There is little doubt that a significant factor at this level is the degree of expectation of fair treatment in the employment market and in the political system. The immigrant generation itself consciously arrived with certain very restricted expectations in mind. The Turkish workers in Germany, the Netherlands and elsewhere knew the conditions under which they were migrating; the Pakistani and Bangladeshi villagers did not expect to be welcomed with open arms – in sharp contrast to the early Jamaican immigrants to Britain. In Britain, the open offer of citizenship and political participation, even after all the restrictions which have been imposed over the last two decades, created an expectation among the young generation of a degree of local and national political involvement which, in the implementation, turned out not to be as straightforward as expected. Thence, the outburst of frustration centred around the younger generation, which was triggered by Salman Rushdie's notorious book. It is no coincidence that this outburst came at a time when we saw in Western Europe the coming of age of the first major generation of Muslims born here or brought here while they were still very young. And this coming of age happened when we were experiencing the highest levels of unemployment seen since the 1930s.

At the *European* level we are seeing contradictory trends. On the one hand, the continuing development of European Union structures around the Single Market and the Maastricht treaty is tending to emphasise the commonality of European heritage as against immigrant ethnic minority communities. On the other hand, the very existence of the common Europe is making it easier to network among the various Muslim groups within the EU borders. But the restrictions imposed on the movement of third-country nationals mean that European converts to Islam and Muslims of Commonwealth origin in Britain are particularly, although not exclusively, well-placed to activate such networking.

The growing tendency towards attempted co-ordination of European policy, even when not successful, has advanced especially in the area of law enforcement, particularly as regards internal security. The publicly expressed justifications have referred to concerns about terrorism and smuggling, especially of drugs. While there have obviously been instances which fit into such categorisation, it is equally clear that the line between suspicion against individuals and against groups has been crossed frequently by politicians and journalists. Since the end of the 1970s, Muslims have often become a group target in such circumstances. This has most markedly been the case in recent years in France since the military clampdown on the FIS and other Islamist movements in Algeria. But there have been overtones of similar processes across Western Europe following terrorist attacks or crises on the international scene, for example in connection with the Gulf war of 1990–1. In Eastern Europe a perceived growth in Soviet Muslim populations and their increase in the Red Army were elements in the agitation of, for example, the Baltic states for independence from Moscow. There is little doubt that the role of the Muslim populations in Europe in domestic and international policy-making is going to be of continuing significance. However, the key question will be how far such roles are earned or ascribed: in other words will their role be one of their own making, in interaction with their wider social and political contexts, for their own enlightened self-interest, or will it come to be one determined by outsiders' perceptions, fears and misunderstandings?

The *international* arena relates directly to this last point. Historically, both in ideas and in reality, Muslim communities have tended to relate both to their particular situation and to the world-wide Muslim community, the *umma*. The nature of communications in the modern world has given the solidarity of the *umma* a tool of a practical strength which traditionally only the annual pilgrimage at Mecca was able to elicit. The speed of these communications means that the *umma* can now be touched within hours rather than the months or even years which were required a few centuries ago. In the past it was only events of truly catastrophic significance which registered in the records of the Muslim community world-wide; events such as the Mongol sack of the caliphal capital of Baghdad in 1258, against which the Crusades in their own time were but puny border raids of only local irritancy.

Today, it is the events of the Gulf, Bosnia, Palestine, Ayodhya, Somalia and Algeria which are immediately relayed into all our living rooms and call on sympathy or provoke revulsion. The degree of settlement and of self-confidence among the Muslim communities in Europe are factors in how they perceive and react to such images. In Britain, it is remarkable how Muslim communities of South Asian origin have been moved to anger and action by the events in Bosnia in 1992–3, reactions which were almost completely absent a decade earlier when Israel invaded Lebanon in a civil war which was very similar both in its process and complexity and in the immediate victims.

Perhaps the most fateful dimension of this aspect of the international scene in the early 1990s is the way in which Islam is in some quarters, especially from across the Atlantic, being trumpeted as the 'new enemy'. The Orwellian requirement that there be 'an enemy' is in serious danger of being met, as Orwell himself imagined it, namely as a fictional creation and ultimately a self-fulfilling prophecy. While the need for an enemy to succeed the Communists appears to be strongest in the United States of America, the ground to receive such appeals is fertile in Europe. It is here that Muslim minorities are most awkward, because of the circumstances and causes of their immigration. It is here that the Muslim world can be perceived as a real, not just imaginary, threat with the countries of emigration and refugee sources lying just across a sea which historically has united as much as it has divided. Here it is that the collapse of the Communist empire could easily come to be regarded as the trigger for a new mass migration, *Völkerwanderung*, from the East in which the 'peril' is not yellow or red but Muslim. But for precisely such considerations European countries, both East and West, must have a deeply vested interest in rejecting the simplistic enemy image agenda currently being propagated. It is medieval in its roots and in its branches, and we are no longer in the medieval world; there is too much which binds all the regions around the Mediterranean together in common interests. And these interests can only be cultivated through agendas and projects discussed and developed coolly and co-operatively 'in theatre' rather than from distant heights.

We started with a subject of marginal and specialised interest among a few individual scholars and observers, with the occasional policy-maker being attracted in recent years. We started with an esoteric corner of sociology and ethnography, where a few church people probably were more knowledgeable than any scholar or civil servant. I venture to suggest, with other contributors to this and similar volumes in recent years, that the field of Islam in Europe and its relationship with the wider concerns of relations between the Muslim world and the West, Islam and Christendom, is one which not only will not go away but will become one of the main issues of the turn of the millennium.

Index